The
Laid
Daughter

A True Story

The Laid Daughter

A True Story

HELEN BONNER

Kairos Center

1995

Kairos Center

4608 Finley Drive
Austin, Texas 78731
Phone: 1-800-624-4697
FAX: 512-453-8378

The names in this book
have been changed
to protect the privacy of others.

Colophon is a trademark of the Kairos Center

The Laid Daughter: A True Story

Editor: Jan Huebsch
Cover design by Kairos Center

Published in 1995

Library of Congress Cataloging-in-Publication Data
Bonner, Helen.
The Laid Daughter: a true story / Helen Bonner, Ph.D.
256 p.   22.5 cm.   "A Kairos Center Book"

1. Incest
2. Psychological trauma
3. Literature—short story study
4. Women's studies
5. Journaling
6. Autobiography
7. Title

RC 560.153 B68 1995   DDC — dc 20   95-76617
                                                CIP

ISBN 1-884178-22-7 HBK
ISBN 1-884178-23-5 PBK

The Laid Daughter

Helen Bonner

Leda's Daughter	7
Kidnapped	20
Learning from the Fathers	34
True Confessions	56
Free Woman	71
So Many Men	90
To The Dark Continent	108
The Border Years	131
Fifty, Refocus	154
Fast Forward, Rewind	167
Winding Down, Winding Up	180
Sneaky Snake Meets the Bitch Queen	193
American Auschwitz	218
Coming Home	240
Afterword	254

Leda and the Swan

A sudden blow; the great wings beating still
Above the staggering girl, her thighs caressed
By the dark webs, her nape caught in his bill,
He holds her helpless breast upon his breast.

How can those terrified vague fingers push
The feathered glory from her loosening thighs?
And how can body, laid in that white rush,
But feel the strange heart beating where it lies?

A shudder in the loins engenders there
The broken wall, the burning roof and tower
And Agamemnon dead.
                    Being so caught up,
So mastered by the brute blood of the air,
Did she put on his knowledge with his power
Before the indifferent beak could let her drop?

William Butler Yeats

1

Leda's Daughter

I am Helen. Helen? But she was the daughter of Leda, a woman so beautiful she was raped by a swan who was the Greek god Zeus in disguise. So am I the daughter of Leda, a raped beauty? Was my father like a god to me? Does he still, even dead, have power over me?

I had just taught the myth of Helen of Troy in a class, and afterward, I found myself asking those questions. Disturbing questions. Questions I didn't want to look at. They stirred some deep-seated anger I didn't understand.

Having lunch with my friend Susan, I tried to avoid my feelings by making light of them.

"Leda, the first woman to be goosed."

Susan gave me a quizzical look.

"Joke." I said, fumbling the wrapping off my pulpy hamburger. I always enjoyed having lunch in the Student Union with Susan, who taught business classes.

"Did you know Helen was kidnapped as a child? Because she was beautiful. Later, at probably all of sixteen, she was married off to a King..."

"Because she was beautiful," Susan repeated with world-weary irony. "Of course. What's new?"

"Then Paris carried her off—because she was the most beautiful woman in the world..."

"As if that weren't a matter of opinion," Susan interrupted, jealous of even mythical competition. Susan had been homecoming queen in high school. She could still carry off the look, even now at fifty, if the light was right.

"Yes. Well, then he hauled her off to a foreign country, where it seems she made the best of it, 'till her husband's brother burned and sacked the place and took her back. "

I laughed ruefully. "Great literature! Every woman's model for success."

Susan was watching me with close and warm attention. "The face that launched a thousand ships," she said.

"Yes. When I was a country kid, I liked to say I had the face that launched a thousand pickup trucks."

Susan laughed. Her glance swept over me. "You've launched a few Cadillacs since then."

"Yeah. And a van. And a Honda, a Volkswagen bug, a Mercedes...." I pretended to start counting them off on my fingers. But it wasn't funny, remembering back. The pain, the loneliness, the odd sense of failure.

How did beauty fail me? I looked down at my plate, while my hand went up to check the gray streak in my hair.

"Helen?" Susan broke in.

"What?

"You got that look again, as if you've gone underground."

I surfaced. "Oh...I was wondering what was it like for the famous Helen, watching them taking their pick of the women, all the time quarreling about who got which one. Then being hauled back to her home after ten years, like used merchandise. Was she supposed to act like nothing had happened?"

"It's just a myth."

"It's not just a myth!" I said. "Those old stories carry weight."

"Something's bothering you, isn't it?"

"No. It's just...sometimes I hate those old patriarchal horror stories."

The truth was, I didn't know what bothered me so much. And I didn't want to know.

I reached over and helped myself to some french fries, dipping them in ketchup. "Did you know ketchup is full of sugar? Everything is now, baby food, cereal, yogurt." I dabbed ketchup off my chin.

"Whatever happened to Helen in the end?" Susan asked. "Didn't she end up getting bitten by a snake? Or was that Cleopatra?"

"Cleopatra." I loved her curiosity.

I tried to lighten up a little. "She had a little more power over her life, but she still ended up getting bitten by her own snake. I can understand how that happens, I've done it a few times."

Susan winced. "Snakes." She glanced at the clock and began to gather up plastic and paper. I dumped our trays, and we hurried toward Stanford Hall.

"I need to stop by and get that book from you," Susan reminded me as we went up the stairs.

In my office, I looked for the book of short stories she wanted.

"What's this?" Susan was looking at some doodles on my phone pad. I had drawn a snake coming out of a jagged fracture, then scribbled over the top of it. Images from dreams. I tore it out of the pad and threw it away.

Susan looked puzzled. "Sorry, I didn't mean to be nosy." She took the book. "Thanks. I'll return it." Giving me a quick hug, she hurried off to her own part of the campus. With her light steps, mass of curly hair, long bright skirt, she might have been one of the students.

I gave myself a mental goad as I closed my office door. If I kept going on about the Greek Helen like that, Susan would think I was weird. I had an hour to change my mindset enough to teach Homer's *Iliad* like the great epic poem it was, instead of going into a rage over it. I made up my mind to conduct the class professionally, keeping it safely on Homer, on the poem, and away from my hot spots.

While searching the files for my lecture notes, I realized that my overreaction to certain kinds of violence was increasing. Like most people, I had learned to accept the barrage of news stories about war, mass murders, brutal killings of all sorts, but rape unleashed tremors in my psyche that erupted like volcanoes.

That night on TV, a woman told how her talented and beautiful daughter was raped and murdered. The program showed pictures of the girl, of the place where she stood by her stalled car, pictures of the two men who pretended aid, then dragged her, begging for mercy, to the nearby woods.

I cried as I watched, not just tears of sympathy, but deep wrenching sobs that tore me apart, long after I had turned off the program.

Another time I had been lying in bed with my lover when the radio announced that a Highway Patrolman in California was arrested for the murder of a woman he had pulled over for speeding. He'd raped her, then dumped her body on the desert. I pushed Ken away and crawled out of bed enraged with him, as though he were responsible for what had happened to that woman. "Goddamn these men, they pretend to take care of women, we trust them, then they abuse us!"

Ken was angry and hurt. "Did I ever rape you?"

"No, of course not."

"Did anybody ever rape you?"

"No."

He pulled on his pants and jacket. "Christ, it wasn't even in Minnesota."

"Well, I'm from California," I retorted, realizing it still made no sense at all. My rage was as astonishing to me as to him. He went home, and we broke up shortly after. Sundered by the image of violence.

Then there was Bible Study. A strange place for violence to unhinge and enrage me. Last Wednesday night, they were already reading *Judges 19* when I slipped onto one of those metal folding chairs, grabbing a paperback Bible off the stack.

"...there was a certain Levite who took to himself a concubine from Bethlehem of Judah. And his concubine played the whore against him, and then..."

My hand shot up. "Wait a minute. What's a Levite?"

Debby (who over twenty-one could call herself Debby?) looked mildly surprised. "Well, a Levite is kind of a priest, I think."

Another woman consulted her Bible reference book: "A member of the priestly Hebrew tribe of Levi, to be specific. One assigned to lesser ceremonial offices under the levitical priests."

"Thank you," I said. But I wasn't satisfied. "What was the legal status of a concubine in those days?"

"Well, in polygamous societies, as most of them were two thousand years ago, she was probably a kind of second wife."

"A wife with inferior social and legal status," the reference reader said. "The word damsel refers to her later, and damsel is a young, unmarried woman of noble birth."

"Well, we've got to move along." Debby commenced reading. "And his concubine played the whore against him, and then arose and went away from him to her father's house to..."

I interrupted again. I couldn't help it. "I'm sorry, but I can't just race through this. What does it mean, that she played the whore against him?"

Some of the women were giving me looks now. "We're never going to get through Judges," muttered the white-haired woman next to me, looking at her diamond-studded watch.

"My Bible words it differently," a younger woman said, "It just says she whored against him...but we all know what a whore is, don't we?"

Laughter.

"I'm not sure," I said. I was thinking how much language changes in two thousand years. But it was more than that. I was feeling that volcano building up under me. I forced myself to quiet down and let the reading continue.

The story went on to say how the Levite, after a few months, goes after her, "to speak lovingly to her," and to take her home. They spend the night in an unfriendly village, finding hospitality with a former countryman. But "certain wicked men" demand that the countryman turn the Levite over to them. The horrified host begs them to leave his guest alone. "Seeing that this man has come as a guest into my house, do not commit this shameful act..."

As Debby droned through the words, I could barely restrain my horror at what I was hearing: "Behold, here is my daughter, a virgin and his concubine; I will bring them out for you, and you may humble them, and do with them what seems good to you; but to this man you shall not do any shameful thing." I was horrified. She read on, unfeeling, unscathed.

"But the men would not listen to him; so the man took his concubine and brought her outside to them; and they raped her and abused her all the night until the morning; and when the dawn began to break, they let her go."

I looked around the circle of women's faces; they seemed suddenly dead, stopped in time, as lifeless as the imitation wood table top. Couldn't they acknowledge what they were reading? Did they not understand it? Were they inured to it? I wanted to scream at them, "Doesn't this bother you at all, what you've just heard?"

Debby's voice rattled on. "And her master rose up in the morning and opened the door of the house and went out to go his way; and he saw his concubine lying at the door of the house, with her hands upon the threshold. And he said to her, 'Get up, let us go.' But she did not answer. Then he put her on the ass and the man rose up and went on to his own home..."

"Was she alive or dead?" the white-haired woman asked Debby, in an irritated voice.

"Well, I don't know, it doesn't say here..." An edge of curiosity was creeping into her deadened tone.

Another woman, adjusting her glasses lower on her nose to peer at the print, said, "Well, she must of been dead, because it says here he took his knife and cut her into twelve portions...I *hope* she was dead." There was uneasy laughter.

Unable to contain my rage and sorrow, I stood up, slamming the Bible shut. "Don't you hear? He cuts her body into twelve pieces, which he distributes to all the tribes of Israel to show what has been done to him. To *him!*" The women looked at me in shocked astonishment. Not knowing what else to do, I left.

All the way home from the church, I cried for the concubine whose own husband sacrificed her to protect himself. I cried for the virgin daughter who was sacrificed by her own father and never even mentioned again. I cried with a vaguely understood impotent rage.

In my office the next day, I looked up the word *whore.* As I had suspected, the original definition of the word was: *To worship false gods. Or the desertion of the worship of God for the worship of idols.* The girl in Judges 19 had probably been a believer of some other God or Goddess, as was common then; she had probably refused to give that up for some wandering Levite.

Remembering the story, I felt tears welling up again. I felt a muscle in my jaw harden. What was that story doing in the Bible? Was it there to threaten women? To unite Hebrew men in common enmity? How come in a Bible study class, no one bothered to tell the truth of it? How come women listened to it in compliant silence? But most of all, why was I the only one who was so angry?

My dreams had been telling me for a long time that there was something I had to deal with, something I had been holding back with all my strength...and that story was triggering it.

Just the night before, I had dreamed: *I go back to visit the house. A bathroom on the third floor has a new toilet in it, but it looks old, with a round meter plaque in the bottom with people's names on it, but I can't read them. A man, tall, thin and dark haired, tries to push his way through the window, saying it is okay, but I slam the white porcelain cover on, covering the bottom half and go downstairs to see if it was really okay.*

On the second floor I see Susan's purse with some pictures. I'm looking through them to see if I'm in any when she comes back in, looking for them. Embarrassed, I confess I took them out of her purse. She says, "No, you didn't," and gives me a big hug.

My dreams were mostly nightmares: I was being controlled by a dark mafia or military police, held hostage, a child was forced into a trunk, its hands cut off. There were dying babies, falling bodies, dark figures breaking into old houses. I recorded them faithfully in my journal for the day when I might understand them.

In my office that day, a glint of light caught my eye, and I looked up to see it coming off the lake outside my window. The surface of the glass threw my reflection back against lake and sky, my own rather worn but still stubbornly beautiful face. With my newly permed hair, I looked a little wild. In fact, I had always been a little wild.

Well, the wild side was getting out of hand, I thought, and pushed my disturbing thoughts away . I pulled out the class file and entered student grades in the green spiral book.

When I drove home that night, I stopped at the mailbox, always with that vague unrealistic expectancy that something special would be there, a letter from some perfect lover somewhere, a surprise gift from my kids in California. But there were the usual ads and bills.

Ken and I were going dancing, and even though it had been as flat as gravy with us lately, we still loved to dance. I eased the car down the drive, avoiding the early spring mud puddles, pushed the electronic door opener, and pulled into the garage. A woman's garage, Ken had said once, noting how spacious and empty it was.

By the back deck, I saw newly opened daffodils, and reminded myself to buy more bulbs in the fall, since they were doing so well. Tucked under the corner of the screen door was a white envelope. "Oh-oh." I took it into the house, put it on the counter that divided the living room from the small kitchen area. Through the wide front windows, I saw the beginnings of a sunset taking shape behind the university on the other side of the lake. Those sunsets were my salvation, my hedge against loneliness.

I put a cup of water into the microwave and got out a tea bag. Then I sighed and opened the letter.

Dear Helen,

It just isn't working for me. I'm sorry.

Ken

Oh. I took my tea out on the front deck and stood looking at the sunset fanning out across the thin cover of clouds, light pushing through the holes in long golden streaks, like in the old religious paintings of resurrections.

It wasn't as if it had been the love of a lifetime, I told myself. But what about the good stuff? What about how much fun we had dancing, and singing little songs on the way home, and sex, how could it be any better? I remembered getting to a party late because we'd been making love on my living room floor. I remembered how we laughed when the William Tell

Overture came on the radio, just at the height of things. Later, all Ken would have to say to make me laugh was, "Listen, they're playing our song."

We had fallen into bed together on our second night out, felt comfortable and natural together. We laughed, danced in the kitchen. One night we played cards while we drank a whole bottle of wine, and he shaved my legs when we went to bed.

Later he had proposed to me; I said if we still felt that way about each other in two weeks, I would say yes. But two weeks later, lying in bed, he said, "I feel like just hopping on a bus sometimes."

I stood watching the wind lap up waves across the lake until I was too cold to stay any longer, then went inside and picked up the phone. I hesitated. Put it back down.

It was over. I had known it for weeks. He hadn't treated me affectionately since we had taken a trip together. He told me, as I made arrangements and paid for a rental car, that I acted like I was the one with all the answers, always the one in charge. I said it seemed to me when I was growing up that the one who paid for everything was always the one in charge, and in this case, it just happened to be me.

The trip was a disaster. The last morning, he went for a walk while I was still asleep, then came back and threw himself on top of me unexpectedly. I yelled, "Get off of me! What are you doing?" I then apologized in tears, but the damage was done.

Well, it wasn't like a lot of time was lost with Ken. We'd only known each other a few months. But Les and I had four years invested before it fell apart, and with Joe, it was three. No matter how hard I tried, I just couldn't seem to keep a relationship.

I did not cry.

I put on a jacket and walked the old railroad trail that went across the Mississippi River and around the south side of the lake. Trying to lift my mood, I diverted myself from my pain by paying close attention to the mallards and wood ducks that were still arriving every day from their long winter away. A great blue heron fluffed up at my approach, then lifted on heavy gray wings and flew away, squawking. I jogged awhile, halfheartedly, my steps sluggish in the sandy path.

At home, I sat in meditation trying to settle down, concentrating on my breathing, taking long deep breaths.

I felt better. I picked up the paper. A film I'd read about was showing. *Casualties of War* was based on the true story of American soldiers who capture, for sex purposes, a Vietnamese girl. Even though I normally

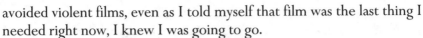

avoided violent films, even as I told myself that film was the last thing I needed right now, I knew I was going to go.

As the dark images played themselves out on the screen of the girl being dragged from her family, of the violent sergeant shaming his men into raping her, of the helpless sobbing girl curled up against the pain, I shook and trembled with her. I had to go to the Ladies Room several times because I couldn't quit crying. But I couldn't leave either. I groped my way back in the dark, nearly empty theater, wanting to see if the sympathetic soldier could rescue the girl, wanting to see the worst if he didn't.

On Monday I told Susan, "They were supposedly there to help and protect the innocent, but instead, they exploited and killed her."

"Why did you go? You knew what the movie was about. You were probably feeling bad already about that jerk throwing you over."

"I don't know. There's something...something I've got to look at, something connected with me and men who are supposed to be protectors, like that California cop."

I stirred cream into my coffee, checking Susan's response from the corner of my eye. She must have thought I was getting really weird.

But Susan just looked at me expectantly, so I went on, my voice trembling. "I have these dreams. In one I go to visit my father, but there is a policeman guarding his place. He abuses little girls, the policeman says. No, he likes little girls, I say and go on in. Then I am standing in a bedroom with two bricked up beds, one on each side."

My hands were noticeably shaking now. I couldn't look at Susan. "It doesn't take a trained psychologist to see what that dreams about. It's about some part of me that guards the old house, guards against me finding out what's under the bricks."

Susan looked me straight in the eyes. "I had a friend who had some terrible things happen to her before she was five. She had no memory of it, but it turned up on hospital records." I could only stare at her. Not me. My childhood was okay.

I left feeling more anxious than ever. I shouldn't be talking about these things. I shouldn't have gone to that movie. I wouldn't go to any more like that. I would turn off the television if something came on that was disturbing. What if something even did happen back there? It was so many years ago, what did it matter? I was fine. I had a good job. I did it well. I had good friends. Leave it alone. Back in my office, I pulled myself together, dismissed the worry from my mind as I began reading my students' midterm exams.

But alone in the house that night, as I sat in meditation, I saw the door to the basement of the house that we lived in when I was small. I let the image stay. I imagined myself going down the forbidden dark stairway. Suddenly I became that small child. I could smell the damp cement and wood shavings. Then I was lifted, playfully laid down on my back on a table. I was laughing at first. I remembered other times, being tickled until I lost control, but this was not tickling; it was the pleasure/pain of being diddled, fingers titillating my genitals until I gave over to wild thrashing. My thighs began to twitch spasmodically. Then my mouth took on a shape of its own. The upper lip stretched grotesquely wide over my teeth and down; the lower lip pulled in over my teeth, my jaw pulled down, and I was choking, gagging on something in my throat.

I came out of the meditation struggling for breath. Not my father! It couldn't have been my father. I'd adored my father. But the experience, the reaction of my body, was so real, as if it were happening right now. My heart was beating like a bird's, my head was splitting. I sat on the bed, rocking myself, reeling with the horror of it. I would have been very small, because we left that house when I was six. The object pulling down my mouth, gagging me, felt like a huge penis.

Scribbling rapidly, I described the experience in my journal. Then I put Beethoven on the stereo, sprawled on the couch with a book of short stories, and when I woke the next morning, I had forgotten all about it.

In the following days, I obsessed over Ken. How could something that started out so well end so badly? I'd been with so many men, and it always started out good, and ended up like that. There had to be something wrong. I was as good a person as anybody else; I had kept a marriage together for ten years, raised two fine sons, made a career for myself, bought my own home with my own hard-earned money. But since my second divorce twenty years ago, I couldn't seem to put together a relationship that lasted, and I couldn't keep pretending it was always somebody else's fault.

Then I had another dream:

I am with a dark, good looking, cold man. I see him cut up a woman with a very sharp knife, but she gets away and hides in the dark. He finds me, and I continue to travel with him, making him think I am on his side. I see a young girl, her throat has been slit, but it has healed over and is not even scarred. His knife is very sharp. When I get a chance, I grab the knife and stab him, but the knife just goes in straight and comes back out, doing no damage at all. He comes after me and I escape but I know he will find me, and either I will kill him or he will kill me, over and over.

It wasn't even a nightmare. It was matter of fact. "That's just the way it is," I wrote in my journal.

I knew that the man was my father, who was handsome in a dark, cold way, uncomfortable with feelings, yet with a surface charm. The slit throat of the girl meant that I could not talk about whatever happened, could not allow feelings to pass from my body to my head. My father and I pursued one another in the psychological world behind my sexual life, where I was alternately the killer or the killed.

It was no use going into therapy, I told myself. I had been in therapy. I learned a lot each time, but never got to the root of it, down to the critical mass.

But the pain at Ken, my overreaction to films, myths, Bible stories, my nightmares, all told me I could no longer avoid looking at this. It was destroying my life. I had to know, beyond doubt, what had happened back there.

The next day, I made an appointment with a highly recommended hypnotist. I drove the eighty miles to his office determined to settle it "once and for all." I did not tell the receptionist anything about myself, just that I wanted to undergo hypnosis.

When I sat down in the comfortable office of Larry Anderson, I told him confidently, "All I want is to find out what's at the bottom of some memories and dreams I've had most of my life. I don't have any real problems. I don't need any more therapy; my life is fine, better than most."

I laughed to show how messed up I thought most lives were. "Just hypnosis. Whatever comes up, I can deal with it. I just need some help getting to it."

Larry, a young bearded man with a gentle manner, refused. "You want to get hypnotized and go home? Helen, I can't do that. I can't just open you up like some tuna can and send you home with whatever we find. Besides, we need to establish a safety zone for you or you won't feel safe enough for hypnosis." Reluctantly, I agreed.

The first session was spent going over the working rules. "We will proceed at your own pace," he assured me. "There will be mutual respect, no violence in the office." That startled me. What was he expecting? That I would go nuts?

The second session, we went through the top layers of my life, my work, my two marriages and my many relationships since. I told him nothing of my early memories, and he made no inquiry.

After that session, he said quietly, "How about this for a goal? How would you like to bring your polar opposites, the head and the feelings, closer together?"

I laughed. "That'll be the day." When I got in the car, I heard an old song in my head. *The good ol' boys are drinking whiskey and rye and singing 'That'll be the day that I die'.*

As my next appointment with Larry approached, there were more dreams. In one, a voice said threateningly, "Nobody tells." I woke mornings with images of shattered glass doors and old men in sailor suits. I woke gagging, sick and angry, wanting to hit and kick. The mind might lie, I thought, but the body knows something. I was going back to what was stored in the body, and I didn't like it.

Next session Larry said, "I think we're ready, if you still want to try hypnosis." I did. He asked me to imagine a place where I would feel safe; I imagined my beautiful lakeside home. "Now imagine someone nearby that you trust." I trusted him. Then, using simple counting techniques, he led me inward and downward to my inner house.

Again I saw the door to the cellar steps. "How old are you?" he asked. "Two."

"Where are you?"

"In the Richmond house. I am sitting on the kitchen floor. Daddy picks me up. I am happy. I love my Daddy."

I could hear my own voice, childlike. I could feel my hands twist the arms of the chair.

"He carries me down the cellar stairs and puts me on a table..." I started to twist in my chair, to lose my voice.

"You're safe here, Helen." Larry's voice came through as though from a great distance. "There will be no violence in my office."

The child voice continued. "He tickles me, we are just playing...." I begin to cry, a tight childlike plea. "I love my daddy."

I feel my body twisting the other way, my head pulled back. The child cries louder. "He's not tickling me anymore ...he's.... he's...." She can't say the words. The child is twisting, pulling her legs up, thrusting her arms out to her sides, hands flailing. Her mouth is pulled wide, distorted, her lips stretched tight as her face turns, twists away. Her body freezes, her mind sees nothing but blankness, darkness, as if she has been suffocated. As if she is dead. Then she is gagging, sobbing, trying to crawl away.

Larry's gentle voice came through. "Who was it, Helen?"

I came to myself, opened my eyes. The kindness I saw in his eyes brought me back to the present. "It was my father," I said, and as I said the words, I felt an immense relief, as if I had been carrying those forbidden words around more than fifty years.

I made a great apologetic effort to get myself together. I straightened my shoulders, blew my nose, wiped the mascara off my face. Then I looked around the room and noticed for the first time that there was a teddy bear on the couch. Embarrassed, I looked at Larry.

"I don't know if any of that is true," I said.

"I believe you," he said quietly. "I saw you struggling."

My friend Susan was waiting in the car. As I crawled into the passenger side, vulnerable and shaky, I said, without looking at her, "It was incest. It was my father. It only happened once." I expected shock, loathing, disbelief, but when I brought myself to look up at Susan's face, there were tears in her eyes.

I thought it was over. It was only beginning.

2

Kidnapped

The day following hypnosis, I felt vulnerable and fragile, as if my shell had been pried off. I felt as wounded as that child had been, and as soiled. I wanted to stay curled up in my house, but I had promised an old friend that I would come to his house for lunch. When his wife had been dying of cancer, I was one of her Hospice visitors.

I picked some wild strawberries from along the walking trail, a tiny handful of fragile pearl-sized berries, and put them in a jar for Carl. At his door, he took them from me and gave me the friendly hug that had been traditional with Hospice. As always, he smelled of freshly pressed clothes, put out for him by his housekeeper.

The big house loomed around us. As soon as I saw the plates and glasses and napkins laid out so carefully on both sides of the formal dining room table, I wondered if I would be able to play the pleasant, polite, and charming guest that he expected.

I couldn't follow the line of his conversation; my shattering experience was all that I could think about; how slimy I felt, how broken and valueless, as if it had been only yesterday the incest had happened. I could hardly hear him as he chatted about the jelly he had made from grapes in his backyard, or the ingredients of the soup he was placing before me. I felt like someone floating under water.

The sun shone through the window behind him, through his close-cropped white hair as he bowed his head to say a blessing. Relics of his past surrounded us; pictures of treasured children and grandchildren, trophies from his days as a dentist, his wife's plate collection, his golf trophies. Hardwood floors, crystal chandeliers, Victorian chairs and family heirlooms. What could he, with his neat orderly life, know about the sordid turmoil in my past?

"I need to tell you," I said. "If I don't seem quite myself today, it's because I'm in therapy. It's been very difficult." I couldn't keep my chin from quivering.

He passed me the bread, with the silver butter knife neatly laid across the plate. "Trauma and food don't go well together. Shall we eat first?"

He placed next to my plate some pages of manuscript. "Some old poems I resurrected from my high school days," he explained. "I was an English major before I went into dentistry, you know. I thought you might give me some comments."

"Yes, I'd be glad to," I said, scanning them. "Sonnets. Sonnets are not easy to write. Fitting the form can make them forced, unless you're Robert Frost."

I spooned some vegetables out of the broth, tried to eat. I was thinking, he doesn't want to hear about it. People don't want to hear about it.

He spooned salad onto the plate next to his larger dish, glancing at my empty one. I realized that I had put my salad on the wrong plate. I was so preoccupied I could barely function. Finally, I couldn't hold it back. "It was incest," I said.

"Oh...we were a bit worried about that with one of our friends' children for awhile. Her father seemed overly affectionate with her."

I was relieved to have my announcement taken so lightly, rather than abhorred, but at the same time, I was uncomfortable for the same reason. This wasn't just "overly affectionate" I was talking about.

I listened to him talk about his family, about his last Hospice meeting. Then I said, "I've got to go."

When he saw me to the door, he leaned and brushed my lips with his. I hardly felt it. He had never done that before. How strange that his response to what I had said had been a kiss. I dismissed it from my mind.

The next week I again made the long drive to see my therapist, who resembled somewhat the bearded gardener of a dream that I had one Easter, kind, gentle, respectful, even a little awed by the enormous complexities of the human mind.

"Twenty years ago I tried to tell a therapist what happened to me," I told Larry. "He was a Freudian, they all were then." I heard the anger and bitterness in my voice. "He told me it was normal for little girls to fantasize such things about their fathers. When I told him how my mother whipped me, he didn't think I made *that* up." My lip flattened in contempt.

"Later when I read for myself what Freud had written, all that penis envy stuff, when I saw how he refused to believe what all those women were telling him, turned it into penis envy, I was sick." I corrected myself. "*He* was sick."

Larry was even kind to Freud. "He had a lot of it wrong, but he did show us how the roots of most trauma can be found in childhood."

"What parent couldn't have told you that?" I retorted, scornfully. "I believed him, he was the therapist. I stuffed it back down for another twenty goddamn years!"

"You're pretty angry."

"Angry! Sometimes this anger, this rage, gets so big, I feel dangerous, I could destroy the Empire State Building with my bare hands."

"Who are you dangerous to? Who might you hurt?"

The question took me off guard. I collapsed into tears. "I don't know...somebody, anybody."

Larry waited. After awhile, I said in a small voice, "I had this dream last night. I'm putting some tiny people in an oven along with some paper, bread wrappers, funny papers, picnic plates. They are just supposed to be hidden or something, but then I get the oven too hot and I start looking for them to see if they're all right, but the paper catches fire. It's all going up in flames. I find some of them but they are not people now, they are worms, and they've been burned in the fire. I am horrified. I grieve.

"Everyone else says they were just worms, forget it. I say no, they were people, a family. I ask, doesn't the mother even grieve? No, a woman says, they were just worms. In the dream, I cry bitterly." I was weeping now.

"What does that dream mean to you?" Larry asked.

"This anger has been heating up to this, this explosion, this conflagration. Under all my nice memories of Sunday funnies and picnics was the truth: my father had done that to me! Now I've lost everything, a father I adored, a mother who would protect me. How can I even have confidence in myself as a competent person who knows who I am?" I looked at Larry. He sat quietly, with no answers. "I've lost all that, and I can't even grieve."

"My father made me feel like a worm... I have opened up a can of worms...and now they are worms."

I was quiet for awhile, then in a low voice, I said, "I'd like to burn the house down, with everybody in it except for my brother and sister."

"Your mother too?"

I thought about my mother, lying in bed with cancer, month after month. I wondered if my mother had known what my father had done.

"No. Not my mother. She suffered enough."

I sat looking at the floor. I was exhausted.

"Before you go home, I want to tell you what I am putting in your file, so you'll know," Larry said. "What you've been going through is called PTSD—Post Traumatic Stress Disorder. The Vietnam vets taught us about it. When what they went through was just too terrible to live with, the mind blocked it out. Sometimes their memories took twenty years to break through the surface, some never will."

I understood that. My own son had been in Nam. When he came home, he would not talk about it. He lived with rage that seeped through the cracks for years. I had seen him writhe on the floor with headaches. His wife said he threw himself off the bed still when helicopters flew too low over the house. "PTSD."

"Yes. The mind has enormous capabilities to cope," Larry said. "Its twists and turns are not sick, but attempts to protect us from what we are not yet ready to handle. You were evidently ready to handle this. It takes a strong person to face it, to go through it again."

I appreciated the respect I heard in his voice. I didn't at that point have much of my own.

As we continued with our weekly sessions, Larry's absolute trust in me gave me the trust that my confusions were not pathology, but the attempts of the mind to bring me eventually to safety and healing.

When summer came and I had a break from classes, I withdrew from almost all social life, too preoccupied with my past to deal with the present. I calmed myself by doing hard physical work. I pulled worn carpeting off the floor of the hallway. I bought ceramic tile, cutters and mixing vats for grout. The task was satisfyingly symbolic, I thought, laying down a hard tiled surface over the old floor. Then I patched my battered canoe with strips of fiberglass that reminded me of bandages. I was putting bandages on the wounds of the past, binding up the leaks in my life's vessel.

Carl drove out from town with tools and assistance. Bringing me a power sander, he would stay to fix a lamp or to play Scrabble with my roommate and me. Ann, a student at the university, was a tough Scrabble player. Carl was even more competitive. He kept a complete record of every game he'd played for sixty years. Every word played, every score! I enjoyed the family feeling the three of us had.

Carl took me to play miniature golf at his family's lakeside summer home. When I went for a checkup, he drove me to the clinic and waited to take me home. When I needed to have car repairs, he picked me up. I was grateful to have the kind of help and attention I had not had in years.

One night when we were watching television, he put my hand on his crotch. I moved my hand away, telling myself that it was just an accident. Then he kissed me goodnight, a funny tight little buss. I sent him out the door. "Carl, I'm in therapy. I'm not ready for anything with men, not you or anyone else."

Ann looked at me questioningly when Carl came down the walk the next day bearing flowers. I had just told her how sickened I was by his unwanted attention the night before. I shrugged helplessly as I went to open the door.

I told myself I was unreasonably critical. Here was this fine man who cared for me and I was going to mess it up. What was the matter with me? Did I only want relationships with men who treated me badly? Like Dick? Who held out on me, like Les? Or had nothing to offer me, like Ken?

In July, he calmly laid out his financial standing. "By the standards of this community, anyway, I might be considered wealthy. If we got married, I would be quite happy to support you to write full time, or if you wanted to go on working, I could certainly provide all the services of a good wife." He laughed, remembering I once said I could use a good wife.

"Thank you, Carl. But I love my home. I couldn't leave it."

"So keep it. We could have two houses, this one and mine in town. Or three! There's the lake cabin. I have a condo in the city, too. It's yours as a wedding present. You can keep it, or sell it to pay off the mortgage on this house."

I was stunned. He was offering me more security than I had ever had in my life.

"Carl, it's too soon to even talk about this. We haven't spent any real time together. I'm still in therapy. I don't even know who I am right now, much less who I'll be when it's over."

That night I had a dream: *I am looking at an Assembly bill with Tom Bane, my former boss at the California State Assembly, head of the Rules Committee. "But this bill gives one man the power to run the entire state!" I say in the dream. "That's right," Tom says with pride. His wife, a pleasant and competent person, explains why that is good. "You won't need all those others," she says.*

A few nights later, watching television, Carl suggested we pick out an engagement ring. I was unable to say anything at all. I went on watching the program like one who hadn't heard.

The next day he asked if I had heard him, though he knew I had. "You looked like a frightened little girl. You, this competent professional woman." He laughed.

I talked to Larry about it. "He is twenty years older than I am, but he's a good person. He was wonderful to his wife when she was dying, took care of her hand and foot for months. He wants to make my life easier. He's very bright. He writes poetry."

"You sound happy with him. What are your concerns?" Larry asked.

"I'm afraid I'll just shut down on him like I always do with men who are good to me."

"Well, you can move slowly. Check it out. There's no rush."

"He wants to take me to his getaway condo. We've never spent a night together. What if I'm repelled? What if I have a flashback?"

Larry reminded me that I knew how to deal with flashbacks now, how to breathe into them. "They don't have to frighten you into shutting down."

At home I went to bed listening to tapes Carl had given me, romantic, sexual. "The fires of Eden still burn in this heart of mine." I floated to sleep imagining myself being loved and loving. I put my doubts out of my mind.

But my journal reflected two different voices. In neat precise penmanship: *July 23—First sex-like stuff with Carl. Felt good.* In jagged scrawls: *July 28—I'm tired of this couch groping. He has to leave me alone.*

Instead of taking that conflict into therapy, I ran away from it. I told Larry I wouldn't be able to continue therapy. I was going to visit my family in California, and after that, classes started. "I think I've mostly dealt with it now, don't you? It only happened once."

He asked me about my tendency to dissociate, to disconnect from events in the present by focusing on something in my imagination. "I doubt if I do that any more than anyone else does," I said cheerfully.

"Good luck then, call me if you need me," Larry said. I thanked him for everything he had done for me and left therapy after only three months.

In California, having dinner with my son and his wife in their sun-filled dining room, I told them I was thinking of marrying. Scott stopped eating.

Joyce's eyes, always round, opened wider. "What?"

I laughed at their surprise. Joyce tilted her head, as if to straighten something crooked. "I thought you were still in therapy for this incest stuff...."

"No, that's all finished. It's gone pretty fast...maybe because it only happened once."

Joyce was a woman who liked to keep things straight. Now she tilted her head the opposite direction.

"Only happened once? Isn't that rather unlikely? Why would it only happen once?"

"I don't know. Maybe he got caught, maybe he felt bad, I don't know. It's not like you suddenly remember everything." I was uncomfortable. "Scott understands, he's had flashbacks. It's like that, comes in pieces."

Joyce considered that. "Well, tell us about this Carl guy."

"There's not much to tell. We don't know each other very well yet. We've never spent a whole day together, haven't slept together."

"Why not?" Joyce asked.

"I'm not ready for that yet."

As Scott listened, his long face took on the hawklike expression he sometimes got when he was focusing intently. His Vietnam experience had sharpened that.

"What I've noticed since you got here, Mom, is you look deeply sad." He waited a moment for that to sink in. "Even when I know you're having a good time, being here with us and all that, your eyes are sad."

I picked at my salad, pushing it this way and that. "Yes. Well, I still feel pretty weird and disconnected after the incest breakthrough, but Larry thinks I'm doing okay. I'm determined to be normal."

"Normal?" Scott repeated, with a questioning squint. "What's normal?"

"I'm not going to let what happened screw me up any more. It screwed me up before because I didn't know what it was down there. But now I know. So maybe it's not too late, maybe I can do this man-woman thing right, like other people." I laughed apologetically. I knew how hard it had been on my family, over and over opening up to some new man, hoping for the best, watching him disappear a few months or years later.

Scott touched my hand. "Mom," he said firmly, as if to get my attention. "You think you're fixed now. It's all done. But it doesn't work that way."

When they went off to their State jobs the next day, looking like magazine success ads, I watched them from the living room window. I always felt tenderly cared for when I stayed at their house. Even though Scott had gotten the worst of things as a child, he had somehow found a way to forgive me.

My other son, Mike, shielded himself from entanglement in my life by refusing to hear about it. My time with his family had been focused mostly on my granddaughter. Lea and I both liked horses. I decided to try and draw a horse for Lea.

I got out Joyce's drawing paper and colored pens, feeling deeply unsettled. Using my left hand, I drew only scribbles at first, then a house emerged, the way a child would draw it, square, with simple square windows and a black door. Over the top, I drew a huge red penis. Looking at it, I felt dizzy and unaccountably frightened. I scribbled a black felt tip over it, in jagged strokes, over and over, until the shape disappeared.

I wadded up the paper and threw it in the fireplace on some scraps of kindling and set a match to it. The fireplace started to smoke and before I could get the damper open, the house was filled with smoke. Guiltily, I opened all the windows and doors, fanning the smoke out like it was something evil.

Then I drove to the Arden Mall and in one of the finest stores, looked through the women's dressy suits.

When Joyce and Scott came home that night, the house still smelled of smoke. "I burned some papers," I explained. "I forgot to check the damper."

"You don't have to look so guilty," Joyce said, laughing.

After dinner, I showed them the suit I had bought that day, a very expensive suit, off white, with a satin collar and satin-covered buttons. Joyce and Scott looked at each other in astonishment. It was the kind of suit one would get married in.

When I returned to Brighton, Carl met me at the airport. He took me to a jewelry store to pick out rings. I felt strangely high, lightly hysterical, even made odd jokes.

"Diamonds?" the clerk asked. "A stone?"

"How about granite."

The clerk gave me a puzzled look. "Isn't that what they make tombstones out of?"

We picked out a simple silver ring. "What would you like engraved on it?" the clerk asked.

"How about return to sender?" I said. Carl laughed, while the clerk's forehead creased in bewilderment.

I told Susan, "I don't know what's happening, or why. I feel like Cleopatra, floating downstream on a barge."

Susan laughed. "Carl's marrying you. You're not marrying Carl." Susan had a good marriage. She was glad I would be settled into Brighton, be part of the community, part of a respected family.

Carl called several times a day now. When I didn't stop by his house, he dropped by mine. He pressed for a wedding date. "Carl, it's too soon. You've got to give me time. Maybe next spring." He pleaded health insurance issues. If we waited past his next birthday, his health insurance would go up.

I felt pressured. We quarreled about it. He wrote a prenuptial agreement to guarantee me financial security for the rest of my life.

I left work early one Friday and we drove to a justice court in a neighboring county. "This is just a formality because of the insurance," I reminded him. "We are not really married."

But after the simple ceremony, with the ring on my finger, the women clerks congratulating us—"What a handsome couple!"—I felt married. I left with my hand through his arm, feeling like the bride on top of the cake. I felt cherished, cared for, protected.

As we drove to his condo to spend our first night together, I could feel tension rising. Carl put his hand on my thigh, rubbed it back and forth on my nylon stocking. "Carl, don't do that when I'm driving."

He took his hand off with an exaggerated, naughty boy, motion. "We're married now, you know."

"No, we're not. Carl, I don't know what I'm going to be like at the condo. I haven't had sex since the lid came off the incest. I don't know how I'll be about sex anymore."

"I find it very amusing, actually, how this very experienced woman becomes this frightened child." He patted my leg.

At the condo, I hurried into my swim suit and went down the stairs to the pool. It was late, and the complex was silent. Only a few lights shone from the patios onto the palms that reached toward the overhead dome. The palms, the tropical plants, the warm waters were real enough, but the place had an ominous artificial quality, as if it were made of plastic. I swam laps for awhile. Carl came down. "It's getting late. Aren't you coming up?" I wrapped in a towel and went up the stairs through the palms and azaleas.

I closed the bathroom door and locked it, stood in the warm shower a long time, dried my hair, put on a short satin night gown, a mere wisp of fabric on thin straps. Then I pulled on a heavy robe.

When I left the bathroom, Carl was waiting with his toothbrush and shaving kit.

I avoided his grasp as I passed him, sat on the edge of the bed, listening to the toilet flush, the water turning off and on as he shaved. I tried to distract myself by looking around the room. I focused on a large Chinese chest at the foot of the bed, concentrating on its brass intricacies, on its mysterious exotic carvings of cranes and water lilies.

When Carl bounced into the room, happy and eager, wrapped in a small towel, he startled me. For a moment, I became a terrified child. I burst into tears. Carl put his arms around me and held me, rocking back and forth, as I had told him to do if I had a flashback. "But I loved my daddy," I whimpered between sobs. Over and over, "I loved my daddy."

As I breathed deep into my belly, long slow breaths, the room around me swam into focus. Carl wasn't distressed. "Nothing to worry about," he said. "Just a flashback. I'll sleep on the couch."

The next evening he took me to the finest restaurant in town, looking handsome and dignified, his silk tie blending nicely with his fine wool jacket. As I sat across from him in my Designer Circle slacks and silk jacket, I practiced the role of the younger wife of a wealthy gentleman. I worked very hard not to remember the night before. We touched glasses across the table. My new ring sparkled.

Back in Brighton, we returned to our separate houses, occasionally going out or watching television together. One night, we watched an old drama about a wealthy elderly landowner who had taken in his orphaned niece. Carl leaned heavily against me, one arm around me, the other hand stroking my leg. As the scenes of evil seduction unfolded, I began to feel ill. I pleaded a headache and hurried to my car. On the way home, my vision became so blurred and distorted, I had to pull off the road. Waves of nausea passed over me. It was the program, I knew that. But Carl wasn't an evil count seducing a young girl, I reminded myself, as my breathing evened out and I moved back onto the road.

"I am not going to allow my past to ruin my future," I wrote in the journal.

I agreed on a small wedding in California during my Thanksgiving break. That same afternoon while I was playing the piano and Carl was reading the paper, my vision went askew, a jagged headache cracked down. "It's a migraine," Carl told me. I'd never had one before.

"I am freaking out with anxiety," I told Susan at lunch. "I don't know if I can do this."

"Everybody feels that way before they get married."

"I'm just going to mess it up again."

"You'll do fine."

The wedding was beautiful; I in my white suit, feeling more like fifty than sixty, Carl looking the elegant elder gentleman, in his black suit and vest. We were surrounded by both our families, delighted for us—the single college professor finally settling down with the comfortably wealthy widower. "How fortunate that they found each other to share their later years." I enjoyed the role, Jackie to his Onassis.

As I sat next to Carl in the dining room of a small hotel in Sacramento, I realized it was exactly like one I had recently dreamed about, with art galleries along its halls. In the dream, I kept looking at the pictures while my friends ordered for me. Is that what I'd been doing? Looking at pretty pictures while my friends ordered my life for me? Now our friends and families banged their forks on crystal goblets for the bride and groom to kiss. The back of my neck felt pressured, tight. I smiled brightly, turned to Carl lovingly, and we kissed.

Afterward, I felt some relief. It was over, done. I was a wife. We traveled in California, returned to a big reception in Brighton, with all my colleagues from work and his big fun-loving family.

At Christmas, we took a cruise to the Bahamas. I sent cards of the cruise ship to all my friends. I got up early in the morning and jogged on the deck while Carl read the paper. I went on shore for a snorkeling expedition while he did crossword puzzles. I took short walks with him in portside towns.

Back home again, I spent long days at the University. It was pleasant to come home to a warm house with a fire going and dinner cooking, pleasant to have friends to dinner, to visit with his family. I wrote friends, "I can't imagine living alone and lonely again." I smiled a great deal. I was attentive and pleasant to Carl, played many evenings of Scrabble with him.

Dreams continued to haunt me. In one, Carl and I are in the church we were married in, but I am caught carrying drugs. They look like M & M candies. I try to pass them off to my partner, but his pockets are transparent. I know what the dream is telling me: I have been drugging myself with sugarcoated pills, while Carl's pockets are transparent; I have clearly been bought.

Nights became difficult. I had no interest in sex. He liked to dance in the bedroom, singing fragments of old romantic songs from the thirties. "Tea for two and two for tea..." "We're happy in my blue heaven." I found his attentions tolerable, even pleasant sometimes, as long as the lights were out and music played at our bedside.

Although he talked a great deal about how virile he was, how his impotence was temporary, it became more and more evident that it wasn't. My incest memories made oral sex repugnant to me, so frustration was building.

One night, when Carl was especially eager, pulling me into his arms, throwing himself on top of me, I let go of my resistance and allowed myself to respond wholeheartedly. After several fumbling attempts, he could not enter me. I was let down, angry at the big build up. I covered my disappointment, patiently reassuring him, "Sex is not that important."

That night I dreamed:

I am on a battlefield of dead soldiers. One soldier starts to rise, and I see a woman is with him, a plain woman, a plains woman, rising from the dead. As they slowly lift themselves, I see under them a little sheep dog coming to life. I say to myself in the dream, I've seen this movie before.

I knew it was the plain reality of my own self, my own animal self, rising from a field of impotence, of dead soldiers.

I began to avoid Carl. I stayed in the bathroom for long periods in the morning. I stayed at work late. I read late in the night after he went to bed, pleading class preparation.

One night, as I was undressing for bed, I heard him coming up the stairs. I rushed to get into my nightgown before he saw me. Was this the same woman who had been comfortable on nude beaches, who used to run around the house naked, who was inordinately proud of her body? Just as I reached for my gown, Carl crowed from the doorway, "Caught you!" I wanted to run screaming from the house.

Instead, I crawled into bed and turned on the radio, forcing myself to think about the music. By the time he had brushed his teeth and tended to his bedtime chores, I had half drifted off to sleep. When he leaned from his side of the bed to kiss me, I jerked awake. "No!" I cried, my heart racing. He pulled back in mock astonishment. "You'd think I was going to rape you."

"I'm sorry, " I said, my heart still pounding. "You startled me."

After lying wide-eyed for hours I got up, went to the other room, and sat in meditation. "Holy Spirit, help me," I repeated, over and over. The answer came to me as clearly as a spoken voice. "It will have to get worse before it gets better." I cried when I told Carl about it. "I don't want it to get worse."

He did not seem to comprehend the seriousness of what I was saying, only laid out the morning cereal bowls, as usual. I often felt that he did not see, did not want to see, what was happening to us.

Yet at some level he did. He became anxious. His attentions intensified. He followed me about the house. If I was reading, he wanted to know what it was. If I went upstairs to rest, he followed me up.

"What are you doing?"

I would sit up it bed, "What do you think I'm doing? Why do you wake me up to ask if I'm asleep?" Then I would feel guilty for overreacting.

He doted on me, asking if I had enough warm clothes on when I went out into the icy winter, if I'd taken my vitamins. When I protested, he sang, "Take good care of yourself, you belong to me."

I pleaded with him to focus on some other interest. "Please, I need breathing room,"

"This is just love, my love" he said, patting my hand. "This is what married people do. This is how we care for one another. You're not used to it, that's all. You've never had it."

I considered the possibility that he was right, that I would get used to it.

In February I was travelling to Costa Rica to make a presentation on women writers at the International Women's Congress. I felt like I was fleeing from Carl as I carried my suitcases out to the car at five o'clock in the morning. I could barely manage to go back inside to give him a farewell kiss. He was sitting at the dining room table in his blue terry bathrobe. "Do you have your tickets? How about your camera?"

"Carl, I have been packing for trips like this for years. You're not my father. Please, stop it." I calmed myself, sighed. "Yes, I have my camera and my tickets."

It was still dark as I drove to the airport. I wrested myself from my guilty preoccupation to look for the turnoff that would take me to the airport. My headlights glanced off snowy fields. The road was clear, the asphalt shone black. That early in the morning, there were no cars on the road, except far ahead, coming toward me, one wavering set of lights. I couldn't imagine where they were coming from; my road ended shortly ahead. I saw the stop sign, saw the other car suddenly swerve in front of me. It took a split second to get my foot off the gas and onto the brake. I was on ice. Black ice. I plummeted forward, hit the rear of the other vehicle, and my car careened off the road into a snowbank.

I pulled my seatbelt off, plowed through the snow toward the other car. With relief I saw its passengers spill out. No one was hurt. I even caught my plane to Costa Rica. But I could not forget that moment when my foot would not move fast enough.

One night when I couldn't sleep I wrote a poem, or rather, it seemed to write itself:

> *Sometimes a great sadness*
> *a deep deep canyon and*
> *I'm afraid I've left the river forever*
> *suspended on this narrow wavering*
> *curve of bridge—too far now*
> *to jump—a desperate plunge—*
> *No suicidal I*
> *wait 'till it comes to rest*

then take another step—

setting rope and lathe swaying again—

and yet again

that jut of land—rock of Gibraltar—hulks before

linked to the river

below

but by so great a distance.

I did not understand the poem as I wrote it. But I recognized some familiar feelings. I felt myself clinging to the delicate suspension bridge of my marriage, felt the yawning disconnection from my essential self, felt the great sadness.

I made an appointment with a recommended therapist closer to home than Larry was. It was clear now that the secrets surrounding the child of the past were not completely dealt with. I was trying to build a life over the top of something unrecognized and destructive.

"It's incest issues," I told the receptionist this time. "It's urgent. They're ruining my marriage."

3

Learning from
the Fathers

It would be two weeks before I could see the therapist. Even a day seemed too long. But how could I claim emergency status? I was doing my job well. There was no violence involved.

Carl and I had agreed to postpone any sexual activity. Still, everything he did irritated me. "I feel like a cat shut in a box with a dog," I told Susan, nearly in tears.

Carl's family invited him for a week in California. "I don't want to leave you when you're so disturbed."

"Oh, go, please go. I'll be fine. I'll go back over to my place. Ann's away, and there's a lot I need to do there." I could barely conceal my relief.

An hour after leaving him at the airport, I was shoveling the snow off the back deck, making hot chocolate in the kitchen, sprawling on the couch, watching the sunset blaze down through the clouds on the other side of the frozen lake. It was Friday. I had a whole weekend to myself. I went to sleep peacefully that night with Vivaldi's *Four Seasons* on the stereo.

I dreamed: *The child roams the dark house. Moonlight falls through mesh curtains across the polished hardwood floors. Each piece of furniture hovers, coming to life at night; the stuffed armchair, the massive encircling couch, the tall lamp with its outcurved arm. Crocheted doilies gleam like snow. The silk fringe on the lamp shade ripples. She stands entranced, a heavy hammer tugging at her wrist, its head dragging on the floor.*

She walks through the kitchen, the chrome toaster reflecting her image, round face and square cut hair, rounder in the curves of the toaster. The teapot with the whistle on the spout is on the front burner. She reaches up to touch it. It is cold.

Down the hall, dim lights shaped like flames, high above her head, light her way on either side. She stops in front of her parents' bedroom. The door is slightly open. As she looks, it opens further, as if to let her through. She enters. There is no moonlight here. The shades are down. From the hall, light spills across the carpet, across the chenille bedspread, leaving black balls of shadow behind each tuft. Under it, her father and her mother sleep close against each other, one mound.

The hammer pulls her toward the bed. Her arms surge with power, they feel huge, larger than her body. Her mother stirs. "Baby, is that you?" Her voice high, like a sleepy song.

The child backs away, the blood draining from her hands.

In the hall, she lets the hammer go. Softly, the head falls on the carpet. The child goes into the bathroom and standing on a small wooden stool, turns on the faucet. With both hands she holds a cup until she feels water spill across her fingers. When she drinks, it spills over her chin, down her neck, onto the front of her print flannel gown. She wipes her chin with her sleeve and goes back to bed.

I woke from that dream with a guilty start. The wind whipped snow against the bedroom windows, howled across the frozen lake. I reached for the bedside lamp, looked around at the familiar room, the pine dressers, the flowered chintz curtains. I pulled the down comforter over my shoulders, relieved to find myself in my own bed, alone, in my own house.

The red letters of the clock told me it was a dark three o'clock. I reached for my thick terry robe, wandered down the hall to the kitchen, turned up the thermostat, put a cup of tea in the microwave.

In contrast to the stormy night, the house seemed to wait in stillness, my strewn books and magazines, the wool throw over the couch. I picked up a *Time* magazine, opened it to the cover story, *Date Rape. One out of every four women has experienced rape....* I threw it back down. Although my helpless rage was always connected with rape, I reassured myself I had never been raped. "I'm one of the lucky ones," I often said.

But that child in my dream was so angry she wanted to murder her parents. Was it, I wondered, that one incident in the basement with her father that made her so angry? Would that alone create such a destructive pattern so many years later?

In a cabinet, under a box of gift wrapping, I found my father's tattered photo album, lay it open on the table. I took my tea out of the microwave and turned on the light over the album, which had most of its black pages torn from their string bindings. Before he died, my father had torn the pictures from the album pages, leaving written explanations lost in fuzzy black felt smears. I sat down and tried to read the pencil marks, etched more than fifty years ago, on the backs of white-edged snap shots.

With a magnifying glass I looked again at a picture of myself as a two-year-old. My plump little body is planted firmly on a tricycle, my face is open and round as the sun, as warm. My eyes as clear as the sky around me, my smile as innocent as the chipmunk my round cheeks resemble. Clearly untroubled, unafraid, unconcerned, unselfconscious, unconcealing, the bright face turns to the photographer in nothing more complex than delight with the ways the pedals go down under the push of her sturdy legs and make a wheel turn.

She is both me and not me, I realized. I compared that picture with another snapshot, taken a little later. Wearing a short cotton dress, I am sitting on my father's lap. One of his hands encircles my round buttocks, the other clasps the bare inside of my thigh. My face is clouded now, an eyebrow pulled tense, knotting the forehead, a look of bewilderment, puzzlement, confusion. One foot twists awkwardly inward, as if pulling against itself. I am perched, rather than settled; my body pulls upward like a frightened bird.

Images of cracking tile, breaking glass, flash across my mind. A headache twists until my vision blurs, turns the photo into a split and fuzzy image. I remember a dream when a voice told me, "The squirrel has the secret of the ancient man."

I ask the child in the snapshot, Were you his little squirrel? His little love bunny? His soft furry animal? Love bucket? I hear a child laughing. I feel euphoric, my back is straight, my feet solid on the pedals of my tricycle. There is sunshine and blue sky and light everywhere. I feel light.

"Daddy's little Peter Rabbit," my father's voice says, laughing.

The child happily repeats, "Daddy's little Peter Rabbit. Daddy's little Peter Rabbit."

The man laughs again, but this time there is something frightening in it, innuendo, an embarrassed sneer. My chin quivers. I want to go back to the euphoria of innocence. "Daddy's little squirrel." I feel my mouth and cheeks pull up, round, squirrel cheeks, then my mouth distorts, twists. I feel the sweat of big hands on my bare round thighs. A flash of heat comes over me. Then my hands go clammy, the room goes dark and cold, and the tears and nausea come. The clear mind, open as the skies, is gone. I can't get it back again.

I leaned into the table, my feet twisted under the chair, trying to recover myself. Breathe, Larry has told me. When the flashbacks come, breathe, deep from your belly. I breathed.

Another photo showed my mother in a neatly tailored coat and hat, standing on the front steps of a small frame house with black window trim. My father worked for the refinery back then. When he walked up those steps after work, I would run with my mother to meet him. Mother always got there first, but he still had another arm to scoop me up, and we would go into the house together. Mother had been only sixteen when she married. Hardly more than a child herself, married to a man seventeen years older.

I examined another picture torn from the album. My father sat casually on the edge of the fender of a car, his black hair sleeked back from a sharp face with deep frown lines between his eyes.

My father liked to tell the story of how he met my mother at the skating rink when she was only fifteen. She'd been the best skater there, he said, swooping by in her short skirt, spinning, looping backward. He bought her a candy apple at a window black-edged with cigarette burns, sticky with root beer. She had laughed over the roar of the roller skates. Helping her off with her high white skating boots, he teased her about her little feet. She pulled off her knee-length stocking and showed him. Her toes were doubled under from wearing shoes too small all her life. Her old man was so tight he wouldn't even buy her shoes.

"I already knew I had to rescue her," he said. "When I took her home, I saw the curtain move, and her old man's gopher eyes glaring at me. I glared back. We each knew a dirty mind when we saw one."

He laughed, embarrassed. "I didn't want to marry her so young, but the old tyrant whipped her and shamed her 'till I couldn't bear it." I pictured my father in a boxlike black coupe, pulling up to a small frame house in the dark of night, my mother darting to meet him, white ribbons flying.

"Little girl," he called my mother. He would come home; "How's my little girl?" The house smelled of furniture polish, and my father's shoes made white marks on the waxed floors. Mother always kept house like that, everything ironed, even the sheets, even our underwear.

He would toss his white cap onto the back of a chair, rakish. He liked to play up his dark good looks by wearing white. "I wanted to walk up those steps always like the man who made her eyes shine at the skating rink."

Was this a family where the kind of things I remembered could have happened? I picked up another photo, a scrawny six-year-old standing stiffly, arms at her sides, eyes squinted shut, broad defensive smile. One leg has bandages taped on it. I saw through my magnifying glass, what looked like cuts below the bandage. Now the small face was clouded, troubled, as it revealed itself to the photographer, and to me, as I went looking all those years later, for the truth of my life.

Knowing that much can be safely revealed under the guise of fiction, I went into my office, pulled out my writing files, looking for a story I had written some years ago. I had never been able to come to grips with it; it couldn't seem to speak for itself. Still, it had vitality and power; I had never thrown it away, hoping someday to finish it. There were parts of it about the two-year-old, written as fiction, but where does fiction come from, except from our experience, reshaped? I skimmed through the pages of type, and then found what I was looking for...

She was a sturdy child with thick hair scissor-cut in a straight Dutch bob. Between the circle of her chubby legs and white high-topped shoes, she struggled to make her inept hands stuff a Jack into his red checkered box. He spilled hopelessly over the edges, grinning. She solemnly pursued her task, pushing the lid down again and again. The clasp would not hold.

Her father picked her up. She felt very tall, so close to the ceiling. She put her chubby fists together to show him her wrists, though there were no marks. "Mamma hurt me. Mamma hurt me, see?"

"What's she trying to say?" he asked, frown lines cutting deep into his forehead.

"She was being a nasty girl. I made her stop, that's all."

Her father held her away from him and shook her. Her legs dangled as if they were sewed on. He looked sternly in her eyes. "Bad girl. Don't say bad things about Mommy."

She never knew what she had done wrong, back then. Her mother could become, at any moment, a witch, terrifying, like the one in Snow White, beautiful even in her powerful fury, eyes black with rage. "I told you not to do that! Do you want me to cut off your hands?"

I could still hear the shrill voice. I remembered twisting away, trying to free my hands, trying to ward off the stinging blows of the twisted wire hanger. I continued reading.

The bedroom door would close behind her mother's printed cotton dress and she would be left alone to whimper until her arms went numb. Light filtered through the window shades, slanting across a chintz dresser skirt with pink roses and pale green leaves.

She would wake to the feel of her mother's hands, freeing her deadened wrists. The witch was gone, and in her place, Snow White herself, soft, smelling of bath powder, murmuring, "There now, it's all right now," taking the child into her lap, rubbing life back into her legs and arms.

I put the story down, haunted by its connection with the child in the dream. If my father molested me, and my mother whipped me for my sexuality, small wonder the child wandered the house with murder in her heart.

Like a detective, I went through a cardboard box of tattered, handwritten journals, kept for years, looking for connections, looking for something, anything, in the brief flat accounts of my daily life, my occasional desperate visits to therapists, that might help me now.

I found entries made twenty years ago, notes scrawled by hand in a spiral binder, often difficult to read, sometimes broken by black angry scribbles. They told of visits to a psychologist when I was teaching in El Paso, Texas. The journal showed that even then, I had been trying to open the forbidden door to the basement.

In Dr. Fosworth's office this morning, remembered being two, sitting on the kitchen floor, looking up at my mother at the stove, her back to me. I wanted to reach up to her, but knew I was not to bother her. Behind my right shoulder is a basement door. Something terrifying is behind that door. What is it? Fosworth asks. I don't know, I say.

I was in El Paso five years. How could I have left my family and friends in California? First for a job in El Paso, then for one in Minnesota. Was I thinking they could only love me at a safe distance? Or that I couldn't love them if they were too close? I had never been able to hang onto anyone, neither sons nor lovers.

The therapist had one explanation:

Lucretia Borgia, Fosworth said after I told him how I'm attracted to men until they move in then I back off. You want to emasculate them, he said, That made me laugh at first, then I cried. He said the only things we're afraid of are the things at the subconscious level; we've got to relive them. I said, but this is all conscious, I remember it, the problems are still there.

A vivid dream after the visit to Fosworth gave a different explanation:

I am in some sort of booth with another woman. The end of the booth is a separate sealed-off section and a child has gotten in there and locked herself in. We call the main building for help but it seems they are very slow getting there and she must be gotten out at once. There is a key hole about in the center, round and worn like a crankshaft hole. I tell her that if she puts her arms through this place and turns them, we can get her out. I know this means both of her arms will be cut off getting her out, but it must be done. She does this. I reach in and pull and one arm comes out and I toss it on the floor. Though I know it will horrify my partner, I'm busy getting the child out. She is not screaming or crying, just doing as she is told. She is out cold when I get her out. I ask my partner for the two arms. Sometimes they can sew them back on. I wrap the arms up with the child, in butcher paper. The uniformed men finally come from the main gate. I'm angry. They are too late. I pick up the wrapped package and holding the child who is stiff and hard, I wail for what's happened to her.

As I read the dream, I felt that wail from deep in my own soul.

I knew my dreams were messages, metaphors for the psychological-spiritual inner world, revealing the truth that my rational mind denied. The dream confirmed that something had happened back there which forced the child into isolation. To get out, the child must give up her arms, her ability to reach out, to grasp, to hold.

But the smaller child in last night's dream had powerful arms. I remember feeling that those small arms could kill. Did the older child have her arms cut off, her feelings cut off, because those strong arms could kill the only ones she loved?

I picked up another photograph. Sturdy and awkward, a self conscious twelve-year-old, still in braids and bobby sox, clowns for the camera. I found another story I had written about that twelve year old. I sat in the snowy night, alone in my house by the side of a frozen lake, with the picture and the story.

Learning From The Fathers

We lived in Clarksville then, one movie theater, two churches, six bars, two drive in restaurants, one on each side of town, next to the gas stations. We were on our way home from the movies, my sister and I in the separate world of the back seat, saturated in romance after three hours in front of a huge screen in a darkened theater. My father drove, as always, my mother sat looking straight ahead, a foot or so from him, worn leather purse between them on the long front seat. We could have walked, we lived only a few blocks from downtown, but nobody walked then. To walk would mean you could not afford a car. Our black '38 Ford was ten years old, but it was kept like new. People always notice whether your shoes are shined and your car is polished, my Dad said.

My body was still living in the fantasy of the screen world; my hair was not braided but cut and shaped to fall softly around my face, my thin lips were red and lush, my eyes were the wide and innocent eyes of June Allison. Somewhere out there, beyond the street lights and the gasoline stations was Van Johnson, wholesome, gallant, freckle faced, protective. Not like the boys in school, who held my elbows together behind my back to see if I had breasts yet, laughing as my face flamed red.

I don't remember where our brother was, probably at the roller rink, arching into a backward circle, teeth bared in a knowing smile for the adoring girls, whose short plaid skirts whipped smooth against their thighs as they skated. He'd taken me once. I'd been startled at how different he was from the silent sullen teenager who sneaked up the basement stairs to avoid our father.

As we approached the White Spot Cafe, my father put out his arm to signal a turn, and I realized with pleasant surprise, we were going to stop. My mother worked there in the daytime, just until things picked up, my father said, and he usually stayed away. He was embarrassed that his wife was working, but he had a good job now, a real job, driving a beer truck through the winding hills to the little crossroad stores and bars.

Still assuming June Allison's domestic beauty, I climbed eagerly out of the car, glad I was wearing my new coat, red with a black velvet collar. My father, holding the car door open, eyed me critically. "Stand up straight. And button your coat." The feminine frothiness slid from me like the mirage it was. Standing straight and buttoned, my sister and I preceded our parents into the bright lights of the White Spot, slipped onto the red and chrome stools around its gleaming chrome bound horseshoe counter. My father, putting the menu aside with a flourish, ordered "Two cherry cokes and two coffees, Florence."

"Comin' up, Ed," Florence called back, continuing to lay out coffee cups and apple pie a la mode for the only others there, an elderly man wearing a plaid Pendleton shirt with a tie, like my Dad and his wife, almost absurdly smaller than he. Her gray white hair was rolled in a severe bun at the base of her skull. Her lack of makeup and her cube heeled shoes told me they were probably Seventh-day Adventists.

I traced the smooth curve of an empty Coca Cola glass, played with the ice and straws, eying the banana split picture on the wall. I knew without being told that would be too much money. Mother sat quietly, hardly saying anything to Florence when she brought our order. When we stopped in after school in the daytime to see what our chores were, she and Florence were like a couple of girls, smiling and close with each other. Florence was probably ten years younger than Mom, about twenty two, her blonde hair rolled loosely under a net, her broad forehead smooth, sure of herself. "You got kids that big?" she'd say. "Gee, you musta' been a baby yourself when they came along."

"Sixteen with the first," my mother said, looking kind of shy, yet pleased and proud. I didn't like the way my mother was when she was at the White Spot with Florence, girlish in that white uniform with the short skirt and low white shoes. She was never that way around home; there she was Mother, making sure the buttons were sewed on Dad's shirts and dinner was ready when he got home from work. Or like now, with Dad, in her best blue Saturday night dress and black platform shoes with very high heels, drinking her coffee carefully so not to spill the heavy cup. Dad lit her cigarette with his monogrammed lighter, and she leaned into his hand, taking long graceful drags. The smoke drifted, exotic, alluring, foreign as the Camel on the package.

Then, though no car had pulled up outside, the door opened and a woman came in, about my mother's age, a pretty woman. But there was something terribly wrong, something that made her leap into focus as she stood staring silently at us, her red hair torn from its pins and straggling over her face, mascara smeared around her stunned and stricken eyes, muddy fingers, broken red nails, groping at the place where her yellow dress was torn from its lace yoke.

For a split second of silence we stared at her. I thought someone would leap forward to help, to wash her face and comb her hair, to bring her fresh clothes. Others would gather to hear her story, the way they did back when Dad was working in the orchards and Mrs. Osborne fell off a ladder. But no one did.

The couple on the other side of the counter looked at each other. The old gentleman made a slight motion of his chin, directing his wife to turn away, as if shielding her from something unpleasant.

Florence's hand, gripping a white towel, halted on the counter, my father's heavy restaurant cup stopped for a fraction of a second on its trip to the saucer, coffee spilling slightly from the edge. Mother's hand went to her own short carefully waved hair, as if it too might be tangled and muddy. A moth flew into the neon light behind the woman's head, flapping and flapping.

I knew there had been some kind of mutual recognition among the people in the White Spot, an instant when everyone was of one mind. The air was charged with it. The moth beat itself against the light. It dipped and fell.

In silence, the woman moved forward a step. The waitress reached a finger into her change apron, motioned to the phone booth outside under the street light, lay a nickel on the counter. No one looked at anyone else. As the woman left, I saw mud across the shoulders of her short stylish wool jacket. One silk stocking sagged around her ankle. I wondered what happened to the other. Her high heel, bent awry, left a distorted island of mud on the shiny black and white tiles.

Florence resumed wiping the counter. My father, embarrassment in his voice, asked loudly for a napkin. Mother, her cheeks burning under discreet oblongs of rouge, stared at her saucer. The old couple ate their pie.

Through the fluorescent signs in the window, I saw the woman tug at the warped wooden door of the phone booth, confused and ineffective.

I wondered at the enormity of what she must have done, had allowed to happen to her, to be so silently and brutally cast out by these good people. I felt her terrible isolation, her disgrace, her awesome aloneness. I saw her accept this unspoken shunning; it spoke even in the curve of her shoulders as the booth closed behind her. And I decided that whatever it was that had happened to her, I would never never let it happen to me. I would wear my hair like June Allison, and it would never happen to me.

I wrote that story exactly as I remembered it, and until I wrote it, I had no conscious awareness of the significance of the incident. At some level, I already understood the unspoken ways women learn about sex and violence, how they were expected to respond to it, how they learn who is to be the victim, who is to be blamed, who is to be protected. The memory had remained in my mind, with all its details, the way a hook remains in the mouth of a fish, trailing a broken leader.

As I read the story again, looking for clues to my own psychology, I realized that the patriarchy in which I grew up, the rule of the fathers, all by itself carried cause enough for powerless rage.

And what about the mothers? What did I learn from my mother? A story I wrote about my teenage years, after my father and mother had saved enough money to buy a little roadside bar and restaurant, showed how girls learn to be women, how they are taught guilt.

Roadside Trinity

When Mary first came I was pumping gas, not usually girl's work but patriotic with a war on. In my photo album, the one I decorated with a wood-burning set, I look long and gawky in denims and tee shirt, pointy breasts like dredged hills, first permanent exploding like the sun around a solemn face. I liked pumping gas, liked the smooth, round handle in my palm, liked watching the gas surge into the glass, heavy red liquid flowing deeper with each long stroke of the handle. Never thought about why.

In those days you could get a beer in the store while I filled your tank, cleaned the windshield, checked oil and water. Road got steep going into the mountains, and water could boil off before you got to Kyburz. You could maybe take a punch or two on the board for 5¢, win a box of Samplers or a gold horse with a clock.

When Mary rolled up in an old '37 Ford pickup truck with the door off the driver's side and one headlight gone, the radiator was boiling, steam pushing through the cap.

"Boy, I don't think there's one thimble of gas left," she laughed. "Worrying since Kyburz." She slid off the seat, where springs showed through torn leather, laughing like she had just done something special.

I looked up at her, me, a tall string bean myself. I always felt so big around my five-foot mother, but this woman was nearly six feet tall. Not mannish, though. Her print dress was poured full in front and her waist wasn't small but curved into broad, smooth hips. As she swung through the screen door, I could see Bud look up from his beer, then drop his head, maybe because he had a paunch and dragged one leg when he climbed into the cab of his Peterbilt.

The screen door slammed shut behind the cotton dress that came just to the middle of her sturdy knees, sheathed in nylons with seams very straight, showing off the curve. Even though she'd been driving all day on those springs, her blue dress looked crisp as new snow, and her heavy hair kept a neat roll in an invisible net.

I'd never seen a woman driving a truck before. Maybe she'd never seen a girl working pumps before, either. I folded back the side of the hood and was reaching for the radiator cap when she rushed out, Dr. Pepper in one hand. "Don't touch that, Babe, it's still boilin'." She got the hose, ran water over the hissing radiator herself, keeping dress and chalk white shoes clear, laughing. I liked the way she looked out for me.

When she went back in, I could hear her talking with my father, whose voice brightened when there were pretty girls around. Soon, I figured, he'd be telling her stories about how he used to race cars when they still had board tracks back in Indianapolis.

The truck took four dollars worth of gas. I was afraid I shouldn't have filled it. Most people filled up in Placerville where gas was cheaper. "Took fifteen gallons," I said to her, as if I needed to blame the truck.

"Could I give it to you in a few minutes, hon?" she asked, not at all mad. Then she and my father went to the office in back, where Coke cases were piled to the ceiling, adding machine tapes curled across the desk, and credit books lined a homemade rack, names printed neatly as if in deference to neighbors going through hard times. There was only a curtain over the door. I could hear my father say skeptically, "Got to be twenty-one to work behind the counter. I sell beer."

"Turn twenty-one tomorrow," she said, too quick.

My father laughed, came out, and said, "Put the gas on the books." I knew then he liked her because we never put gas on credit. Groceries sometimes in winter when people got laid off from the lumber mills or orchards, but never gas. "They can stay home if they're broke," my father would say. I wrote up the four dollars, and she signed across the yellow-lined pad, Mary McMurphy, so strong that her name sprawled black even across the carbon, where my own writing barely came through.

My mother didn't like his hiring Mary. When they closed up that night, I listened while I swept coffee grounds across the floor with a push broom, putting slugs in the arched-rainbow jukebox, playing "You Belong to Me." Mom was cleaning the grill with a brick wrapped in burlap. "We don't need any more help, honey, with the girls watching the pumps and keeping the cabins made up. We already have two good waitresses."

"Business is growing," my father answered in his best Chamber of Commerce voice. "Look at this register, best day yet. Time you quit working so hard, let Mary do some of that." He sounded proud to offer her an easier life. Mom's freckled face flushed with pleasure, but she had to make sure nobody would think for a minute there was really going to be any indecent leisure. Brushing her hand across her forehead, she pushed at escaping strands of hair, though there were never any escaping. She wiped her already dry hands on the print apron she'd made of leftovers from kitchen curtains.

"Well, it would be nice to put in some fruit trees where the new house is going to be. Make Helen some new skirts for school. Her knees are already sticking out. If that one gets any taller...." She shook her head in despair of my future if that happened.

My mother was always saving. Gifts put away for some special time, best dishes saved for company, best dress saved for monthly dances at the Timberino Hall. Bedspreads crocheted evenings square by square saved in lined drawers for the day when the new house was built, away from the noise of the loggers that rolled to a stop from eight in the morning to eight at night, logs thirty feet long and ten feet across dwarfing our little 8-Mile House with its red, white, and blue Standard Oil colors.

Both my father and my mother had something held in about them, like they were walking the fine edge of a precipice and had to watch every step, though Dad did it with more grace than Mom. But Mary was different. Mary was like those frisky dolphins in the nature movies, swimming alongside a ship, having fun, knowing which way to go. She was bigger and more outspoken than women are supposed to be, nearly a foot taller and forty pounds heavier than my mother.

I knew my mother didn't like her, didn't quite trust her, though she never said a word against her. Except the time the liquor salesman, Mack Moretti, took Mary in the back room to tell her a story. Mother said if it was a story he couldn't tell in front of ladies, Mary shouldn't hear it either.

I thought Mary was the most beautiful woman I'd ever seen. I liked to talk while she cleaned up between the lunch hour rush and the dinner rush. She didn't treat me like a kid, just because she was seven years older.

"Hon, what would you do if you could do anything you wanted?" she asked me once, while she wiped hamburger grease off a home-typed menu.

I laughed. "I dunno. Rob a bank, steal Judge Morgan's Packard convertible, bludgeon Nasty Kasty, my math teacher."

"Where'd you get the idea if we did what we wanted, it would just naturally be bad?" she asked.

"I dunno."

I wasn't paying too much attention, fixing a float with vanilla and Squirt. At fourteen I was a walking sponge, listening a lot, not putting much back out, trying to figure out how things fit together. I paused to think about what she said. "That's just the way it is," I ventured. "If people do whatever they want, something bad always happens."

I closed the ice cream box and put the scoop in the water jar. "Or maybe they just teach us that. When I was a kid, they made me go to the dumpy green church off Mosquito Road, you know the one. All those old people kept asking me if I'd been washed in the b-l-o-o-d of the lamb. Spooky."

Mary just laughed. She didn't have much in the way of religion, though she said the usual things, like "God knows," or "God bless," but she said them with brightness, different from my mother who would say, "Only God knows," with her eyes all distant and cloudy, like there was something dark or cobwebs all around.

I sat at the counter, noticing how Mom's Naugahyde stool covers were beginning to come loose around the bottom. The store was quiet at four in the afternoon. We could hear the squeal of the last truck, braking for the turn below our place. That was before they put in the freeway with the access road too far down for business, but that's another story. And what I wanted to say was how much I liked the afternoons when the store was quiet and I could just listen to Mary talk.

"You know what I think?" she said. I knew she'd tell me anyway. She was like that creek that comes right out of the rocks in the canyon. "I think way back somewhere people got awful scared, scared of plagues, scared of starving, scared of saber-toothed tigers. They passed it on to their kids, who passed it on to theirs, and pretty soon, they didn't even remember what they were scared of anymore. You know, like rabbits when the wolves have been gone for years."

I'm thinking now she was free of the guilt that grows on people like cobwebs in a closed house.

When Mary came to work for us, small meannesses of the other two waitresses diminished at first. Minta and Mrs. Matthews, faces showing dark shadows of forty years' endurance, both waitressed to care for large families. They commiserated over their twin burdens, husbands who never earned more than enough to buy their own beer. Minta's white blouse always had a button missing or a gravy splash. Mrs. Matthews had so many shirts and pants to iron that there was no time left for her own clothes. She would wear the same uniform a whole week, if my father didn't get after her.

When Minta and Mrs. Matthews started their complaints, Mary would just laugh and strut to the sink, dumping a load of heavy restaurant ware, swishing a clean towel across the counter. Her lively eyes would shine. "He'd be out on his ear in a week if he was my old man, 'less he had something very special to give me," winking at me. "Must give you something special if you're putting up with it all these years, Minta."

Minta would laugh like a kid getting caught. "Yeah, guess he does at that." Her tired face would brighten for awhile.

The men came just to flirt with Mary. "Hey, Mary, I'd give up my dog and my old lady and go to Hell forever for a night with you." She'd laugh, swish a cloth around the counter. "Now, Mack, you wouldn't know what to do with a woman like me if you had one. I'd straighten out your wandering ways for sure." Mack would grin like the biggest rogue in the county. She had a way of making music of work, kidding, turning over hamburgers, butting milk shakes onto mixers, effortless, moving from motion to motion like a dancer.

When fall came and we felt the coming snow, I sat behind the stove, pretending to do my homework, learning other things. I listened to my father's stories, over and over. The one about the black man he saw running down the street one hot summer night in Indianapolis, head way out in front of his body like a rooster, his throat cut ear to ear, running, my father said, like his body was trying to keep up with his head.

Behind the stove, I learned things my mother never talked about. I learned from the waitresses who was pregnant and who was running around with whom. I wondered how girls could let something so awful happen to them. I learned about unions when the man came and tried to sign Mary up. She gave him a pony toss of her head. "What do I need with a union? Gene pays me good, gave me a raise after a month. If I get sick, I know he'll pay me just the same. Gene doesn't need a union to tell him what's right."

My father smiled, went on laying rows of cigarettes in the glass case, giving the union man fair chance. My mother, doing dishes in back, heard it too. After Mary left, she said, "How come Mary got a raise? Minta's been with us over a year. Where's her raise? ... Helen! Will you turn that jukebox down, please!" That was the closest I'd ever heard her come to yelling, so I turned it way down.

"Minta isn't worth half what Mary's worth," my father said. "Won't keep her counter clean, won't keep buttons sewed on her blouse, customers don't like her nearly as well." My mother didn't say any more but her nose got that pinched look it sometimes got when she had to remind herself that good women don't argue, especially with their husbands.

A few days later, I noticed my mother had started to walk like Mary, swinging her behind, sticking her front out. Moretti, the liquor salesman, ran a comb through his hair, leaving rake marks in oiled rows, slicked down his pencil moustache with his little finger, as he watched her. It didn't look right to me, a tiny woman with not much in front or rear anyway, and besides, she was my *mother*. But I never said anything.

None of us ever said what was really on our minds except Mary. Mary would say, "Hey, isn't that sweater beginning to fill out there? Watch out, kiddo, I saw Mack lookin' you over like a ripe pear." She'd wink at me, and I'd be embarrassed but at the same time feel special as a scraggly colt turning into something beautiful. She started calling me the Personality Kid. When I got chosen for the high-school play, she was the first one I told.

I was so busy with myself that I didn't really notice, though everybody else did, that Ernie Rutherford was coming by more than usual. There were so many men, highway patrolmen, radios fussing, the bread man singing. "I'm Gonna Get You on a Slow Boat to China," fruit workers with white sulfur spray on lace-up boots. Who would notice one man around a lot? Especially Ernie. He was such a quiet guy.

Ernie was the sheriff of El Dorado County, and my father was unofficial mayor of 8-Mile House, so Ernie gave him a deputy star. They worked together when the locals got into trouble. "He's a good boy," Ernie would say about some kid who had helped himself to a car after the Saturday night dance. "Just a few too many hormones. I can keep him out of jail if you keep an eye on him, Gene." My dad would let the kid take the pickup to town for supplies, or have him build a woodshed, anything to make him feel important. Usually, they'd turn out all right.

I liked Ernie. He looked like Alan Ladd in the movies, calm and sure, but way too old for me, nearly thirty. Anyway, Mrs. Matthews said Ernie was hanging around more now because there was something going on between him and Mary, but I never saw it. She treated him like anybody else, kidded him about wearing a gun, keeping a jail. Ernie would just grin and drink his coffee and tell her about the apple trees he planted last spring or about the new colt out on his ranch.

Mrs. Matthews talked more and more when Mary wasn't around, the sheriff being married and all and the closest thing to a hero our little town had. She said Mary'd been seen in Ernie's car, up on old Visman Road, nearly every day. I didn't believe that, and even so, I didn't see what was so bad about it. I rode my horse up there all the time. You could see for miles, hills squared with plowed orchards, bare now, but all white blossoms in spring. Couldn't blame Ernie for wanting to show her that.

When Minta and Mrs. Matthews would talk about it, my mother would get quiet, put the cream back in the refrigerator carefully, as if it were an eggshell. She never said anything and neither did I. "If you can't say anything good," my mother often said, "then don't say anything at all." I suppose now that's why she was such a quiet woman.

One day I came in flushed and excited from riding my horse in the orchards. For the first time I'd really let him go. We tore through plowed rows, scattering leaves and limbs, moving from a hard, jouncing trot to a long, rolling gallop, my hair and his mane flying, the closest I've ever come, then or now, to flying across the crest of the world.

My father and Ernie were alone in the store. Ernie was sitting red-faced, flustered, with a cold cup of coffee in front of him. My father gave me a look, sending me to the back room to do dishes. He was saying something to Ernie about remembering his redheaded wife and Mary's reputation. I wondered why my father was so worried about Ernie's wife. I remembered when Ernie had married the wife of the previous sheriff, my father had said, "Darned if she didn't divorce old Jack when he lost the election and go after Ernie, him as innocent as an eighteen-year-old. Can't say I blame him. Breastworks like a U. S. Fort." Now I heard him saying, "Maybe you better not hang around here for awhile, Ernie."

Mary never seemed to notice that Ernie stayed away. She was her same self, cutting up, swinging around the counter, eyes dancing. I hoped that meant she wasn't seeing Ernie, hadn't been doing what people said.

"Too bad she doesn't show any interest in Bud," my mother said. "Such a nice boy. He'd do anything in the world for her." Unable to keep judgment entirely from her voice, she added, "Besides Bud's single." Sheep-faced Bud. I couldn't believe it.

"Bud's all right for his kind," my father said, "but no match for Mary." Mother gave him a sideways look, tucking her hair under her ears. "You think she's so much," she said, over the sound of the brick scraping the grill.

A few nights later I woke to my parents' quarreling. "I can't help it if he just leaned across before I even knew what he was up to. You know what these Italian salesmen are like," my mother said. "Besides, it was only a little peck." Their voices didn't sound like them at all, exaggerated like stage characters.

My father said, "I figured as soon as I went to Sacramento for a day he'd try something. Well, that greasy-haired Don Juan sure as hell's not going to be hanging around here anymore."

They'd left the door ajar and in the mirror I could see my father lift his chin to get at his tie. He didn't look mad. He looked like a feisty dog that's just run off some stray.

"You're making a fuss over nothing," my mother said, reaching up to redo the knot. There was a glow about her, as if some of that pinched flesh had been plumped out.

"And quit walking that way," my father said, "Like some kind of whore. No wonder."

"You like it well enough when Mary does it," my mother said.

"Mary's Mary," Father said, as if that settled it. My mother looked pleased.

I learned a few weeks later, sitting behind the stove with *Forever Amber* under my Civics book, that Ernie's wife was getting a divorce.

Mrs. Matthews said, "She timed it just right. Election's in September. Now his chances of getting reelected are about zee-row. With her charging adultery and a member of the Eastern Star to boot. He can just kiss that job bye-bye."

"Dunno," Minta said, "Everybody likes Ernie. They know he done a good job, and they know his wife is like a whore when she's had a few drinks."

When Mary came in, Mrs. Matthews tied her scarf tight under her chin, so tight you'd think it kept her head from falling off.

She said to Mary, "Well, I hope you're happy."

She stiff-legged on out, making sure Mary had no time to respond. Surprised, Mary raised her eyebrows at me, then went to scrubbing pots just like nothing had happened.

Setting the table in the back room that night, I said, "Mom, is Mary really wrecking Ernie's life like Mrs. Matthews says?"

"Don't be gossiping about people, Helen. There are all sorts of things we can never know the reasons for." She was charitable enough, but her lips were tight, and her eyes got a faraway look, thinking things she would never say.

I set the plates evenly around the table, laying knives and forks exactly the same distance from each other, carefully. I wished Mary would quit doing things that made people talk about her. I wanted her to get back on the right side.

That night I dreamed I was riding out of the canyon. The road kept sprouting branches ahead of me, like tree limbs, but I would just take any one and go on. My thighs felt huge and fleshy, and the horse hot and rough against them. I was naked, but I wasn't embarrassed. Then Champ got a stone in his hoof. Panicky that someone would see me, I jabbed at it with a paring knife, until the cavity was filled with blood. I screamed for my mother, "Help me!" An old cart went by, my mother pulling it. She didn't see me. On the cart, Mary lay dead, a puffy pile of flesh. I woke with my wrists hurting. I'd cut off the circulation, lying on my hands.

On their day off, Minta and Mrs. Matthews came in wearing dark heavy coats. Mother waited on them, pouring coffee and putting out napkins. "We don't want to work with her," Minta rasped through tight lips. "A woman who breaks up homes and a man's job like that." Leaning across the counter in their black coats, they reminded me of crows.

"None of our business," my mother said, nostrils narrowed as if scenting something on the evening wind.

I felt sick. Muttering something about taking Champ to be shod, I pushed through the screen door, which hadn't yet been taken down for the winter. It made a rickety slam behind me. Near the stable, I picked up a dry manzanita branch, whipped it against a pine until it broke. I tossed the end into buckbrush, stirring up a musky smell. Then I saw Ernie's car, parked off the dirt road. It made me furious. Down the path toward the reservoir, I saw him and Mary, walking slowly and naturally as the sun that was dropping over the ridge.

Mary's voice drifted back. "I'm sorry she's hurting, Ernie," matter-of-fact, as if none of it was her fault.

A few mornings later, my mother left the breakfast table to answer the phone. Three rings meant it was for us. When she came back she stood before my father as if laying before him some terrible evidence. Ernie's wife had slit both wrists. "Blood running clear down the wall under the phone," she said. "Drunk. Couldn't save her."

My father stared a long time at the table, grey-faced. My mother sat down across from him, silent, her new white shoes tucked neatly together under her chair.

Mary came in for work that day looking fresh as always. She didn't sing, she didn't joke, but set about getting the potatoes peeled for the hashbrowns. My mother stayed in the back, washing clothes. I could hear the washer—shump, thump, shump, thump—and the squawk of the wringer as she fed clothes through. Dad kept filling the coolers.

No one mentioned what had happened. I sat at the end of the counter, close to Mary. I wanted to talk to her. I wanted to touch her. I wanted her to cry, tell me she was sorry, anything to show she was not a dangerous woman.

Seeing my troubled face, she asked quietly, "What's going on, Kiddo?" She didn't smile, but I heard the same spirit in her voice, the dolphins next to the ship. I didn't think it ought to be there. I looked at her and hoped my eyes would say that. I didn't know how to talk. She was the only one I ever knew who did.

Mary dried her hands and leaned on her elbows so her eyes were level with mine. She was so careful, as if she knew what she said now was the most important thing she might ever say. Her eyes were alive with light, bright and direct, with as much dignity as I have ever seen.

I looked away.

She touched me, briefly, on the arm. "Hon, listen to me. We all of us every minute have to choose our lives, and just ours. We can't choose anybody else's. They've all got to make their own choices, and she had a right to hers, too, even if she chose anger and spite."

Her eyes wouldn't let me go. The washing machine thudded against soiled clothes. Unaccountably I remembered my father's story, the man running with his throat cut.

I looked down. "But, Mary," my voice came out small and hesitant. "You can't just do whatever you want, you have to think of other people."

She reached out to put her hand on my shoulder. "I know this must be real confusing, Kiddo, just when you're starting to—." I jerked away. I knew she was going to say something about becoming a woman. I didn't want to be like *either* of them. I stumbled out the door, heading toward the canyon. I passed my mother hanging up clothes, reels shrilling as she pulled in the line. She didn't see me. Through my tears, I hardly saw her either.

Mary quit. Some say, the most spiteful, she and Ernie went to Nevada that same day and got married. Nobody in Placerville spoke to either of them for a year or so, but they didn't go to town much anyway. They had enough to do, trying to make a living off that ten-acre ranch. After awhile, people forgot.

Then the freeway opened, with a chain link fence between the highway and the 8-Mile House. Business plummeted to just the locals. On an early summer afternoon, I filled Mr. Matthew's dusty '35

Chrysler with regular, watched it find its way to the access road like a black beetle.

On the other side of the chain-link fence, summer traffic sped to Lake Tahoe. People looked at me from behind glass, distantly curious. Dust hung lazily in the air as I pumped the gas back up, the round end of the lever fitting smoothly in my palm, red gas rushing into the glass with each stroke.

I think of the blood running down the wall under the phone, and the man running in the hot city night, head separated from his body. As the gas surges toward the top of the cylinder, I am unaccountably afraid. My father is coming through the trees from the house, my father, always larger than life, small now under the looming pines. Not knowing he is seen, he walks with his head down. I pump slowly, not wanting to finish. The gas froths up about the four-gallon line.

I think about Mary. I often do. In my mind, she grows with time, like a clear light, closer and closer. I see her getting out of that one-eyed pickup truck, laughing and broke, chalk-white shoes and sturdy body disappearing into the store, twenty years old and looking for a job.

I tell my mother I'm going riding. She looks up from the towels she is folding, looks past my shoulder. "Like Mary," she says, her face pinched and small. "You remind me a little of Mary."

I am quiet, defensive. In another voice, she says a surprising thing. "I always wished I could be like Mary."

I ride Champ into the canyon, sun slanting through dark branches like cathedral light. Ahead, I see the reservoir where Mary walked with Ernie, and the smell of buckbrush is heavy in the air. I gather the reins, prod Champ, he leaps forward. Dirt flying, we gallop over the crest into the orchard. Long-legged and easy, he rises up and down. We float through corridors of pear trees, blossoms scattering, limbs whipping our thighs.

That story was about a woman who knew there were other ways of responding to life besides passive acceptance, even if you were a woman. When I wrote it, I was impatient with years of Father, Son, and Holy Ghost. I wanted to hear something about Mother, Daughter, and Holy Spirit. Mary was a Holy Spirit to me. Every time I read it, I could smell the buckbrush growing under the pines in the foothills of Northern California. I could reconnect with the introspective self conscious girl I was then, and sometimes still am.

Is it truth or fiction? I wondered. We make stories of our lives, whether we write or not. After my father left the refinery, we did move to the mountains, and Mary did come to our roadside business, bringing such a breath of freshness to my life that she still lived in my memories. But a lot had been left out. Left out was my brother John, who was in the Navy at the time, and my sister Beverly.

I envied Beverly. Small like Mother, dark like our father, with a gift for choosing just the right pleated skirt, just the right matching sweater and blouse, she looked like the teenagers in the magazines, white bobby sox tucked neatly over trim well shaved ankles, hair piled in deep waves, bright new lipstick gleaming on her small, pretty face.

With her insecurities hidden under an aloof and mysterious manner, Beverly immediately attracted the attention of one of the best looking boys. "A Senior," I marveled, as we washed the dishes. "And he has his own car!" Beverly's face showed nothing as she wiped off the counter and polished the copper bottom of our mother's best pan. "It's not a real date," she said. "It's just a hay ride."

Our father set down strict rules for dating; he had to meet and approve of Beverly's date when he picked her up, and she was to be in by eleven. While I swept the store, those prohibitions were repeated for my benefit, even though I was not dating yet. The lecture was accompanied by dire warnings: "If you ever get yourself pregnant, don't expect to come home." I didn't dare question that, just kept pushing the broom around the counter stools.

"I don't want to find you pushed out of a car, lying in a ditch somewhere," he said. I was confused and frightened. What did he mean? Were the shy and awkward boys I knew somehow not what they appeared? Were they like werewolves, becoming something else at night?

Beverly came home an hour later than the curfew. I was lying in bed, awake, listening to Dad shuffling the pages of his newspaper, almost palpably watching the clock. Through a crack between the window and the shade, I watched a car arrive with half a dozen other teenagers. I saw Dad go out to meet them, carrying a shotgun. He didn't listen to their explanations; the hay wagon had broken down, there was nothing they could do. He knew their type, he told them. Mortified, Beverly scurried into the house, shamed and embarrassed. She said nothing as she undressed and got into bed. For days she could not bring herself to go to school.

Our father's terrorist tactics had the desired effect on me. "What do you think I am?" I would demand indignantly if a boyfriend tried to get beyond "necking."

Dad would shine his flashlight into our eyes the minute we pulled up in front, or if we managed a moment alone before he switched on the porch light and caught us kissing, he would harangue me all the way into the house. "Tangled up like worms out there. Whore!"

I would fight back, or leave home and stay at a girlfriend's until he apologized. He never pulled a shotgun on my boyfriends, though. I thought that was because Beverly mattered more to him than I did.

Forty years later, remembering, I shook my head and put another cup of water and a tea bag in the microwave. It would soon be getting light. I sat down and tried again to read the pencil marks, etched more than fifty years ago, on the backs of white-edged snap shots, explanations lost in fuzzy black felt smears.

Clues, I was looking for. A response to that child wandering through the dark house, her rage in one hand and her love in the other.

4

True Confessions

My adult years began like the story that I later wrote for *True Confessions* magazine. It was, as promised to them, a true confession, or at least as nearly so as I could make it at the time. I remember being surprised that the illustration in the published copy did not look like my young husband and me.

The "tickler" to the story read: *With so much love, we should have been the perfect family.* I had called the story, *We Didn't Know it Was Child Abuse,* but the editor titled it:

We Never Meant to Hurt Our Little Boy

All through high school, I was interested in Jimmy, though we didn't go together until the last year. I always admired the way he quietly went about succeeding in a lot of things, as if to prove that even though his father was known as the town drunk, he couldn't be judged by that.

Jimmy was the best player on the second-string basketball team. He was also one of the smartest guys in our class. He was great at languages and math, and if his father had any money, he would probably have gone off to a university instead of having to study aircraft mechanics at the junior college. But that was okay because he liked airplanes. On top of that, he had the kind of sullen James Dean good looks that I found attractive.

He had been in my freshman English class, but I was too busy playing Miss Popular to notice him. When I was a Senior, my mother died, and soon after, I let Jimmy know I was interested in him. I'd stop and talk in the hall and all that. He was flattered. After our first date we were a steady pair.

A month later we were in my room while my sister was out. We'd been lying on the bed, listening to records and kissing and kissing and kissing. Then Jimmy's hand began caressing me, and it was like fire. I didn't even want to stop him.

Everybody says how awful the first time is. Well, it wasn't for us. It was wonderful. It was like all the loneliness just dissolved in the excitement and heat of our togetherness. And how I loved the holding afterward—the peacefulness of lying in each other's arms while the sun filtered through the leaves outside the window, through the faded blue curtains, and across the bed.

Finally, we were sleeping together so much we figured we might as well get married after graduation. We talked about having children someday. I'd always wanted three. Jimmy said that was okay with him, but not for a few years. We got a little two-room apartment, and I went to work as a telephone operator to help him through school. Only a few months later I had trouble with my birth-control method, and soon afterward I discovered I was pregnant.

When I told him the news he looked as if he'd just been sentenced to be executed. He threw himself across the bed, face down. "That's the end of school," he said.

"We'll still make it, one way or another. It might just take a little longer," I tried to reassure him. "My folks had us before they were ready, and they got by. My father even said it was the best time of his life, when I was little."

Jimmy didn't say anything.

I sat down beside him. "I'll get an abortion if you want me to," I said. And I would have, even though I didn't want to. He gave me a scathing look. I'd forgotten until that moment that his mother had died of an abortion when he was only five. "Honey, it's different now," I said. Nothing would happen to me."

I put my arms around him, and lay my cheek against the back of his head. He liked it when my hair spilled down across his face. He turned over and grabbed me tightly. I held on to him, and the first thing we knew, we were pulling off our clothes, making wild, abandoned love— lovemaking that always made it seem that nothing else mattered....

I smiled to myself as I read. Our lovemaking had not really been all that wonderful, but the story had to be sold. I continued reading.

Jimmy got a job in an auto shop, cut his classes down to half time, and I quit my job. I fixed up an area in our bedroom for the crib and baby things, and planned on moving it into the living room at night. I thought we were doing just fine.

But from he moment I brought Scott home from the hospital, Jimmy refused to have anything to do with him. He wouldn't even hold him while I took off my coat.

"He'll get over it," our friend Phil said a couple of weeks later when he and his wife, Paula, were visiting us with their nine-month-old baby.

Though Paula tried to comfort me, I had seen her concerned look after dinner. I had just fed Scott and tucked him back in his crib. He was crying a little, the cranky way he always did before he went to sleep. I could see Jimmy was getting tense. "Can't you do something about that squalling?" he said, throwing his cards down.

"If I pick him up now, he'll just start again when I put him back down," I said, feeling helpless. Scott did cry a little more than Brian did, and any crying at all just sent Jimmy into an unreasonable rage.

Phil picked up the cards and dealt a fresh hand. The baby continued to cry. I could see that Jimmy's mind wasn't on the game. The blood vessels were starting to swell in his wrists. Suddenly he pushed the table back, sending coffee slopping all over the cards.

"Hey, take it easy!" Phil said, reaching out to touch him, but Jimmy just brushed past and stormed out.

Tears of disappointment stung my eyes as I walked the baby, his downy head warm and fragile against my cheek, his cries subsiding to halting intermittent bursts. I didn't understand Jimmy's attitude. My own father had been especially good with babies. I guess I just automatically expected Jimmy to be that way, too.

I pushed back my tears and tried to listen to what Phil was saying. He was Jimmy's best friend from high school. Besides, he and Paula were the first in our graduating class to have a baby. His words were reassuring as he proudly picked up their son and swung him over his head. Brian squealed with breathless, trusting joy. I longed for the day I would see Jimmy look at our son with such pride and pleasure.

"It just takes time, " Paula said, giving me an understanding good-bye hug. "For weeks Phil was afraid to even hold Brian." She gave Phil a loving glance as he tenderly tucked his son in a blanket and carried him out the door.

After they left I walked Scott, holding him against my shoulder, patting him gently, hoping a burp or the lulling motion would quiet him before Jimmy came back from wherever he was. Walking around the block in the dark, I supposed. Or down to the corner for a pack of cigarettes. He'd been smoking much more since the baby came.

From the front window of our apartment I could see Paula and Phil in the parking lot, loading Brian and all his accessories into the car. Paula still managed to look as sleek and calm as ever, her pretty hair catching the light as she swung into the front seat. Phil closed it behind her in a protective gesture, walked around, and eased into the driver's seat. The car, a wedding gift from his parents, disappeared around the bend. Jimmy had been too upset to stick around and say good-bye, even though we probably wouldn't see them again for weeks.

When Scott was nearly a year old, some new friends of Jimmy's invited us to meet them for lunch at a restaurant near our place. John and Ginny were both going to the University, and Jimmy wanted to make a good impression. He dressed up in his best slacks and white shirt. "I don't want them to think I'm just a grease monkey," he said, tying his tie. No one ever would. When he dressed up he was really a knockout. I dressed up, too, in high heels and a sun dress. As we walked out the door Jimmy reached over and wiped off Scott's drool with a handkerchief.

At the restaurant Jimmy was trying to tell John about his plans for a future in aircraft engineering. Scott sat in a high chair, banging on the metal tray with a spoon, and practicing new sounds. I could see Jimmy tense, but he went on, explaining how the instructor had chosen him for an outside engine repair job. "He knows all he'll have to do is check it over once and sign it off," he finished proudly.

Just then Scott's cup of milk toppled and splashed on John's shorts. The waitress moved in with a towel and cleaned things up while John and Ginny waited awkwardly, trying to smile. After the mess was cleaned up Jimmy tried again to explain what was so special about the engine job. Scott, confused by all the strangers, especially when the waitress had snatched a cup away from him, looked like he was going to cry. Hurriedly, I gave him his spoon back, and he banged it happily. Jimmy reached over, took the spoon out of his hand and tossed it in front of me. "For Christ's sake!" he snapped.

The abrupt gesture and the loud words frightened Scott further, and he burst into terrified wails.

Jimmy lunged from his seat, grabbed Scott from the high chair, and carried him, screaming with fright, through a sea of staring customers. Ginny gave me a pitying look. I excused myself and went out. As I approached the car I saw Jimmy fairly toss Scott into the back seat, then crawl in behind him. I heard Scott screaming. After a minute,

Jimmy, red faced, went back to "apologize for the kid," while I climbed in the car to quiet our frightened son.

At home a few minutes later, changing Scott's diaper, I was horrified to see huge scarlet welts the shape of a hand across his soft white buttocks. In the bathroom, with the water running so Jimmy wouldn't hear me, I cried and cried....

The story went on to describe Paula discovering the bruises, confronting the narrator with the seriousness of the problem, and naming it child abuse. The narrator defends her husband. One hot night soon after, he erupts in rage again, takes it out on the child, and she finally tells him to get out. She gets a poorly paid job, has trouble getting child care, is miserable and overworked. Then...

One hot and humid Sunday afternoon I was standing at the stove, canning some peaches I'd gotten on sale. It wasn't going well. By the time I'd bought the jars and the sugar, it cost more than buying tins. Then, after all the sticky hard work of peeling and pitting, the peaches were breaking up in the pot and turning a strange brown color.

Scott was clinging to my legs, teething and fussy. I was trying to keep the peaches from burning and scald the jars at the same time. The job required concentration. Scalding water was dangerous. Absently I moved him away. He toddled back and clung to my leg, whimpering.

"Scott, stop it!" I said, giving him a shove. He fell, hitting his forehead hard on the vents of a heavy metal fan. Blood oozed in lines from rising welts on his forehead. As I knelt down beside him he stared at me, his eyes wide in disbelief. I knew exactly what that expression meant. I was the only one he had trusted, and now he could trust no one.

In the story, the mother realizes that she, too, can be pushed to her limits, as her husband was, that they both need help. After taking parenting classes under the tutelage of a kind and understanding social worker, the two are reunited and become happy and considerate parents.

That's the way those kinds of stories have to end. There is a formula you must write by to create valuable little teaching stories, telling the readers how it could be, maybe, in their own lives.

But my own story had not ended that way. It ended with long and bitter quarrels, reconciliations with nothing solved, another unplanned child, and finally, the children's father leaving to go back to school. I had left that marriage, I realized now, with no insight at all into my contribution to the disaster, no realization of why I had chosen the man I chose, or of my own dysfunctional role. His behavior had made it easy for me to believe my only problem had been my husband. Now all I had to do was get a better one.

That pursuit went something like another story I wrote for the confession magazines, whose lead read *kisses that led to terror...*

Our Dangerous Love Affair

When I met Cap, I was twenty-seven, but I didn't have any more experience than a teenager. A small-town girl, I had married at seventeen. Nine years and two children later, there I was, newly divorced and no wiser about dealing with the single life than I'd been at seventeen.

Even before I met him, Cap Capston was a glamorous figure to me. I'd read his columns in the Weekly Observer. Then I got a job as typist at the newspaper, hoping to work my way up to reporter someday. The publisher, Bob Hendrix, explained that the editor was away on a Wyoming hunting trip. Of course, I was curious about Cap as I typed the column he had sent postmarked Jackson Hole. But I thought he was probably an older man like Hendrix, married, with a family and all.

I wasn't prepared for the man who walked in that Monday morning. He was handsome in a rugged, outdoorsy way, his face glowing with good health and the triumph of a successful hunt. He wore a red hunting cap pushed back over his thick hair. With is broad boyish grin, tanned face, and lean body, he looked about thirty-five. It came out later that he was forty-two.

As everyone in the office gathered around him to hear his stories about the treacherous Jackson Hole country, I went about my business, typing, filing, making myself inconspicuous.

I was used to going unnoticed. As a child, my rather severe parents had never thought me pretty. A high-school marriage hadn't helped my self-esteem. We had children before we were ready. To make amends, I spent little time or money on myself. I sewed all my own clothes, scraping by with cheap material, so they looked homemade, I'm sure. I always wore flat-heeled shoes, to apologize for being almost as tall as my husband. He never complimented me, and when others did, he scoffed. I had not yet learned that he downgraded me because of his own insecurity.

I actually felt good when he was gone. I could enjoy my sons instead of trying to hush them all the time. I could do some of the things I liked, instead of always trying to please him. Finally realizing there must be a better life than what we had, quarreling, angry and resentful, I got a divorce.

On credit, I bought two nicely tailored skirts, a sweater, a blouse, and a jacket. I also bought my first pair of high-heeled pumps. I had always liked my hair the way it was, long, simple, so I left that alone. Pretty? I didn't know. But I knew I looked my very best.

Even with the tiny salary, I felt hopeful and excited about my new job. I typed up ads mostly, and short fillers out of the files. Bob Hendrix dictated some letters, slowly enough that my high-school shorthand came back. Some days I wrote letters to the advertisers and sent out bills.

I didn't know what life would bring now, but it already felt one hundred percent better than before. I could go home each night and enjoy supper with my two boys, instead of dreading my husband's arrival.

My second week, because they were shorthanded with Cap gone, Bob even gave me an article to rewrite, news style. I had worked on the high-school paper, so I knew how to do it. Though it was only an ordinary article about a wedding, I was proud to see it in our next issue, with only a word or two changed.

When Cap came back that Monday morning he noticed me by the file cabinet. I heard him ask Bob about me. Bob introduced me in glowing terms. "Helen has all the work I can give her done by two, and then starts looking around for more. She's got the makings of a cub reporter, too," he said.

I probably glowed with pleasure. Cap looked at me with appreciation, but I could see that it wasn't just business. His eyes and his smile showed his interest. I tried to be cool and sophisticated, but I knew I had attracted a very important and attractive man.

The next afternoon he told Bob he was taking me along to Carson City to interview our congressman about a new dam. Bob gave us both a strange and inquiring look, but Cap already had the camera slung over his shoulder and we were out the door in a whirl of excitement, Cap's usual style....

Reading the story, I skipped over the slow dramatic buildup: my heroine learns Cap is getting a divorce, but is still deeply connected to his small children. She enjoys how well he treats her children in the absence of his own. She tries to overlook how much he is drinking. They predictably end up in bed after a suitably moral interval. Then she reads a letter in which his wife begs him, for the children's sake, to try once again. Helen breaks off their relationship, and starts dating someone else. After that...

ap came to work each day looking worse and worse, with dark circles under his eyes. We carefully avoided anything personal, but the air was heavy with tension. I kept my distance, though the evenings, after our warm nights together, were so cold and lonely I could barely stand to let the boys go to bed.

A few nights later Cap stopped me as I was putting on my coat to leave the office. His eyes were dark, his face haggard. "I've got to see you right now."

"Cap, please. We made a decision." I tried to keep my voice friendly but firm. I walked out to the street, and Cap followed, just in time to see Jay arrive at the curb. As I got in Jay's car, I was sorry Cap had to see us. But I thought maybe it was better that he did. Now he knew it was really over.

Late that night I was awakened by the phone ringing. I looked at the clock—four a.m. In the dark, still apartment, the phone seemed to be screaming. I got to it, knowing there was something terribly wrong.

It was Cap. His voice was hoarse and nearly incoherent. I didn't understand him at first. "My wife killed herself," he repeated.

I didn't go to work that day. I went about my household chores with careful exactness. They were all that held me together. I sent Scott off to school and kept Mike with me. I needed one pair of trusting eyes to get me through the day.

That afternoon the sheriff came to ask me questions. He was polite and respectful, but I could tell he was trying to find out if Cap, or even I, had killed Cap's wife. I said, "Can't you tell whether it's suicide or not?"

"Police work isn't like the movies," he said. "These things are rarely that clear cut. The bullet didn't go in at the angle we would expect if she were pointing the rifle at herself." He explained details too horrible and grisly for me to hear. I could tell they had grave doubts but no evidence. Finally the sheriff admitted, "Chances are that no one will ever know the truth about last night at Cap's."

After he left I was stunned by the implications of what he had said. I remembered so many things Cap had told me about his wife—that she didn't like hunting, was afraid of guns, and would never even touch one herself, even for target practice. Could such a woman load a hunting rifle and rig it up so she could pull the trigger with her toe?

I remembered her strong, worn face, her cheerfulness. But I also remembered all the loving attention Cap had given me and my fatherless sons.

Cap came. I was prepared to take him in my arms and comfort him, but he didn't want comforting. He had a strange, frightening, feverish look about him as he walked in the door. It was a look of triumph. "She did it for us," he said, "so we could be together."

I was horrified. I could only look at him. Where was his grief? Was he, too, in shock?

He turned and went back out the door.

I spent the night struggling with my fears. I remembered all the things I had not wanted to see before. I saw a man whose drinking and promiscuity had sent his wife of twenty years away with his children. I saw that just when he needed to be faced with the consequences of his behavior, I had stepped in, seeing him as the answer to my problems, just as he saw me as the answer to his. He wanted the youth and glamour and naive adoration I represented. But he loved his kids too much to give them up, and he couldn't just substitute mine in their place.

What if she hadn't killed herself? What if Cap had killed her? Could I love a killer? But if he hadn't killed her, didn't he need my love all the more?

Early the next morning, as I was trying to make myself presentable enough to drag to work, Bob Hendrix called to tell me that both Cap and I were fired. The newspaper couldn't take the scandal, he said.

I burst into tears. Two weeks before I thought I was on top of the heap, and now I'd lost it all.

And the worst part of it all was the guilt. "I'll never be able to sleep again without the vision of that woman's face before me," I said.

Jay just listened. Finally, when I seemed to run out of tears, he said, "What about you and Cap?"

"How can I turn my back on him now?" I asked.

"Look, guys sometimes see things that women don't," he said. "Cap was drinking heavily and seeing women a long time before you came along. It was a problem between his wife and him. You just happened to be there for him to grab on to. If it hadn't been you, it would have been somebody else."

"But it *was* me," I said.

He stood up, looking sad and helpless. He gave me a little pat on the shoulder. "Well, I have to get back to work," he said.

Shortly after that, Cap came roaring up in his station wagon. I went out to meet him, and to my amazement, he handed me a beautiful four year old girl. "You killed her mother," he said. She looked at me in terror as her father drove away.

A few minutes later, he came roaring back, snatched her away, and said, "You don't deserve her."

I thought we were both going crazy.

I sent my children to the sitter and asked her to please keep them late. I didn't know what I was going to do. Cap solved it for me. He came back late that night, driving a car from a rental agency. He was wearing gloves when he came in the door. Looking at me with a strange twisted smile, he said, "I've come to take you with me."

He lunged for my neck with his gloved hands. I fell backward over the coffee table, screaming for help. By the time he could get to his feet and corner me again, the neighbors were running to my door. He jumped in the car and took off, tires screaming.

An hour later, he was dead—hit by a bus while driving on the wrong side of the road.

For a long time I couldn't sleep with the lights out. I felt guilt ridden, too sad to see anyone. My father stopped by. He was no comfort.

"I thought you were smarter than to get into something like that," he said.

My ex-husband even came, ostensibly to see if I was all right, but really to let me know he thought I got what I deserved....

The story ends when, after a suitable mourning period, Jay gets her to see that the guilt belongs with Cap, and they build a friendship with a promising future. That's the way those stories have to end, there is a formula.

But that's not the way it really was. The way it really ended, I felt like a woman with a curse, a woman whose love could not be trusted and who could not be trusted to build a good life for her children. I went looking for shelter for myself and my two boys.

I found, after a short period of terrifying poverty, another job, where I met a solid young engineer who took the three of us on picnics, and I married him one year later, among flowers and lace and the celebration of our friends. And it was what I wanted, years of safety and security, a nice life.

Until the dream of poisoned air: *She lies fully clothed across the king-sized bed. Outside in the rock garden, bees circle lazily over brilliant crimson azaleas. The sun shines across the sloping lawn, the great oaks of Lakeview Hills. But inside this room, she dreams she is suffocating, she cannot waken, cannot call out. She hears her husband's steps on the gravel path outside the sliding glass doors, tries to lift her head, to open her mouth to call out to him, but her sleep holds her in the closed* room, filling with poisonous air. Then her two sons are with her, and she is holding them, dying, in her arms.

I sat up on the bed. Outside the sliding glass doors, the azaleas bloomed in the rock garden, though my husband was not outside the window as he had been in the dream. The air was fresh with spring breezes, not poisoned as it was in the dream, and my two sons were out working on their MG's. Another dream of suffocating, unable to call out, unable to be heard.

The dreams were warning me: *Get out, get out of this stifling marriage. You are poisoning your sons with the atmosphere of superficiality. This practiced formal ballet of a marriage.*

Our marriage was perfect, we never quarreled, never disagreed. We were a real estate ad couple: he was tall, handsome in an aloof, dignified way. I was the well-dressed suburban wife. I had managed to get a college degree, fitting classes around my job at the State Capitol, and now had a full time job as a Social Worker. I kept the house spotless, spent weekends planting and weeding our parklike property.

True, my husband did not share my love of plays and movies and good books, but I had Mike for that, Mike who learned *The Music Man* by heart when he was ten, who was so enraptured by *Laurence of Arabia* that he could talk of little else for weeks. We had gone through a lot together—the divorce, my scramble as a single-mother to support them.

Now that I had remarried, my son Mike and I were more like friends now, companions. I would tell Mike about my frustrations at work and he would tell me about the girl he liked at school. As he got older, and my husband became even more involved in his work, Mike and I spent more and more time together. His buddies said, "Wow, is that your mom?"

My other son, Scott, who had gone through more years of abuse with my former husband, was going through a difficult time. He isolated himself in his room, coming out secretly at night to become the neighborhood cat burglar. I was terrified, though my husband only said, he'll be all right. He was not their natural father; I did not expect more of him. With the help of an exceptionally understanding parole counselor, Scott *was* all right. The behavior had stopped, though Scott was still withdrawn and angry. I had an anxious fear that his past had left him deeply hurt, and felt both guilty and helpless.

In all, the poisonous air of the dream seemed an apt metaphor; my ailment was invisible; I could not find words for the symptoms.

I had told my husband a year earlier that something was very wrong; I wasn't sure what it was, but when I thought of the future, I saw only a black tunnel with no ending, a deathlike darkness. No joy, no hope, nothing to look forward to. If our marriage wasn't better in a year, when Mike was in college and Scott in the military, I would be leaving. My husband looked mildly surprised; after all, we were surrounded with everything we had both worked for ten years to achieve, but then he rapidly recovered his usual aplomb, and did not mention the matter again. Nor did I.

When the year was up, I told him as I put his pancakes and bacon out on the breakfast bar, that I would be leaving. Again he looked surprised, so I knew that he had just dismissed what I'd said earlier as something that would go away, as he did with most disturbances. Now he said, "I think we should go to a marriage counselor, get some help," and went on reading the morning paper. I saw myself in the mirrored surface of the chrome coffee maker, perfectly coiffed, my polite smile unaltered. I wondered who was under there.

In California, those were the first years of the encounter groups. Our marriage counselor, Gary Mart, put us in a 24-hour intensive with 20 others, most of them like ourselves, handsome expensively dressed couples in their thirties or forties. We sat on cushions on the floor while Gary used big colorful markers to write on butcher paper. "The rules. Get rid of the veneer. Tell the truth. Stick with feelings. Say I, not you." He did some diagrams, talked about intimacy, what it was and wasn't. High above us were shelves with colorful balls, dolls, teddy bears, cars and trucks. I felt as I had in kindergarten. Everyone else seemed to have a lot to say about their feelings, I didn't even know what mine were.

In the afternoon, the entire group, at some signal I hadn't seen, piled onto me. "Poor kid, poor thing," they mocked. I pushed them off with more strength than I knew I had.

Well into the night, we lay on the deep rugs, with sounds of a fountain nearby, while Gary led us through a guided fantasy. As a virgin to groups, I entered the fantasy entirely. Gary's voice led me to an imagined path where my mother stepped out of the woods to give me a gorgon's head. In the dark cave at the top of a mountain, I found a sword to defend myself, and a chalice to offer others. While some participants remained unmoved, the experience was more real for me than my stilted stylized life.

By dawn everyone's polite veneer had worn off. "You're the loneliest person I ever saw," one woman told me. "You're dead from the waist up," Gary said. Others joined in. "You're dead from the waist down." "I'd like to take you to bed." "You're the last person on the face of the earth I'd go to bed with." "You're too needy." "You couldn't open up with a crow bar."

I sat and took it. Women were crying in corners, men were pounding pillows. People were groping in corners with other people's mates.

I was being forced to look across the room at my husband. "Tell him the truth," Gary insisted, "For once in your life, tell him the truth." I crouched in the near dark, glaring at my husband, whose face registered no emotion. "Tell him you don't give a damn about him," Gary coached.

I would not say that. I said, "I don't want to be with you any longer unless you change. I want us to learn how to talk to each other about more than the dog or the price of tires."

He looked back defensively but steadily. "I like myself the way I am." I heard it as a release. I'd given him the chance, he turned it down.

After twenty-four emotionally exhausting hours, we went home. My husband gave me two aspirin and put me to bed, while he finished some engineering layouts for the plant.

But the group had shaken my tottering foundation: I dreamed a dream I knew was not a dream, but a memory: *I am a child, about two. I am holding my dearly loved kitten, Smoky. But he is trying to get away. I can't bear to let him go, so I clutch him harder. He claws and bites. I can not release him. I feel a powerful surge through my arms and hands until the kitten dangles, unmoving, from my clenched fists. When I let go, the cat falls on the ground, limp, lifeless. I hurry into the house and crawl onto my bed, face to the wall. My mother comes in, holding something black at arm's length. I huddle closer to the wall, refusing to turn. "Look at what you've done," my mother screams, poking my face with her other hand. "Turn around here and look at what you've done!"*

"No! I love my Kitty. I love my kitty," I whimper.

I must have cried out in my sleep. My husband came to see what was wrong. "There's something I have to tell you," I said, "but it's very important that you don't ... make me feel worse about it." I moved over for him to sit on the edge of the bed. "I did something awful when I was a kid, I only just now remembered it, in my sleep...." I heard my voice, childlike, tearful, whimpering.

"My god, what did you do?"

I who loved dogs and cats and all animals, I who would rescue rabbits from the neighborhood boys, squirrels from traps, butterflies with broken wings, confessed: "I killed my cat. I strangled it."

He let out a breath of relief, a little laugh. "Oh, is that all. I thought that you must have burned down your house or something." His response was somewhat freeing to me. I had confessed, and I was not condemned.

Dressing for work, I could barely move to comb my hair. I sat in front of the dressing table, staring in the mirror, feeling as though the workshop had left me emptied of everything I had thought I was for the last ten years. Worse, I felt as if I were in the bottom of a well, way way down, looking up at a circle of light far above, and between me and that light was only slick, slimy mud.

"You're too needy," Gary had said. I, who worked most of my life, raised two sons, kept a beautiful house and garden, entertained friends and neighbors, cooked family dinners for 14 on holidays, graduated with top honors from college while holding down a responsible job.

"Too needy." My mouth formed the word in the mirror. "Need. Need." My lips stretched wide and gruesome over my teeth. I was appalled at the image. Want, I thought. Want is a better word than need. "Want. Want," I said in the mirror, watched, fascinated at the sexual sensuous kissing movements of my lips. From now on I would not be needy. I would have only wants, not needs.

Somehow that broke through my depression; I dressed and went to my job with the Placer County Welfare Department.

Driving the county car to a client's house, not too far from my own community, I kept thinking about the dream, about the cat, Smoky. Why had I killed the cat I loved? I remembered a snapshot of myself with a cat. Was that Smoky? Was it a black cat? How old was I? I swung around to my house, pulled the box of old family photos off the shelf and went through the handful I had of myself as a child.

It was not there. I was drawn as if by some force into the bedroom. I opened the drawer where I kept my sheer nightgowns. As if someone else were moving my hands I reached under the scented gowns to a picture frame lying on its face. I took it out, lay it face up on the bed. It was my only framed picture of my mother. My sister had enlarged a snapshot, and given it to me years earlier. Without ever questioning why, I had put it face down in this drawer, and there it had stayed.

Now the face that I had not looked at for twenty years looked out at me. Under my mother's gaze, I felt myself becoming the awkward teenager that I had been the year she died. I felt myself moving away from the bed, not wanting to get too close lest my mother see on my face what I already knew, what my mother pretended not to know, that she was dying. I felt the stiff smile masking my face, felt the urgency to keep it there, not to betray the lie that the whole family was colluding in. At a distance it was easier not to see that my mother held her magazine upside down, that her joints were the size of soup bones, that there was no flesh left on her frame.

I, the woman in Lakeview Hills, suddenly saw the grinning girl through my mother's eyes: the grin seemed to mock her; Ha, I'm going to live and you're going to die. I heard myself say, as my mother had, "Get her out of here. Get her out of my sight."

All the rest of the day was like that: the workshop had broken through to some different place. I could see my clients' pain, fear, and anger under their manipulation. I saw that children could not hold their heads up because their eyes would meet parental despair or fury. I saw my supervisor's unacknowledged illness, the strain of a co-worker's marriage. But it was as if from some great distance, some objective cosmic distance. I felt no need to change it, this dance-like clockwork reality. I had no feelings about it, one way or the other. It was just the way it was.

That night, after my husband and I made love, I really looked at him, and saw for the first time behind his closed, defensive face, behind the "high indifference curve" on which he prided himself. I saw a man who was hurt, worn and tired, and I was filled with tenderness. He saw this in my face, and it frightened him. He sighed heavily. "I'm going to have to get another woman," he said, so quietly I could almost not hear him.

The next day we walked in the wilderness of the state park across the road, a feeling of tender nostalgia between us, though no words were spoken. A new dam had driven the snakes to higher ground. Unexpectedly we came across a rattler, a large one, some five feet long. Before I had time to react, my husband pushed me back and smashed its head with a stone. It was one of those moments one remembers forever, the rescue, as deep in the cells as Adam and Eve. I wished it could save us.

5

Free Woman

I was forty when I left Lakeview Hills. I left behind closets of matching suits, shoes and handbags, dresser drawers full of curlers and hair sprays and scarves, cabinets full of china and crystal and silver. I left behind a tall, dignified husband who stood in silent bewilderment in the front window, looking out at the lawns and oaks without seeing them.

I felt freed by his decision not to change; it gave me permission to shape my own life in my own way. My strongest wish was to have what I had never had: intimacy. The word showed up like a Biblical promise for the hereafter in all the popular psychology literature. Those books fed the hopes of people like me, feeling deadened by conventionality, wondering why they drank and flirted so compulsively at cocktail parties, and why the years ahead stretched out so long and empty.

I was one of the few women in my neighborhood who worked. Most took care of big homes, got children off to school, taxied their kids around, then played bridge with one another. They complained, with just a touch of jaded humor, about husbands who were always at work or having affairs with secretaries. The woman next door, who had once been a great beauty, had taken to carrying a television around from room to room when her husband was away. She broke into angry crying spells at our occasional cocktail parties if someone there was younger and more beautiful than she. It seemed to me a very sad community.

Scott, at 18, wanted more than anything to fly. Almost as confused and naive about Vietnam as his mother, he had joined the Air Corps. I didn't want him to go, told him his options, college or Canada, but I hadn't been much help to him, and thought perhaps he would do better finding his own way. Mike was going to a nearby college. The big house seemed like a dangerously tilted boat, their side of it empty. It was not hard to leave.

I moved to a small apartment, three tiny rooms, and was so happy with my new freedom that I danced — danced in front of the mirror, danced in front of the tiny stove, danced on my way to the car. I no longer drove too fast, and I now always fastened my safety belt. I wanted to live. I wanted to know who I was; what I would choose when I had only myself to consider, what kind of home, what kind of furniture, what kind of colors, what kind of music, what kind of life.

When I visited Lakeview Hills to see Mike, I always walked through the garden, visiting the apple trees I had planted, the azaleas growing among the rocks by the pond. I missed the family, the growing things. The house I didn't miss; it seemed so unnecessarily large, so eerily hollow, like an empty bus station.

On my days off, I usually drove up to my cabin near Lake Tahoe. The cabin, roughly built and primitive, satisfied my longing for the genuine. I would sit on a boulder, staring into the giant pines that sheltered it. I would walk along the tiny creek in the meadow, watching the silvery trout dart for cover.

One weekend I went to an outdoor workshop at the Tahoe Institute. Fifteen people packed into the Dardenelles, a chain of small mountain lakes. The hike in was easy, since the Institute packed in on mules our sleeping bags, tents, and all of our food. We took our time, stopping along the trail to examine bleeding hearts and mariposa lilies among the rock crevices, or mosses and tiny monkey flowers on the banks of meadow streams, where we drank cold clear water from tin Sierra cups. We got acquainted on the way; two families of four, a matched pair of blond college kids, a widow about 60, an amiable man about 40 who used to be a cop but now managed an inn at Tahoe, and Jerry, the psychologist who ran the Institute, along with his wife.

I was nervous about what would happen in the daily group work, but excited too. I chose a spot in the boulders above the main campsite to pitch my tube tent, laid my sleeping bag out in the shade of a hundred-year-old sugar pine, then relaxed in the late afternoon hour before dinner, taking in the smell of pine needles and mountain alder, watching a striped chipmunk flirt with my open backpack.

I congratulated myself on my campsite; two boulders formed a secure backdrop, the open space would allow me to watch the stars at night, the pines would provide afternoon shade, and I had an eagle eye view of the main camp. Below, the lake lay serenely blue amid glacier-carved granite and sandy beaches. I saw no signs of other campers. Near the inlet, the camp kitchen was already set up on heavy Forest Service tables. The fire pit of circled stones was already heaped with kindling and logs. The rest of the party was scattered around the woods. I could see them establishing their territories, erecting tents, setting out clotheslines draped with blankets. The kids had already headed for the closest beach, peeled off their clothes and plunged, screaming, into the cold, snow-fed water.

While I stood surveying the clearing below, a man emerged from the woods who had not been with our group earlier. He moved quickly and effortlessly, even though he carried a sixty-pound pack on his back, and had an eager little beagle on a leash. His battered brown felt hat had wilted yellow flowers in the brim, and his jeans had flowered inserts sewn in the bottoms to make room for his hiking boots. He had a scruffy beard, above which his wire-rimmed glasses glanced gold in the sun. There was such energy about him, energy like that of the eager little beagle, but more solid, more purposeful; he seemed to radiate life. I realized he must be the Berkeley environmentalist, Dick Larkin, who would take us for nature walks. I watched him sling off the heavy pack, let the dog off the leash, and stride toward the welcoming kitchen crew, his voice, his laughter, deeply resonant through the trees. He fairly radiated attractive energy.

After dinner the group gathered around the fire. On stumps and logs, we listened to Jerry tell us the rules of the camp: no soap in the lake, use the garbage containers, be on time when the groups met after breakfast. Then we sat silently watching the flames or studying the coals, a little shy with each other. Jerry talked quietly with Dick, who was replacing a broken leather strap on his pack. From my shadowed place, I watched the sure practiced hands drive a needle through two thicknesses of leather, pausing to arrange kindling under the logs so they would burn fresh and hot.

He wasn't a big man, probably one hundred and sixty pounds at most, and spare from climbing. He laughed often as he talked, a warm laugh that invited people in, yet had the sure dignity of someone who knew exactly who he was. Someone asked him how he liked his work. "Who wouldn't like to take Berkeley coeds into Desolation, with their brand new Camp 7 sleeping bags and their cute little boots?" He gave me a sly grin. "Teach them how to take care of the environment and maybe a few other things, if they ask?"

The next morning the married couples worked with Jerry in the group, both of them having trouble with their marriages, having trouble with their kids. Jerry led them through some Satir exercises, where they acted out their habitual roles in the family: blamer, placater, fixer, the irrelevant one. Watching, I wondered about my own role, half dreading and half anticipating my own uncloaking.

After lunch, we carried our towels, our sunscreen, and our beach blankets down to the sandy stretch along the sunny side of the lake. The young blond couple were out of their clothes and into the water in seconds, the eyes of the married men hanging like hungry tongues on the heartshaped white buttocks of the woman. The children were next, nudity so natural to them. It was refreshing to watch them race to the water, as if freed from more than their tight clothes. Taking my lead from them, I shed my jeans, panties, and tailored shirt and edged into the cold water, feeling the shock of it on my sun-warmed thighs and belly. I plunged under, coming up gasping, but exhilarated.

Lying on a sun-soaked boulder, I felt fresh, renewed. Nearby, people talked and laughed comfortably. The widow, unconcerned about her sagging breasts and belly, her thin hair, sat quietly by the water and studied the flitting shadows of pontoon-footed water skippers, letting her grief heal.

As the afternoon shadows cooled my rock, I gathered my sunscreen, sun hat, sunglasses, and towel. I noticed Dick had come in from a day-hike, was leaning against a pine at the rim of the beach, drinking water from a tin cup and looking at me. Casually, I gathered up my clothes, but I did not cover myself as I walked away.

That night at the camp fire, he sat next to me, lacing his heavy boots with leather strings, asking teasing questions. "No husband? Women who look like you always have husbands. Lawyers. Or doctors." He took my hand, looked hard at the place where the rings had been. "What did you do with him? Throw him out?"

He didn't really want answers. I didn't give him any. He kept my hand, tucked it into the deep pocket of his jacket while he finished lacing the boots and talked with others across the fire. It was an intimate moment, my hand deep in his pocket, along with a soft bandanna, a rather large nail, something that felt like a whistle, a book of matches, an intimacy known only to the two of us, hidden by the flickering shadows.

When the group met in the meadow next morning, it was my turn to work. I knew what to expect; Jerry would ask people to sculpt themselves into the position they usually found themselves taking in their family.

I stood alone in the center of the clearing, both frightened and excited. "Which family?" I asked, hearing my voice break. "My childhood family or the one I just left?"

"Choose."

I thought of myself as a child, felt my shoulders curve inward, my neck move forward as if my head were too heavy to hold. "Where are your mother and father?"

I pointed at a couple sitting on a boulder some distance away.

"Any sisters and brothers?" I nodded.

"Where are they?" I shrugged, I didn't remember, it was as if they were not there.

Jerry walked around me, commenting on my body position. "The irrelevant one," he said. "This child felt she was irrelevant to the family, unnecessary, perhaps even unwanted."

I felt dizzy, almost faint, as I heard the words. I was glad when Jerry said, "Okay, now sculpt your recent family."

I felt my entire body posture change. I stood straight, even stiff, and borrowing two boys from another family, I placed them one on each side of me, my arms sheltering them like wings.

"Where is their father?" Jerry asked.

I shrugged.

He walked around us, looking at my changed posture, my chin high, my hands claiming the shoulders of the boys. "Well, she sure isn't irrelevant any more, is she?"

I laughed, and let the boys go. Jerry asked me to stage my family in terms of how they managed conflict "Who was the blamer, who the placater? Who the irrelevant one?"

I considered. Jerry said, "No, don't think about it. Just let the body tell you."

My arm shot out, pointing a blaming finger.

"And who are you blaming?" Jerry asked.

"My husband," I said.

"And who is he?" Jerry asked. "Sculpt him."

I chose a man standing a long way away and placed his body in the way my husband always stood, relaxed hands, relaxed body, high defensive chin. "Now he's the irrelevant one," Jerry said.

When I was off the "hot spot," thinking about the implications of it all, I wondered where the placater was. My mother had been the placater, usually. After she died, I had taken on that role, trying to hold the family together as it fell apart. After that, I was constantly trying to placate Jim. Sick of that, I had become the blamer. I knew none of the roles was productive. I wasn't sure I knew what else to be.

The next night, Dick led me away from the fire. He held a candle lantern with tiny holes punched in the rim, its dancing lights adding a fairy-like magic to the night. We walked up the trail to the grassy hollow where his sleeping bag lay in the open, under the stars. As we undressed, he talked about what he wanted, to keep living in the mountains, simply, any way he could. Everything else was secondary. Even the years he'd spent at the university were for one end; to earn enough to free him for the mountains. We made love, laughing softly at the sounds of other lovers scattered through the woods, then slept the whole night in one another's arms, while the wind sighed in the pines and the coyotes howled in the distance.

After breakfast, packed for the trip out, I hauled my sleeping bag down to be loaded on the mules. Dick was tightening the straps of his pack around his shoulders when he saw me. He approached, smiling broadly, his eyes bright behind his glasses. "So here's my lady." I knew this was a man with many opportunities with women; I wasn't going to act the ingenue. He took my hand. "It's hard to say goodbye."

"It was nice, " I said, and giving him a friendly farewell hug, I turned to put my sleeping bag on the pile with the others.

"Wait a minute here," he said, still smiling. "What's this, it was *nice?*" he mocked my casual manner. If he hadn't stopped smiling, if he hadn't told me I'd hurt his feelings, I'd never have seen him again.

That was August. In November I wrote in the journal:

Yesterday Dick and I moved into the cabin. Moonlight flooded the snowy mountains, the river shone as I drove up. He had the fire going. I cooked supper, we ate by candles and felt a little shy. We kept saying to each other, 'We're going to live together!' wide eyed.

This means to me, learning who I am outside the daily restrictions and routines. Will I write my book? No more job. No more bras, curlers, cosmetics, no more feeding my time and my dollars into the system. It means surviving a winter in a cold cabin, with only a wood stove, much like my great grandmothers did. More scary, it means living with Dick, closer than any married couple, because we'll be spending all our time together, nobody leaves for work or watches TV. It seems incredible to me rationally, but somehow within my guts I'm not overwhelmed. It even seems natural. We've been moving toward this since last summer, when he came striding into camp with his dog, his beard, his bright patches, and just seemed to radiate life.

The cabin was small, one open room, a loft, a small kitchen and bathroom at a step-down level. My first husband, my brother and I had

built it for summer use, so it was not insulated, and the Franklin stove was chosen for its open fire, not for heat. Many times that winter I got up to make a fire in a house with icicles on the *inside* of the roof.

I wrote every morning until one, a book about my welfare clients, while Dick cut wood, read, or planned his next outing.

Then I might make bread, or sew, or ski the moraine behind the cabin with Dick. In the evenings, we read. Books and articles were always stacked on the heavy picnic table in the living room. At night, we talked about politics, education, psychology and science. He knew more about everything than anyone I had ever known. We made love in the loft, the fire flickering and snapping below. We talked about our childhoods, our families, our dreams. We made up fantasies and stories for each other.

For days at a time, we would see no one, then we would get in his truck and go into town for groceries, visit friends, eat a special meal at the Casino, maybe even see a movie. Sometimes his Berkeley friends came up to hike, ski, or rock climb. The people from Tahoe Institute became our good friends. The cabin gradually became the place people liked to come for good company, good conversation, good food. Dick gloried in making them envious of his idyllic life.

I watched the ups and downs of our love affair more closely than a pneumonia patient watches the thermometer. If we disagreed, if we quarreled, if he said he did not like something I wore or said or did, I would agonize for hours. Did this mean he didn't love me? If he stayed too long in Berkeley, where I knew he was staying with former women friends, I would make myself miserable imagining his delight in their bodies, always perfect in my mind. And of course they were always freer and less possessive than I. I would fall into his arms in grateful relief when he returned.

Dick never pretended he would give up other women to be with me. He believed it was possible to conquer possessiveness and jealousy, believed that women especially were capable of accepting one another while in a sexual relationship with the same man. I wanted to achieve that, thinking how freeing it would be for me, too, not to make sex more than it was. But I didn't think I could. We had endless discussions about it.

I said, "Why not two men and one woman?"

"I'm afraid I would feel less masculine."

"You don't think I'm afraid of feeling less feminine?"

"But I could help the women with their problem. Who would help me with mine?"

He considered himself to be so complete a person that a woman should be willing to do much more for him in return for being with him, support herself while doing all the wifely chores for him, but not ask him to fix her car, or other chores. "I won't accept that," I said. "If you don't consider me your equal, find someone who is."

But I knew I was too dependent on his affection, his responses; I wanted to be as free as he was. I went to a Bioenergetics workshop at the Institute. I saw for myself how bodies can hold childhood traumas. In the group, a chronically red-faced man would not let himself breathe more deeply for fear of feeling the terror when his father died, leaving him the "man of the house" at age nine. A woman with a narrow band of indented white skin around her ankles could never really "put her foot down" about anything. The body, directed by the mind's past programming, blocked the circulation.

I wanted to work on the memories of my mother, but was afraid that I would become "worse" if I did, even though I didn't quite know what "worse" meant. As the therapist, John Dillinger, worked on my breathing, I returned to the memories of the two-year-old. I felt my mother's fingers pushing and prodding at my face, trying to force me to look at something. The child me could see the black shadow dangling behind my mother. I refused to look at it. I scrambled off the chair, screaming, and crawled under a table, where I huddled, whimpering, "I loved my kitty, I loved my kitty." John held me on his lap and rocked me like a child until I could breathe deeply enough to come out of my hysteria.

He showed me how I held pain and anger high in my chest, keeping it at a shallow level, rather than allow myself to feel deeply. "You hold it there, rather than let it go, rather than feel emptiness in its place. No wonder you can't open yourself up to men, but want them to get through to you, to penetrate you."

He pointed out to the others my frail build, Barbie-like legs, s-curved spine. "Her frame is so light it won't support heavy emotional loads. She has only two alternatives in emotional crisis: turn off and go unfeeling, or hysterics. Like a building with no lightning rod." He turned me around once more. "Hers is a beautiful body by today's standards, but it's the body of a deprived, malnourished child."

I was left alone then, to absorb all that, to recover from a profound sense of emptiness. I had been neglected as a child. So much so, that I clung desperately to my cat, the only thing I had to love. And when it tried to get away, I hung on so hard I killed it. Then my mother had tried to force me to look at the body of the cat, but I wouldn't. For forty years I wouldn't.

I finally sat in meditation, concentrating on deepening my breathing. *Gradually, I feel energy flowing from my clasped hands into my legs, feel my body moving itself slowly, suspended, like a fetus. I feel charges of energy, as if directed by the sun, circling my head and body. My hands and arms float before me effortlessly, I open as a flower opens to the sun. I have returned to the womb.*

After that, I saw all of them, even Dillinger, as overburdened or neglected children, still crying for love, crying to be touched and held, all the puffing up or going hard just cover-ups for fright. I finally went home with a splitting headache and the conviction that my body carried still more secrets.

The next time I was at the Institute, Jerry said, "Did you give Dick hell?" I hadn't, but I did begin to make demands.

When Dick told me that he'd like to fuck Jerry's wife, I told him I didn't want to hear about it. Then I said I wanted his stacks of papers taken off the bed, and was even willing to fight about it until he took them off. Emboldened, I also told him that I wasn't going to keep doing all the household work and the cooking and his sewing. He seemed a bit shook, made some remarks about being used by women, but I held my ground.

I wrote in the journal:

I am not as loving toward him as I was, not as adoring is perhaps the word, but I think he likes me more, calls me comrade and gets me into intellectual discussions.

Dick told me some pretty serious things, like he'd been looking for a woman who was his equal and sometimes thinks I seem like it. I said, "I am, not seem." He says he finds himself thinking in terms of one woman, wonders how he got into this, "Pretty scary business." I told him I didn't trust my feelings to last. He said that would be my loss. I started to cry. Will we love each other in spring? By then I'll be blowing my nose on my sleeve, walking with five foot strides, cursing like a logger, telling guys to fuck off."

Over the Christmas holidays, Dick invited friends from Berkeley, Bernie and Lou, for Christmas dinner. The pipes had frozen and there was no running water when they arrived with a very difficult six-year-old son. I did the best that I could to prepare a good dinner and deal with the unhappy child. After they left, I sank wearily into a chair. Dick said, "Well, you certainly were trying to be the good hostess. I never saw anyone trying so hard to be entertaining."

"You mean rather than genuine," I said, tired and angry. "You mean that as a put-down."

"Not a put-down, just an observation. You went right into your Lakeview Hills mode."

"It was a put-down." I reached for my jacket and then started for the front door.

"You stupid little bitch!" he yelled as I left.

I went for a long walk. Under the cold winter stars, the looming pines, I faced the fact I'd been unhappy a lot, and probably needed to admit I could not live with Dick. His great arrogance, his coercion, my need for his love, my sensitivity to criticism, all combined to make me feel subservient and inadequate.

When I came back, he said, "You're feeling unloved and unlovable." I broke into tears at having my feelings named. He instituted a 24-hour seclusion order; I was to remain in bed, no talking. He would bring me food and take care of the house.

I came out of seclusion loving him again, but terrified I had let a snake into our garden. I had turned cold, hard, unfeeling. There was no way to know when it would happen again. Dick couldn't trust me not to just leave when I got angry. Nor could I trust myself.

Bernie and Lou sent a matted photograph they had taken of me over Christmas. I wrote and thanked them. After I mailed the letter, Dick accused me of trying to set up a separate relationship with Bernie. He was rigid with anger. To my own surprise, I laughed. It was involuntary.

"I'd like to smash you," he said, fists clenched. I felt the smile still on my face. He hit me twice about my head as I tried to protect myself. "Fucking bitch!" I waited, frightened, for the next blow, felt him holding himself back. Then it was over. He reached for me, I went to him, relieved and shaking, and we tried to figure out what it was all about, why I was so delighted to get a rise out of him, why he was so violently angry.

He said I was triumphant because I could go off and leave and say, "Fuck it," and mean it. He admired me for that, but at the same time, hated me. "I feel rotten when you just walk off or turn off, or laugh like you've gotten the best of me." He carried me up to the loft, and I forgot it all in lovemaking.

The following week, we went to the Inn to see Jerry and his wife. Dick left, and when I went to look for him, I found him in the coffee shop with some women. I sat down beside him, thinking I would like to meet them, but he ignored me. Later, I told him, "I felt bad, being ignored like that." He turned on me defensively, storming around the cabin. "I'm tired of doing all your work for you, mending your problems."

When he calmed down, he told me how he felt when I came to "claim him" when he was with other women. I collapsed; all my fantasies that he didn't really want me around, didn't value me, welled up. I felt wounded, hurt, hopeless. I pulled away, my face twisted.

He said, "You look like you're killing yourself. Stop it!" He shook me. "You don't have to be this way. Take some responsibility for yourself here." I heard his words, but his face was fierce and his fist ready to hit. I was immobilized. I could only look at him and ask him not to hit me, while tears spilled down. At the same time I resented that I should have to beg.

Dick was pleased at having pulled me back from my "deadness."

He quieted down. "Look, I don't like what happened either, don't like the way I was. Just see it as my problem, not yours." He said he'd never been able to be as straight with anyone about things he was ashamed of, said he'd never let me go. "But you've got to take care of yourself, Babe."

I said, "What if taking care of myself means not putting up with any more of this other woman shit?"

"We'll just have to work that out as we go."

But I was feeling that familiar cold alienation. What's the matter with me? I asked myself. I can't love.

I had a dream: *I am digging a hole to sleep in. On one side of me is a hole I've already dug but it is full of rocks and uncomfortable. I want a hole that is soft and free of rocks. Out of the corner of my eye, I can see the cement foundation of a house.*

Perhaps out of all that drama a foundation of some kind was being built, I thought, as I read the journal.

While I was living at the cabin, that spring my father died. Over 70, he had made it through what looked like a successful operation. I had just returned from the hospital to the cabin, when a call came that he was failing. I made quick arrangements with Dick, who was going to the valley on other business, to contact me in Lakeview Hills if he couldn't come to the hospital.

Dad was in intensive care and fighting hard to live. I told him I was there. He didn't respond, lying there with his eyes closed, fighting for breath, his pulse half the pace it should be, the bleeps on the scopes almost level. The nurse said, "Do you know who is here?" Without opening his eyes, he said, "Helen."

Shortly after that the nurse told him to relax, to quit trying so hard, and almost immediately he died. He looked angry as if she had tricked him. I reacted in a way I hadn't expected. I found myself letting my long hair down, swinging my head back and forth over his body, my hair brushing across his sheeted torso, back and forth. "Goodbye sweet daddy goodbye sweet sweet daddy" putting my face against that hard gray angry head, already looking skullish.

That afternoon, Mike took me to Lakeview Hills with him, but I found my husband's let's-talk-about-something-else way of responding to pain aggravating when what I wanted was to cry in Dick's arms. But he didn't come or call. I knew my father's death meant a part of my life was closed, finally and forever. Obligations and fears of taking care of or trying to please an angry father were gone, but so too was the comfort of knowing he was there, and the hope of those rare star-like times when we really talked to each other.

I slept little that night. I kept getting my anger for Dick confused with my anger with my father, trying to make peace with my memories of Dad, trying to sort out my good and bad feelings about him. He had never reached out to me when I was hurt, he was too self centered to even see that I was hurt. He often belittled me. But he was the one I had turned to, and he was gone.

All that night I wrestled with grief and anger: grief at the loss of my father, anger that my images of him and Dick kept merging with one another. I poured out my anger to my sister, Beverly, to Mike. "How come he wasn't there when I needed him?"

Driving back up to the cabin with Beverly, we stopped by the old stone house where our mother had died. "It will be there forever," Beverly said grimly, "a stone monument to our father."

When Dick got to the cabin, I greeted him with a cynical remark, and later, in bed he reminded me that he had no way of knowing my father had died. "You could have called," I said. I told him I didn't know if I wanted to get in any deeper with him. He was unreliable. He was now furious with me. With others nearby, he could only throw himself on me, glaring hate, "You green bitch, you dirty green bitch."

I lay there, unfeeling, cold. I finally said, "I think a lot of things you said are true." A fierce winter was descending in my heart.

Depressed. Nothing I want to do, counting my woes, not interested in finishing my book, irritated that Dick still expects me to do all the housework. Tired of hassling it. He asked me to try and say what puts me on these downers. I don't know.

"I don't know?" I said aloud, reading the journal twenty years later. The woman's father has died, she confuses him with her lover, who is a classic abuser, and she doesn't know why she's depressed? I shook my head, and went on reading.

In late May, with the snow finally off the lower mountains, Dick drove to Berkeley for supplies. I missed him terribly, and when he came back, we ran in the meadow and tumbled in the grass and wrestled like kids.

Stepping into the cabin from the chill was like stepping from the night into a warm cave. Dick built up the fire to heat the pot of oyster stew I'd made. The fire reflected in the polished silver base of the oil lamp. With its slender chimney, it shone like a magic lantern. From the stepdown kitchen, Dick brought the enamel coffee pot and set it steaming on the hearth. He cut two slabs of heavy bread, thick with butter, to go with the stew.

I sat on the side of the rough board table nearest the fire, pushing aside the book he'd been reading. He ladled the stew into my favorite bowl, blue and gray streaked pottery, large and generous. He sat opposite me, the firelight glinting off his round gold-rimmed glasses.

He said, "I'm afraid when you're so beautiful when we go out, someone in a Lincoln will drive up and take you away." We climbed into the loft and made happy reuniting love.

Then he told me he'd slept with Anna. I felt like I was choking. Part of me wanted to shove him away, hit him, the other wanted to hold onto him desperately. He said, "I don't understand what she has taken from you." When I tried to tell him, he mocked me. "You're just hurt because you're supposed to be." I hated him, turned dark and rigid with fury.

He rolled me around on the bed, "Breathe! Breathe goddamn it!" I came out of it, mostly because I thought he'd be beating me again if I didn't.

Later I dreamed:

I watch as a car , a yellow Volkswagen, comes around a curve, runs carelessly and out of control over the head of what seems to be a puppy, yet it's not a puppy. It's pink and round and fetus like. I'm angry at the driver's carelessness. I keep saying , maybe the puppy can get fixed up. Someone says, are you kidding? It's his head. You know what brains are like.

I was learning how to have feelings, but at the same time, they were destroying our emerging puppyish vulnerability, so terrifying to both of us.

In July, Dick took a group into the mountains for a week. When he came back, he got a phone call from a woman named Connie, and went back into town. "Just finishing up business," he said.

A day or two later he got a note from her, a romantic verse. He asked me how I felt about it. I said, "Like tearing it to shreds."

I went out to the trash can, and tore it into tiny pieces while Dick said, "Get mad, growl or something." He put his arm around my chest and squeezed me hard. I felt an animal fury rise clear from my toes.

I snarled, "Let go of me!" My feet were ready to kick and my hands to claw. Afterward they throbbed with energy. I was excited about it for hours. *I'm not helpless; I have hands and feet, I can use them.*

I demanded the truth. "Okay," he said. "I fucked her. But it meant nothing. I love you."

When I made dinner, I sang, "Fuck 'em all, fuck 'em all, fuck the long and the short and the tall." I felt free of my desperate need to be his one and only. I asked him to please tell me, making no accusations, if he was going to see Connie again, so I would know the truth. He said he would. I knew my euphoria wouldn't last, but I felt as if something had clicked. *I'll never be as caught as I was. His demand that I give him freedom has given me my independence.*

A month after, he went on a weekend hike alone, and when he came back, a slip of the tongue, "we", gave him away. He admitted he'd been seeing Connie all along.

I felt weak in the knees, all fuzzed in the head, as if I'd been hit. I hated how he'd been lying to me and colluding with another woman. I spent most of the night sitting on a rocky ledge in the moonlight, finally getting through the hate, wanting to hurt him. What did I want? To be controlled by him, selling my peace of mind, my confidence for him?

I stayed away all the next day, lying in the meadow, walking the creek. Under my boots, the grass was paper dry. The creek, golden all summer, was dark now, eating deep into the hollows of its banks. With the snow gone from its rocky slopes, Mt. Tallac looked harsh, the famous cross barely visible. I felt the shadow of the mountain.

The lights of the cabin flickered through the crowding pines. Dick would have the fire going when I got there. The air, cold against my face, made my skin burn, brought it to life.

He would laugh at me, as he'd laughed in the spring when I came back from the green flowered meadow saying April made me feel the urge for change. "You know, rebirth, resurrection, all those Easter things."

He had said I was posturing. Maybe. But I knew the seasons affected me as surely and as physically as they affected the meadow and the streams and even the mountain.

When I walked back to the cabin, Dick was reading. He looked up at me with a tentative smile. I asked him if he had told Connie he loved her. He floundered. "Not exactly. I don't think so," so I knew he had.

I said, "You've taken the last thing that was just mine and given it to her. Everything I've been using to hold things together was fake: you said you fucked her but you love me." I refused to listen to him any more, went out to the kitchen and started sanding the cupboards. *There is such relief in feeling nothing when pain is the alternative.* He followed me. I said I couldn't take any more right then, "Leave me alone." He took my arms and put them over his shoulders. "Hang on to me, goddamn it!" I let them drop. "Stop that!" he yelled.

I said, "I'm not doing anything." He grabbed me, tried to turn me over his knee. I said calmly, "You're making me hate you." He stopped after a few hard whacks.

I said, "You've made the words *I love you* meaningless. I don't ever want to hear them again."

"You fucking bitch!" He grabbed me by the hair, began to drag me around the room. Screaming, I grabbed for the kitchen knife, missed it by inches.

He yelled, "What do you want me to do?" He dragged me into the living room. My hair was coming out in wads. He said, "Think!" Finally, he said, "Will you accept it when I say I love you?" I said yes, lying, anything to make him stop, but thinking, statements taken by torture are not legal or binding. "Did you hear what I said?" he asked. "Are you listening?"

"I'll listen to you tell me how you feel, " I said firmly, "but I won't let you tell me how I feel anymore." Exhausted, we slept as if a truce had been reached.

That night I had a dream: *Dick keeps bringing me these women, and I am cutting and rude to them, all but one who runs away when she can't stand to see him bringing all the others home. I am moving, traveling all the time, and my hands feel huge and heavy, powerful, clawed. Then, lying down somewhere, I see another woman standing over me. I don't recognize her. She seems powerful but not beautiful.*

I wondered, was she the other woman? Or was she an emerging part of myself?

I told Dick I would not live with violence and lying. I was going back to Sacramento; he could rent the cabin from me if he wanted. As I packed to leave for the valley, Dick got tears in his eyes and wished me well. Then he went upstairs, lay on the bed, and cried so long and hard I thought my heart would break. I'd have said anything to make him stop, and I did. We made up. Made love. I felt wonderful, full of peace. Then he began to talk about seeing Connie again, and when it was all over I had gotten nothing I asked for but as good as gave him permission to see Connie all he wanted, as long as he still loved me.

I decided to drive with Mike to New York, to take a break from all the emotion, and to take my finished manuscript to the publishers. Dick, still cherishing his dream of two accepting women, wanted me to meet Connie before I left.

It was rather a comic scene. A very attractive woman, slim tan legs tucked under her, she sat on a log, smoking a cigarette, coolly sizing me up, saying little. Dick danced like a jittery high school boy between the two of us, looking miserable and frightened.

The journal reported in a flat voice:

She said things like, "This is happening to us so fast, we hadn't planned it," like it was the irresistible love affair of the century. She told me what she wanted and expected: Dick and marriage.

I told her I wasn't going to compete with her, I didn't think people were tennis trophies, Dick could make his own decisions, I said if Dick and I made it through this, I'd feel secure, no matter how many women he had. If we didn't, I'd be free of the whole messy business, I was going to New York as planned.

Traveling with my son across the country, visiting friends on the way, I told my tale everywhere we went. Mike must have been sick of it by New York. How confusing for him the whole thing must have been. He admired Dick, some even said they looked alike. His adored mother admired Dick so much she was acting like a lovesick teenager. She admired a man who abused her more than she'd ever admired her husband, who may have been aloof, but at least he was kind.

When we got back to California, I left Mike off in Lakeview Hills, drove up to the cabin to see Dick. Hadn't he said on the phone that "nothing was happening" between him and Connie? It was late when I arrived. He came out of the cabin to meet me, we held each other tight, I could feel him trembling. I thought it was because he missed me. I said, "Let's go in."

He said, "Don't go in there yet. Connie's here."

I brushed off his restraining hand and went past him. I found Connie coolly smoking a cigarette in front of the fire, wearing one of Dick's shirts. "Get your stuff and get out," I said. Connie gave me a "how amusing" look.

I slapped her across the face. Connie looked startled, but recovered. "There's ashes on the rug."

I was prodding her like a cow puncher, "Move, move, move!" Dick was standing in the doorway. "Get your stuff and get out too," I snapped. I raged through the house, calling him a lying bastard, dumping boxes of cosmetics and curlers off the porch, while they stood at her car, exchanging mutual sympathetic looks. I began to pull Dick's papers off the shelves and dump them in boxes.

"Leave them there," he said. He came charging upstairs and grabbed me by the throat, carried me to the floor and pounded my head against it. Then he went outside with Connie. I grabbed his pistol off the dresser and was checking to be sure it was not loaded when he lunged back up the stairs and slugged me full fist on both sides of the face. Then he went back to finish his tete-a-tete, which infuriated me more than anything he did.

After Connie drove away, Dick sat at the table, looking stiff and dry, metallic eyed, and somehow very funny looking, with his chopped off hair and scraggly beard. "You can't even keep your calendar straight enough to cheat right," I said. I was suddenly very tired.

I opened the mail, a note from a friend in Sacramento who saw me as the glamorous writer living in a mountain cabin with an exciting lover. She was complaining about her husband. A letter of acceptance from Grad school, with a teaching assistantship confirmed. That felt secure and positive.

"The TA came through," I said.

"You knew it would. When are you going?" He was hand-rolling a cigarette. The match flared against the loose ends of the paper.

"You know my money's almost gone," I said, not looking at him, opening an envelope, concentrating, as if only I and it were the world. "I have to go back down, go to work, rent an apartment."

He didn't answer that I could work at Stateline if I really wanted to stay.

"Some great things are going on down there," I said. "A seminar on Lessing's *Golden Notebook*. An anti-war rally. The U has a new foreign film festival coming up. I'd like to be there. And I need some of my writer friends to critique my manuscript. A social worker's response too, since it's all about welfare."

I cleared some bowls off the table, rinsing them in the new sink. I'd built the cabinet for it myself; never quite finished, it looked primitive and rough.

"How can you leave this place?" he said.

The question seemed to bring everything together, the spark smoldering out in the rug, the axes in the corner, the loft that loomed above us, the bed in that loft, with its faintly animal smell, books, papers, sewing machine, typewriter. The shingle roof with chinks of sky showing through. And that roof sheltered by boughs of huge pines, their trunks like black pillars outside the window.

I had no answer. There were easy answers. The money I was living on was nearly gone. The book I was writing was finished. And winter was coming.

Last winter had been the best I'd ever known. Cutting logs, Dick on one handle of the four foot saw, I on the other. Skiing on skins up the mountain, camping in the hollow near the peak, waking in the morning wet from our own breath, condensed on the plastic tent. With him, it had been a shimmering white winter, dazzled through with blue light.

But it would never be that way again. If I left, he would stay on here, pay a little rent. Yet if he left, I wouldn't stay without him. I didn't want to remember how cold the cabin was in the winter, when the fire went out. Alive and rich in firelight, it would go dark and soulless as an abandoned mine. I didn't want to remember how heavy and dark the pines loomed when I lay in bed alone. My dependence made me angry.

I resented him, was envious of him, that he could stay, live the life I loved, here without me. I thought of him leaning into the lantern to read by the fire, alone, contented. I saw him bringing the ax down dead center, the wood dividing perfectly as the halves of a peach. It made me angry.

Maybe some day I could become independent enough to live with him. But now, I'd only become a bitch, doing his cooking and resenting it, wondering when he was coming home, who he was with. I'd seen it many times, and so had he. He had put my picture on the wall with crossed American flags under it, his ironic comment on the demands of the domestic female.

"You've never been committed to me," I said.

"Or you to me. You've always planned for when the year's up, the book's finished."

We read for awhile. He was reading a study of the effects of carbon monoxide on Jeffrey pines. I read a poem about a family who went in sorrow to cut down a tree. They found that fallen tree opened up a view of the sunset.

We went to bed. We made love more quietly than usual. I cried a little afterward. "I suppose Carol will be here." There was no accusation. Carol often stopped by. The three of us would drink hot coffee with chocolate and talk about animals. She was a forest ranger. She had wide hips and a small waist, unfit for uniforms.

"I'm not the kind to stay alone much," he said.

I lay awake, his arm under my head. He stroked my hair with the tips of his fingers. "Write in one of your stories, 'Her hair grew long that summer. He liked to wake in the morning with his face against it.'"

The fire burned itself out and the cabin gave up to the cold night. Under our blankets, we lay like the warm heart of it.

Friday, the car loaded with clothes and books, typewriter, guitar, blue pottery bowl, I left. I cried as I drove past the meadow, away from the mountain that always seemed to wait, across Tahoe Valley, up through the pass, following the slow line of cars pushing up the steep grade.

Then I was around the last curve of the summit. The gray rock canyon opened around me. The car rolled easily through it, winding beside the American River for miles. Bend after bend, lower and lower, my heart feeling lighter, the mountains spilled me down.

The Sacramento Valley lay ahead, a warm brown bowl between hills. The sky opened up, blue and endless. I realized with some surprise that here, off the mountain, winter was still a long way off.

6

So Many Men,
So Little Time

The years I was in graduate school, the early 1970s, were the years of great social ferment in the country. Nightly, television played out the horror of atrocities in Viet Nam. My son Scott, a loadmaster in the Air Force, was writing letters that wrenched my heart, letters showing what it does to a sensitive 19-year-old to load canisters of bodies onto cargo planes. He wanted out; his greatest fear was his sanity.

I picketed McClellan Field with young families and students protesting the war. I marched in demonstrations, wrote and distributed pamphlets. I walked up the capitol steps with five hundred other women, candles in our hands, while the CIA photographed us from above. I wrote letters to editors, asking how people could keep on going to their jobs, paying taxes to a government so blindly corrupt and brutal, so unresponsive to the will of its people.

In graduate school, I felt the excitement of the Women's Movement, though I didn't see myself as a radical. I went to lectures with titles like: *Teaching a Woman Her Place* or *Emasculating Language*. Afterward, I would talk for hours with my women friends.

"I've never been ambitious," a married friend said.

"Kathy, you have always been ambitious," I argued. "Look at the men you've married, both of them were successful or on their way up. You just transferred your ambition to men, you let them do it for you, riding on their coattails."

"Well, we all do it," Ruth said. "We've been raised to do it, to take our identity from men, rather than establish our own."

We commiserated about how easy it was to make strong and independent decisions when we lived alone, but how difficult it was in a relationship with a man. We talked about wanting to feel so secure in ourselves we could live with strong men without giving up ourselves.

"But if we're that secure," Ruth asked, "will the men we like want us? They seem to want helpers, not equals." Ruth, a counselor, was newly divorced, and struggling with dating again.

"It's a new world from the one our mothers trained us for," I laughed, with mock trepidation.

I had taken a part-time secretarial job and resented how much of my time it took, and how little it paid. I found I could no longer play the Girl Friday role I had done so well previously. I decided to invest in myself: I would live on the money I had coming from the divorce, and trust that when I finished graduate school, I would get a good job.

It was a high risk, since in California, there were already more highly educated people than there were jobs for them. I decided that if anybody could make it, I could. I was making straight A's, a publisher was considering the book I had just finished, and I was gaining a reputation on campus as an innovative teacher.

I played it up, wearing my professorish tweed jacket over tight fitting ribbed sweaters and narrow-hipped, bell-bottomed jeans. I wore my hair long and sleekly straight; I wore wire-rimmed glasses and the silver spoon ring Dick had given me.

My professors and the writers they assigned us to read were all male. On my own time I discovered Lessing's *Golden Notebook,* and realized with some shock that I had never before read a book that had very much to do with me or my experience.

The ending made me angry, though. Anna, an independent woman, is left alone and loveless, while her friend gives in to a pointless marriage. Are those really the only options? I wondered.

Although my days were full, nights were lonely.

"OK, so I'm lonely and alone," I wrote in my journal. "I want to lose my fear of loneliness. And Dick, Dick, Dick. I want to go to the cabin and see him almost as much as I don't. How can I write with such longing and anger tearing at me?"

Alone in my low-rent apartment, I had dreams that reflected a deep sense of powerlessness and alienation:

I'm a lady politician. I keep practicing my speeches, but when I go to give them, nobody's there. In between classes and speeches, tired, I want to go home. I get there, it is full of strangers. Somehow I've abdicated to them. Leering and unfriendly, they consent to give me a corner to rest in.

I come home the next time to find it all torn up while I was gone, drawers open, mattress gutted, my colorful, beautiful things gone, my music strewn around on the floor. I am demolished with grief.

I thought a long time about that dream. I understood the powerlessness I felt about the political situation. But who were the unfriendly intruders in my house, stealing my joy? I turned my attention outward.

Why should any of us live like we do, in little isolated units, I asked my friends. Why this self-imposed isolation? Scuttling around looking for a partner, putting all our energy on one person? Why can't we live in little villages or tribes like people used to?

Most of my group had lived comfortable conventional lives, with families, good jobs, two cars, and well groomed homes. We recognized the infidelities, alcohol abuse, work compulsion, that often lay behind well groomed appearances. My year in the cabin had taught me that I was happier when I owned fewer things, and more of my own life.

Twelve of us men and women established what we called a bureaucratic commune. We were mostly mature people connected with the state in some way: graduate students, social workers, a psychiatrist in internship.

We leased an old mansion, where we took turns cooking and cleaning, shared the children of the two married couples, worked through the inevitable conflicts in group meetings. We bought wholesome food in bulk and recycled cans, bottles and papers. We planted a garden, wrote poetry, danced wildly in our basement ballroom and swam in our pool, sometimes nude. We showed the children that bodies were not shameful, did not have to be perfect, and would not provoke others to sexual assault.

They were people who were asking the same questions I was: Was there an alternative to the stifling nuclear family? Could we be free and also responsible? Could possessiveness and jealousy and dependence be eliminated from relationships, leaving room for more positive emotions, like trust and intimacy? Could we make sexual choices out of desire rather than obligation, and if so, could we still have long-term supportive relationships?

We believed in love. We worked hard at relating. We took real emotional risks. Open marriage was a goal for two couples in the commune, who spent many hours working through the insecurities aroused by time with other partners. Despite my own experience with Dick, I still believed, though with some skepticism, in the possibility of sexual freedom.

We didn't indulge in the kinky sex our neighbors fantasized for us. We became too much like brothers and sisters for that. Some smoked marijuana or used drugs; some lost interest when they found drugs weren't the shortcut to enlightenment.

I offered the commune's ballroom for a campus-sponsored Women's Dance. I thought it was just an opportunity for women to dance without having to sit back and wait for men to ask them, or give them permission. I watched in astonishment as the evening unfolded. Musicians and sound technicians arrived from Los Angeles, all women, all tall, all wearing their jeans tucked into high sleek boots. I found them intimidating, their long appraising looks, their aggressive style as disturbing to me as that behavior was when it came from males.

As I sat on the steps observing it all, a sparrow-brown woman sobbed on the step below me, clinging to the boots of her partner, who growled gutturally, "Cut it out, for Christ's sake." On the dance floor, women with stars on their cheeks, brilliant red lipstick, and long swirling skirts—super women, they looked like to me—swung their partners out, hands under their breasts, showing them off. At midnight, they flung their shirts and blouses aside as the crowded room heated up, and women danced free from the waist up. Awed by the unleashed erotic power, I could see why men wanted to control women's sexuality.

Unleashing our own erotic power, Ruth and I planned a party for her 40th birthday. We invited all the single people we knew. Ruth's parties were always fun; as a counselor, she knew how to open up ways for people to be courageous and take risks relating to each other. We fed each other with our fingers, talked frankly about our most fulfilling sexual experience, played games involving one another's partners. I wore a long velveteen dress that flowed around my body, softly revealing, and walked through that party feeling like every eye was on me.

Ruth was angry. She saw me as out to prove to other women I could take away from them any man I wanted. "I was just trying to prove to myself that we were free, that we didn't need to belong to any man," I said from my hurt. Freedom wasn't going to come without a price.

My Creative Writing professor, a Catholic intellectual named Petrowsky, invited me to coffee to talk about the themes in his latest book, the nature of sin in mankind, the redemption of suffering. "Suffering doesn't redeem," I insisted, thinking of my own experience. "It just scars."

These discussions, we both knew, were sexual foreplay, and one night, I brought him home. He was a married man and very experienced with women. I was nervous, one lover out from newly divorced. I wanted to know him, to be genuinely intimate with him, not just "a lay."

I made him nervous with my talk, all my personal questions. "Relax, don't be so intense, quit probing." He called me an intellectual woman.

I could feel him keeping his distance. He sat on a chair, rather than on the low bed with me. He seemed not to know whether he wanted me or not. Yet when we were in bed, I found him to be loving and warm. He became tender when he left, tucking me in and tiptoeing out. "He keeps saying the trouble is he likes me, but he needs bitches to love, excite him. The Virgin Mary complex," I told a friend.

At an educational conference, I met a man who invited me to visit the Berkeley commune where he and his wife lived. I loved the big house, with all its windows, I liked the ease of the people, enjoyed helping Will and Shirley strip paint off the fireplace while they told me about their open relationship. They had a party later, and I danced with Will, then Will and Shirley, then Shirley. Will asked me to spend the night with them, and even though I was not particularly attracted to him, I agreed, mostly out of curiosity.

"Shirley was like a priestess," I wrote in my journal. "Softly gowned and perfumed, setting the mood with candles and incense, marijuana. Both she and Will received me like the nervous innocent I was. They were gentle and patient. When I finally gave in to the marijuana, I forgot my inhibitions and enjoyed the splendid eroticism of three beautiful bodies being tossed on a waterbed ocean. Whose hand or lips or leg was whose became irrelevant, just strong hard arms or warm soft skin, small woman's bones, soft lips, fragile head, or man's broad shoulders, powerful legs. I felt like I was making love to both my male and female selves, felt both aroused and cared for."

The next morning, I told Shirley that if I could have been more like her I could have saved myself some unhappiness with Dick. Then I just got in the car and left, not even staying for breakfast. As good as the experience had been, it had frightened me.

I wanted to experience everything, to know all kinds of people, all kinds of situations but I wondered: was I trying to make myself as impregnable as Dick was? Was I "taking on the power of the oppressor?"

Meantime, the Vietnam war went on and on. I would pick up the paper and see yet another picture of women and children fleeing from their villages, flaming napalm clinging to their bodies. One night on live television, the world watched as an American soldier held a revolver to the head of a Viet Namese man, whose arms were twisted behind him. The captive seemed delicate, almost dainty, compared to the big G.I. Before my eyes, the American pulled the trigger; I saw the small body twitch then sag into death, as valueless as a rabbit. It was more than I could bear to think my taxes were paying for that. We kept up our demonstrations.

At last Scott was home—angry, unresponsive, unreachable, confused, hurt—but home. Home to Lakeview Hills where his mother no longer lived, home to see his familiar world falling apart, a scattered family who did not know how to help him. Home to feel so ashamed of the uniform he had worn that I was never to see him in it again.

A few months later the news quietly announced that the war was over. After all the years it had been part of my life, was it really over? Was it only a temporary truce? Had we lost? Had we won? I waited for the celebration. There was none. Only a kind of hushed waiting, followed by a silence, a long silence that would stretch into years, the silence of denial of an entire people. I knew something had changed and would never be the same again. The age of the innocent righteous war, the age of the warrior hero, the age of the United States as rescuer of oppressed peoples, was over.

By then I had met another professor, Jack Lamar. He was soft-spoken, with a quick nervous energy, a mass of curly hair around a strong, patrician face. His eyes were almost girlish, wide and blue, with long lashes. Tentative eyes. He had the quick tentative movements of one who does not want to grasp too firmly until he's sure he won't be hurt. We went walking on the bicycle trail along the river, then dancing in a small Bohemian gathering place. He said, "I have room for you in my life."

He wrote me from a conference in Hawaii, a very perceptive letter. "I see a woman with great energy, very intense, introspective as hell, trying to grow, and willing to risk. But I sense massive bruises and a pushy aggressiveness. I suspect I'm getting ready for more than I can actually handle. My wish is that we can go with gentleness, warmth and patience."

When he returned we plunged into a tumultuous love affair. He too was newly divorced and uncertain about what he wanted. We talked about intimacy with freedom.

We skied and danced, went to hot springs and camped. We swam and sunbathed at nude beaches. People often told us how beautiful we were together, and we would pause, nude, before a mirror, admiring ourselves, a matched pair of forty-year-olds with sleek, trim bodies.

I wanted to experience an honest loving relationship with Jack. Ideally, I wanted us to allow each other total freedom, discovering that we each would return again and again to the other, by choice, and perhaps eventually, find little need for others.

The old mansion swallowed up time like a killer whale. It took time to relate to each of its fourteen members, and to do my share of the household work. I was working hard on my Master's degree, as well, teaching and writing.

I did not want to give it up for a conventional relationship. Jack wanted more of my time. We quarreled, he would walk away. He would come back.

I wrote: *"How much freedom do I want and how much can his jealousy tolerate? I'll see how much I can move his way without feeling either embarrassed at my captivity or resentful of limitations. I will not give up the right to give men at least the attention I would give them if they were women; nor will I drop men who are friends because they have once been lovers. I want to learn to treat men as total human beings, not as sexual partners. Can we handle the insecurity?"*

I received a carefully hand-printed note from Jack: *"Trust my love for you and recognize my caring and concern for us as a couple. Accept that this is new and difficult for me, and be patient with my melodrama, jealousy and conditioning until I've made some changes. Knock off the Lolita thing."*

Both of us were ambivalent. He wanted to see other women, but did not want me to see other men. I wanted him to see other women, but would distance myself emotionally when he did. We wanted to be honest with each other, but honesty led to anger and hurt.

We broke up, we made up, we broke up. He joined our commune. Then the writing in the journal becomes angry and sprawls across the page:

I have been struggling with some deep feelings of doubt about my own self worth, and Judy had some psychedelic mushrooms she thought might help bring some insights. For an hour or two, I felt nothing different, did the dishes, joined others in the basement listening to music, doing massage, feeling very mellow. After a while I realized that I was giving Bob the best massage that I have ever given. The electricity from his body seemed to guide my hands to whatever places most felt stress or pain. He cried like a child in his sleep, and told me afterward that he had a transformative experience: he was three persons in one, boy, man, and all men. The vibrations, literally vibrations, that I was feeling from people told me everything: their fear, their love, their pain.

Jack, unaware we were on psychedelics, came down and asked me to go back to his room with him. I felt uneasy about it, his vibrations were so angry, so cold. In his room, he treated me so roughly that I told him I couldn't stay. He seemed like a devil, leaning over me, furious with jealousy. He pinned both my arms down with his knees and hit me with his fist. When I tried to scream he covered my mouth with his hands.

I feel rage and humiliation every time I look at my bruised face in the mirror. But what's gotten me down even more is the reaction of the house I live in, "Poor Jack, how he must be hurting." What must I have done to make him act like that? No one mentions it to me. The men refuse to look at my black eye. The women seem to find Jack even more attractive. The girl across the hall is sleeping with him. The men huddle with him on the couch as he spits out his anger at what a terrible experience that night was for him, the worst thing that ever happened to him in his life." Shit, he's hit me before, and other women too.

At first I half convinced myself that it was my fault, that I shouldn't have told him the truth about how I perceived him, shouldn't have given Bob the massage. I've been feeling guilty for being angry for being treated in a way that I have never treated anyone. So long have we women been taking this that right seems wrong and wrong seems right.

This morning I have become aware for the first time of the violence done to me by men, and for the first time, I cannot just be tolerant. They have their troubles too." That does not relieve my humiliation and anger. I'm angry with men and women both. Women for their goddamn masochistic support, men because they gang together in their fear of being "deballed." Goddamn, are their balls that fragile, attached that loosely?

But that nightmare evening, Jack's hand over my mouth jarred loose my earliest childhood memory as I lay in my bed after leaving him. *My heart is beating like a hummingbird's. I am a baby in a crib, jumping with fright at noises in the hall, banging noises which mean my father is mad. He is mad because a baby is crying when he's trying to sleep. That baby is me, and a hand, my mother's, goes over my mouth and nose. I feel terror, the air pushes in my belly as I try to scream out. My heart pounds, my head feels like it will burst. The hand comes off. I look up at my mother with a pitiful pleading smile. I am helpless and I depend on her.*

The first humiliation.

Much as I needed to break up with Jack, I felt a great loss, a hard place in my chest where softness was just beginning. A friend told me I looked confused and disoriented. "Did somebody die?" I knew something had.

Meantime, my fantasy of the perfect match, Dick Larkin and Connie, broke up too. Connie called. "I think you should know." They had not had trouble over other women. If he baited her about other women, she would just say, "Go ahead." But small violent incidents escalated until one day when he had told her to pick up a box, she had refused, saying it was too heavy. "He charged down the hill, knocked me down and kicked me so hard in the groin that I'm now in the hospital. I'm just lucky there's no permanent damage."

I saw then that whatever had gone on between Dick and myself, it was not really about other women. Whatever it was between him and other women, it was not love.

Since Dick no longer lived there, I went to stay in the cabin that summer, to heal, to read, to meditate, and to write.

I enjoyed having my sons and all their friends at the cabin with me, filling the place with guitar music and car talk. At night, we talked philosophy and psychology, and the difficult intricacies of love, lying in our separate beds, watching the flames until the fire went out.

If I was ever on a pedestal with my sons, I fell off it that summer. My attractive friend Ruth had come up from the city, just as Dick dropped in, and Jerry had come over from the Institute. Ruth admitted later she wanted revenge for my earlier flirtations, Jerry, as always, wanted to be the top stag, and Dick wanted to claim that title for himself.

I was running around trying to control it all. "All right, we are just going to bed and sleep, just sleep," I said at midnight. No one paid any attention to that, once the lights were off, and by morning, Ruth was furious with Jerry for forcing himself on her, and Jerry's wife was hurt that he had not come home. By afternoon, Ruth and Dick had infuriated me by making love in the loft.

All with Mike and Scott there. They looked at me with bewilderment. I was embarrassed and contrite. "We were certainly not models of new and more loving ways," I told them in apology. "We were careless, competitive, hurtful, and stupid." They agreed.

When they weren't there, I had a lot of time alone. As I walked the mountain trails, I thought about the confusion of the times. All the old roles were changing. In the evenings, I read Anäis Nin's books and was especially impressed by her thoughts on the creation of the female self from selflessness.

Out of the silence of the mountains, the isolation of the cabin, a powerful experience came.

I am sitting cross legged in the meadow, meditating, when I feel my body wanting to move of its own volition. I let it follow its urges, rolling my shoulders in circles, letting my head fall forward to the ground, like an autistic person. I become aware of black tightness in my head that I can't get past, like a door. I stay with it, remembering a dream I used to have, a curtain of undulating weaving lines, making me nauseated. I try to get through the curtain, finally push beyond it, to the anger and rage it covered.

I go back to the cabin, close the door, and let loose. I yell and beat on the bed, no words, just guttural animal sounds.

In my mind, I see my father and mother lying on the bed. I am beating them bloody, wallowing and growling. But my father's genitals keep appearing before me. No amount of hitting on the bed drives them away. I want to tear them away from his body with my teeth, to tear them away then swallow them, one ball then the other, then the soft penis.

I bite on the bedspread, clamp and tear, imagining the soft succulence in my mouth. I swallow them, feel them now between my own legs. I become him; my chest swells, my thumb disappears, my chin lowers on my neck, my brow straightens, waves and waves pass through me and around me. A small voice says, Experience this.

Because I am him, I become aware of what his power means, intimidating all of us, causing my mother to suffocate me rather than have my cries wake him, discounting all needs but his. His eye falls on me. I am him, seeing me, a child in a puckered plaid swimsuit, innocent yet somehow sensuous to him, even then. Looking at me, in his embarrassment, he asks, "Where's Beverly?"

I understand for the first time that his avoidance of me all those years, his scorn for me, was because he was projecting his own sexual guilt on to me.

After that I look at the bed and see my father there, dead and gray. I cry, stifled, twisted sobs for him, lying there so defenseless without his power.

Exhausted, emptied, I wandered in the woods, along the stream, in the sun, all the rest of the day, trying to integrate it, wondering what it meant. Had my relationships with men always been based on hiding the fact that I wanted to rip off their testicles and eat them?

At a workshop in Long Beach, I told a therapist how tired I was of it all, "the man-woman thing." I had a deep yearning to love and be loved, but it was so difficult.

"Yearning is a strength, not a weakness," Erica Kelly said. "Look how much you have to give."

Through body exercises, I felt myself stop breathing when I was asked to tell my partner, "I can show you my needs."

Chuck Kelly pointed out what he saw. "By keeping your breathing shallow, you can just numb out. You say you want intimacy, say you offer it, but it is so terrifying to you, you quit breathing rather than experience the fear. Then in your resulting isolation, you look for someone to break through to you." It was confirmation of what I had heard before.

At that workshop I met a young biologist, Joe, 14 years younger than I. His was the kind of beauty one hears about in romance novels; tall and fair, he had long wavy hair, which fell in curly tendrils across his face. He had clear blue eyes with curly lashes, full red lips. He counteracted this softness by wearing black shirts and pants, a black wide-brimmed hat, decorated with bright silver and turquoise. He seemed to me the perfect balance of male and female.

A month later he came to Tahoe for two weeks of backpacking in Desolation Valley. Into the mountains the two of us climbed, mile after mile, with all we would need for two weeks in our backpacks; sleeping bags, tube tents, dried food, clothing. We would stop at every lake and stream, cool our feet, set up camp early enough to swim in the icy waters. We read poetry by flashlight, talked into the starry night. By the end of a week, we were like friends of the same sex who made love like lovers, tenderly, mutually.

At Stony Ridge Lake, our sleeping bags zipped together, I had this dream: *I am the owner of a large ranch. I seem to be male. I am strong and in charge, but I have a hole through my back, a bullet hole, and because it's in my back, I can't take care of it myself. Everybody else sees it and shies off and disappears. My woman self, a distant figure, goes off trying to find out why I had the hole, if I deserved it, but is no immediate help. I stand near the end of a bar, angry that no one comes to do what needs to be done. Finally a cowboy at the end of the bar, gentle but very frightened, comes to help. He wears a hat like Joe's and has long hair, but when he pulls up my shirt and sees how great my wound is, he does not want to have* to do it. *I know that whatever gets done I'll have to do myself, no one else is big enough to help me.*

I told Joe about it, and when I lay naked, next to his chest, I felt the big hole in my chest close.

I had another dream about building a chicken coop inside a huge barn with a high clean ceiling, about trading stamps and conniving people. I thought it was about conniving trades for love. "Chicken shit stuff." Joe saw it as a dream of unfulfilled potential. I think now it was both.

When, ten days later, we stumbled off the mountain and pulled off our heavy packs, he and Mike, not so far apart in age, played chess, talked about politics, about the environment, about women. When he got in his big Blazer 4-wheel drive to return to Long Beach, they were friends too.

I visited him on occasional weekends. We listened to *The Doors*, worked on an antique chair, read *The Little Prince*. He bought me a lovely turquoise ring. We made up ceremonies and built sand sculptures on the beach. He told me he loved me, wanted me, missed our poetry and togetherness, had never had a relationship as multifaceted as ours. He called me Lovely. "Hey, Lovely. Breakfast is ready." I basked in it like a cat in the sun.

But the risk frightened me. The age difference. We lived 600 miles apart. He was recovering from a divorce and often missed his wife. He needed time before making any commitments. He went on working cruises that lasted weeks at a time, sometimes with very attractive students.

I was living back in the big house, putting in extra time to make up for my absence, finding fourteen people too many. I was almost finished with my graduate studies; I wanted Joe to ask me to come and live with him. He would only say, "You're welcome to stay awhile." Ruth said that when I spoke of Joe, she saw pain in my face.

My dreams told me I was still trying to push things through. *Driving my car in heavy downtown traffic, many stop lights, it won't run right, stalls, stops, I get mad, ram my foot on the accelerator. It stalls. I use a choke, angry spasmodic, it will only run backward. When I try to go forward, it stalls. Angry, frustrated, I ram it into gear, choke out, racing backward, roaring through stop signs and dangerous intersections, knowing I'll be arrested or get hit, not caring, just wanting the damned car to run, not get stuck in the middle of all this traffic.*

I gestalted it out, playing all the parts of my dream. *I'm Helen's car. She keeps tearing around, pulling the choke in and out without really paying attention to how my engine runs, what it needs. I feel rammed through. She's so frustrated, she keeps going backward and we're going to get hurt. I want to be driven carefully, taken care of, there's nothing wrong with me. I can go forward if I'm treated right.*

I played the part of Helen the driver: *I'm afraid if I go slowly, if I stop, I'll be in this terrible place forever. I feel an urgency to have these empty places in me filled. I can't stand them much longer. My child feels beat up and uncared for. My emotional parts feel exhausted and needy and pushed around. My parent is furious and frustrated. Get out there and do it, push, push, push.*

The dream was echoing what Erica Kelly had told me in the workshop. "You don't think you're enough, you think you have to make it happen." Knowing that didn't seem to change it.

On my next visit to Long Beach, Joe had obtained some carefully produced psychedelics, "acid." We were cautious. Knowing the set of the mind is the most important factor in an experience that can either be enlightening or horrifying, we prepared carefully. We bought groceries ahead of time, made sure there would be no surprise visitors or interruptions. We talked quietly, listened to soothing music. Then we took the prescribed doses. Both of us knew the rules for attaining the best results: whatever the experience, don't resist or it will intensify; go with it and it will change.

Joe turns into many different people before my eyes, yet all of them a part of him I recognize. One moment, he is a proud shy 18-year-old, his eyes full of joy, the next, an arrogant prince or 16th Century king. Then he becomes a post-20th Century man, with his black shirt and long blond curls, absorbed with technology, cameras, cars and science, a Los Angeles man. In brief flashes between, he is a clownish boor, an affected girlish prig, in just the right proportion to his total personality.

I look in a full length mirror and see a 20th century woman, large intelligent eyes, long questioning fingers, and intermittently, a waif, a mermaid, a country peasant. All of it is acceptable, all of it good. My eyes fall on a poster of a magnificent wild snow cat, so beautiful I can not leave it. As I stand before it, it changes to an old lady in a shawl, with a voice of wisdom, then to a beautiful fantasy creature with wooden flower eyes and purple shaded ears, jewel bedecked, changing, changing, always fine and beautiful.

Food is an even more absorbing experience; I can see its living cells. I feel the knife and fork waiting to be picked up, feel the fork clinging like a claw to my lip, know the omelette is alive, breathing, see a strawberry devouring a grape, see the tiny cells of the melon, breathing, the orange, bleeding juice and wanting to, waiting to be eaten. The honey drops sensuously into my coffee cup, the cream swirls like living clouds. It is all there to give itself to me. My pleasure in it is all it wanted.

I become fascinated with projection: when I think them old, my hands change before my eyes to an old woman's, veined and speckled, then change back to smooth firm skin when I think them young. Trees outside the window dance in the sun, shelter the house. When I deliberately think of them as dark and foreboding, they lean toward the house, sinister, threatening.

It was night when I felt myself coming into the dark passage called "coming down." We were listening to violent sexual music, the Doors, Come on Baby, Light My Fire; L.A. Woman; 20th Century Fox. Sex was not love now, it was sex, both of us wanting to be the passive one, wanting to be fucked violently. I became a cruel bitch, pinching Joe, dragging at him because he would not control, dominate me. Then we were going through that, past that, and my body was being carried by his body into one motion, gently, like riding a dolphin, filling me with soft joy. We rode on and on, churning like the ocean, like cells swirling and dividing, like sea anemones tossing with the tide.

The next day we were both exhausted. Still feeling some effects of the psychedelics, we talked. Joe wanted to decide how to deal with any future woman he'd be with. I got very anxious, walked down to the beach to steady myself. As with Dick, I wanted him to love me too much, made that far too important. I needed to pull back. I decided to put my energies elsewhere, perhaps teach in Australia? Perhaps the Peace Corps?

Later, lying in bed next to him, I was quiet. He said, "What's the matter?" I smiled and said, "Nothing, I just don't feel like talking, I'm quite content." But I was feeling down, afraid to say it was because he hadn't asked me to live with him, and he was keeping his life open to other women. I pulled away and lay on my stomach, deciding that I wouldn't live with him if he asked me anyway. I wanted to travel, live overseas, stay free.

I knew that this was manipulation and what its effect was going to be: I would pull away angry and not get what I wanted anyway, blaming him, confirming my nothing-ever-works-out tragic fantasies.

My next dream confirmed that: *Someone, a man, is holding a rat in a plastic tub full of water, increasing the pressure to kill it. I take it and say no, it will die by itself in time, don't put pressure on, it's painful.*

Back in the big house in Sacramento, I tried to solve the problem by fantasizing a different partner. Clearly, distancing was preferable to the hard work, the risks, of change. My dreams reflected my ambivalence: *I live in a fine and beautiful old house, but I'm disturbed because the house is being changed, its front is being remodeled, the fine old pillars removed to make room for a sun deck and let in more light. I want the sun and light, but the destruction of the fine old front disturbs me. Inside there is a new window all along the left side, through which I can see the knights riding back from the jousting tournaments, elated and strong. One knight is the father of a girl in my house, a beautiful 16-year-old who has* become newly aware of her power as a woman. She is sure of her beauty and desirability, is dressed in fine womanly garments. Her father feels she is too young for those clothes, I feel she is old enough and defend her. Then a man and I are doing dishes. He has been to a group and he is angry because they have all faced him with the fact that he tries to make people do things his way. I tease him, "C'mon now, really?" He laughs. We shove each other and where we meet, our thighs are warm. The feeling is good and caring and uniting.

Joe and I managed to ride our turbulent relationship through the next few months. He would make the long drive from Southern California; we would ski and talk by the fire and play games like kids together. One game was choosing animal spirits for ourselves. Joe would say he was an eagle, I would say, "You are not, you're a frog," and we would laugh. We snowshoed up the moraine, enjoyed each other. Then he would return to Long Beach, and I, feeling separate and alone, would go to work on rebuilding my independence, not wanting to fall into the painful neediness.

Over the Christmas break, Joe and I made a trip in the Blazer down through Baja California, Mexico, to the inland coast. It was a magical trip, driving through mile after mile of saguaro cactus, desert sands swept clean by ocean winds. We camped on the shores at night, listening to the whales in the bay blowing water through their spouts. Fasting, we experienced the way time slowed down. Small daily tasks like washing one's hair, eating a ripe fig, watching the sun set, became meaningful and fulfilling rituals. In that place, away from time and noise and worldly demands, I had this dream: *I'm leaving one country to get to another, approaching the suspension bridge that gets me across the bay. Several big burly longshoremen bear down on me to keep me off the bridge. They're on some sort of picket line. I'm scared, but I realize that if I scream they will leave me alone. They don't want people to know they're attacking a woman. I keep going, they fade back. The suspension bridge is narrow and has a hand rail on only one side; the other side is open and dangerous. I reach a small island in the center where people are foreign and where I pause before going the rest of the way on the bridge.*

Back home I wrote Joe: "I've been having one hell of a time with those longshoremen as the bridge gets closer."

I was finishing up my University work, graduating with Honors, but the prospect of being out of a job loomed large. There were very few positions in my field anywhere in California.

Money was tight. My husband was dragging his feet about a fair divorce settlement, complaining he couldn't pay even what he agreed he owed. When Joe wrote that he wanted me to come and live with him, I was ready.

In January, manuscript and exams finished, Master's degree in hand, I left the Bureaucratic Commune and went to Long Beach.

Our only commitment to each other was to keep communication open, and be as honest with ourselves and each other as we could. We had learned enough from our pasts to know that communication alone did not guarantee the survival of the relationship, but not communicating would guarantee that our relationship would fail.

We both enjoyed jogging on the beach, gathering mussels on the rocks, gathering grape leaves to feed snails. We spent long afternoons in the kitchen making *escargot*, with lots of garlic. We made weekend drives to Mammoth Mountain to ski. I had weekdays to myself for writing, while Joe went off to work in the labs, or on a marine cruise. I got acquainted with his grad students, learned from their discussions of the effects of pressure and changing temperatures on deep sea animals. I saw the tearing competitiveness among the professors as Joe sometimes came home sick from subtle attacks in Departmental meetings, threats to his attaining tenure. I decided I would not want a place in that world.

Sometimes I would grumble that he was always at work or talking technology. He would complain that I was careless about cooking, imprecise about recipes, indifferent about the proper tools. We would call each other "turkey" or "toad." I would fall into black funks occasionally, he would back off into passive noncommunication. But it would pass. We liked each other.

We enjoyed the role playing we had begun earlier. I would dress up in a sexy outfit, leave the house for a while, knock on the front door as a completely different personality. He never knew who to expect. He would pick it up from there, either capitulating entirely to my bitchy, dominating role, or playing the dominating rescuer if I arrived as poor sweet thing in distress. Perhaps I would tie him up and force myself on him. Perhaps he would take charge, dominating me. We never hurt each other. It was fun.

As time went on and we pushed these games further, I found it more and more difficult to play the dominant one. "It seems to me the slave driver has to work even harder than the slave," I complained. But the problems started when I was the passive one. Tied up, mildly tormented, I suddenly became a wailing defenseless child, begging him to stop, "If you don't stop, I'm going to hate you forever!"

Shaken, he immediately untied my hands and tried to soothe me. "I wouldn't hurt you little one, you know that." But something had happened at a deep level, and I didn't want to play those games anymore. He was deeply disappointed. After that, our sex life became rather lukewarm.

I was not to learn for years that we were coming dangerously close to the dark cellar door of my denied memories. All I knew was Joe felt cheated, and I felt very bad about it.

I landed a temporary job at the Community College and put my energy into being one of their best and most innovative teachers. I organized part-time faculty to lobby for equality for women in the college system, where great numbers were exploited, "freeway fliers" who had to take temporary jobs at several colleges to make a living.

I put out job applications all over the state, came out second or third in dozens of interviews, but nothing permanent came of it. I applied to teach with the Peace Corps.

Joe still hungered after his ex-wife, or less often, the tanned young legs of a grad student.

I wrote in my journal:

I think if I were really committed, our relationship would probably go on indefinitely. If I would decide he came first, above traveling, other men, a job, etc. I have never been committed to a man. There were always reasons: Jimmy was bad to the kids, Cap was frightening and a drinker, Bill was passive and unresponsive, Dick had other women, Jack was too demanding, Joe is too young. But I chose them. Maybe I have some fatal flaw. Maybe I need to accept that I'll always be a rover and quit blaming men for it.

When the Peace Corps offer came through for Sierra Leon, Africa, I faced for the first time the reality of actually serving a stint in the Corps. A two-year chunk would be taken from my life. I would be leaving my friends and family, leaving Joe, Mike, Scott, Nanci, Ruth.

For two years there would be no peaceful mountain cabin, no skiing. I would be dealing with strange and foreign surroundings, dangerous diseases, language barriers. I was angry that Joe made no attempt to talk me out of going. I felt if he loved me, he wouldn't let me go. He called my attitude "suspicions confirmed."

Before I left, Joe and I camped by the Mokeleme River, fished for salmon, chased a rattlesnake out of our camp. We took our second and last acid trip.

Joe became a bearded child in short pants and big heavy boots. Everything became a projection, trees leaned inward beseechingly or rigidly, a mountain turned when I turned my shoulder, became a sphinx filled with moving forms, frogs, horses, people, evolving, the most powerfully beautiful thing I've ever seen. Rocks became serpentine, beautifully scaled, along Chinese garden paths. My own flesh became many things, sometimes corrupt with purple blotches, sometimes splendid, shining, reptilian. I knew I had gone back to the beginning of time.

We hiked out of the canyon, bathed together in the yellow bathtub, scrubbed the dust off one another's backs. Then we dressed in our most beautiful clothes, Joe in a black shirt and jeans, I in a long soft dress.

Wearing turquoise and silver, we took the gondola to the lodge on top of the mountain overlooking Tahoe Valley. Below, the trails we had skied last winter flowed like earthen rivers down to tiny forrested ski resorts, and beyond them lay the magnificent blue expanse of Lake Tahoe.

Over good food and good wine, we pledged our rather bewildered friendship. "For Africa, and for the coming years."

7

To Africa and Back
"O monin O! Ow debody?"

I felt deeply isolated, departing California to live in a foreign country. "The Dark Continent" was a phrase that haunted me. I imagined dark dense jungles, dark sinister people. I spent my last few days alone at the cabin, feeling like I didn't matter to anyone; their lives would go on unchanged, maybe better, without me. Nothing could ease the loneliness I felt, leaving my family, my friends, the places I had known all my life. Later, a friend would send me pictures of my cabin, looking abandoned, the family dog forlorn at a closed door.

My son Scott and my friend Nanci were the last to see me off. Nanci, deeply involved with her young family and a career in college teaching, looked bewildered, like she didn't understand what I was doing. I wasn't sure I had understood myself that I was leaving, until the last moment, saying goodbye at the Sacramento Airport. What a chunk I would be cutting out of my life. In two years my family and friends could marry, have babies, go through divorces, even die, and I would not be there. I didn't understand for years the hurt and abandonment that my departure created in those around me; I didn't think I mattered that much.

At the Philadelphia training site, there were 160 excited young people, most of them right out of college, white, middle class. Almost hysterically fun-seeking, they carried their six packs and wine bottles from room to room, like university freshmen the first day before classes.

During the three-day training, I found the few among them who were a little older. We looked to each other for escape from the fraternity atmosphere of the dorm rooms. We were a colorful group, all of us strongly defined individuals, a bit cynical, a contrast to the wholesome, optimistic new graduates.

I dubbed us Terry and the Pirates, after a comic strip. Emily was a southern beauty from North Carolina who looked like Elizabeth Taylor and acted like Scarlett O'Hara, talkative, witty, and restless. At 28, she had already done one stint in the Peace Corps. After returning to the States, she had taught a while, married and divorced. Life in the States no longer suited her, she said. "I like bush boas better than Holiday Inn lounge lizards."

Emily was already acquainted with Terry, the son of a Massachusetts House Minority Leader, grandson of an oil billionaire. Terry was a small, wiry 26-year-old who had been to Africa several times before and felt a strong affinity for it. He too had been married and divorced, something more than age that seemed to engrave the mark of the "older" person on us.

They called me the California Hippie. We joked together as we sat on hard metal chairs, hour after hour, getting briefed about the scorpions we might find under thatched roofs, cobras in the reeds, boas in the bush. "All Americans, even P.C.s living on $160 a month, are rich." We were told to expect thievery, even from our "houseboys," since this was a poor country and an American camera or radio could be sold for enough money to feed a S'lon family for six months.

We were warned that Sierra Leon had only two seasons, wet and dry. This was the rainy season; Freetown would be rainy, smelly and moldy, wringing wet with humidity. We were warned to keep absorbent chemically treated packing in our camera cases, and that no matter what we did, our clothes would come out of our suitcases sodden. We were told how to guard against malaria, fungi, and disabling infections.

Philadelphia was the last chance to bail out gracefully, and many did, but none from our group.

On the plane I wrote Joe a postcard:

"We're about 500 miles off the coast of Africa. All around me, Peace Corps volunteers are playing cribbage, cards, drinking Gallo and Jack Daniels, eating potato chips and candy, reading the latest Newsweek or Time, joking about Nixon. I hoped the Peace Corps would delay our departure from Philadelphia so we could hear Nixon's step-down address. I am sorry to miss the climax of the Watergate furor; too bad a demand for honest and responsible government occurred just when I was leaving for Africa. I'd like to see it."

When Nixon's address came on, the pilot put it over the speakers. As always Nixon professed his innocence and blamed the calumny of others, especially the press. With that hangdog picked-on tone so characteristic of him then, he reluctantly agreed to step down from the presidency. The entire plane load cheered and whistled.

The new President, Gerald Ford, was introduced. I had never heard of him. "One ass is as good as another," Emily said, polishing her nails by the overhead light.

I felt a little twinge that I would not be in on the political excitement back home as the facts of the Watergate scandal emerged. "If it weren't for the free press, we'd have been an authoritarian state long ago," Tim said. "Newspaper types are a pain in the ass, but if they go, Democracy goes."

When the plane dropped down through the clouds, a rim of light circled the curving earth. We could see the airport on a narrow swatch of land surrounded by swamps and open water.

Farther down the coast, we could just make out the outlines of Freetown, a clutch of buildings five or six stories high, just inland from a stretch of long white beaches. Everything was green beyond that. Sierra Leon, Lion Mountain, rose up in the misty distance, a calm presence over the dense jungles and wet grassy plains.

Freetown, we were told by the guide at the airport, was named by slaves who had escaped their chains and come there to establish a free colony. Its original "cinque," or leader, was a Mende from Sierra Leon, a captured slave who led the mutiny of a slave ship.

The Peace Corps group was taken immediately to Farah Bay College, which looked more like a coastal California condominium, clustered along a hillside, all dark weathered wood and wide windows. It was built, we learned, with boards from one of the slave ships.

It was not raining when we arrived, and the beds in our small dorm rooms were not damp. There were no lizards or mosquitoes. Those conditions would change when we were given our permanent assignments in the "bush," a term used to refer to anyplace outside of Freetown, the only city in Sierra Leon.

"The bush?" I asked.

"I contracted to teach college English. Surely there are no colleges in the bush?"

My supervisor informed me, as if it were a minor point, that the Peace Corps had been unable to place me at Farah Bay. "The teachers here are all male, and in Sierra Leon, men feel it is insulting to be taught by a woman, even an American woman."

"Won't this be a problem in the bush too?"

"College faculty are especially proud."

"But I'm not trained for...."

"Teaching is teaching, isn't it?"

Tentatively, my training site was Port Loko, about 100 miles inland, and all my new friends were going other ways. Meantime, we were herded from lecture hall to classroom to cafeteria, always behind the constantly altered and confused schedule. For the first time in my life I experienced racial discrimination from the receiving end: black administrators and teachers were in charge of white Americans now. They hung around in laughing cliques, looking over their shoulders at the women, especially Emily. In the black culture I was considered old, and because I was slender, I was also a "flat ass." S'lons valued plump women, whose well fed bodies reflected the success of their families and implied desirability. "Something like a woman wearing diamonds in our culture," Emily said.

For entertainment, the talented black staff and faculty performed a musical which made gentle fun of the Peace Corps. Emily drawled archly, "They obviously enjoy the superiority of knowing we do not understand their inside jokes." I didn't mind. It seemed to me it was the whites' turn to be on the other end.

For the remainder of our two weeks in Freetown, we studied language, geography, culture. I enjoyed learning the Creole language, gay and simple and charming. "Good morning" was a song, "O monin O."

"Ow debody?" spoken in a laughing lilt, meant "How are you?"

My body wasn't so good. After sleeping so long with Joe, tight and close in one another's arms, I physically ached at night, like a person in drug withdrawal. I slept with one of his tee shirts pillowing my face. "Monkey babies separated from their parents are more healthy if something with a parent's scent is left with them, so why not people?" I told Emily. She gave me a skeptical look, but said nothing. More than ten years younger than I, her two-year Peace Corps stint had given her far more maturity.

Children followed Emily and me everywhere we went, to the market, on our neighborhood explorations. If I took out my camera, five children would suddenly be in front of it, with wide exaggerated smiles, sometimes holding their goats or chickens. They asked for pennies and nickels and chewing gum. In time I had to quit giving out those things, or there would be ten more bright expectant faces streaming behind me when I walked to the market, twenty more plump hands grasping mine.

Freetown's thriving marketplace reminded me of Dogpatch in Lil' Abner. Men wore blouses with frills at the waist and bright jewelry. They hiked their brightly colored American undershorts over their pants to show off. Some had cut out pictures from American magazines and pinned them to their hats. Brigitte Bardot or Marilyn Monroe or Gina Lolabridgida. I noticed they were never black women.

There were many kinds of beautiful women in the marketplace; big-breasted solid women hawking fruit drinks on the sidewalk, corner-corner girls in high platform shoes and short skirts, and sometimes, most beautiful, I thought, a quiet group of bush women bringing plantain to market, moving sedately in their colorful tie-dyed wraparounds, easily balancing baskets on their heads, graceful as gazelles.

After the newness wore off, I missed my family and friends. Although I did not want the obtrusive attention that men gave Emily, my ego smarted. The alternating heat and dampness made me feel sleepy, sticky, dull. It would be weeks before mail from home would get through to us, and phone calls were difficult and expensive.

Many others began to feel their alienation. Some got sick, some became depressed, even suicidal. One frail young man with the lost look of a Berkeley burnout told me he was considering suicide. Not wanting to be a mother, I said, "Jon, that's your choice, of course, but I don't think that's any way to get what you want."

"Well fuck you!" he said, slouching down the hall.

Emily said with a shrug, "We dryfodomgrab," a typical S'lon expression something like, "We make grab for it," or, "We do the best we can." Jon and a few others left that week.

Emily and I spent two days with a family in Makini, a small village near Freetown. It reminded me of Mexico, with its block houses always midway in construction, waiting for enough money for the next load of concrete or building blocks.

Children, and sometimes adults, often defecated in the streets or gutters, their feces left for the morning deluge to wash away. There were open, much used "peeing walls" in many places. Those too were washed clean daily by the rains.

But the villagers were warm and friendly, and seemed more content than most Americans. They lived in long low blockhouses, with large extended families, often the wives of one man with all their children and relatives. Most houses were not furnished for looks and comfort, but left bare. Their purpose was to shelter people, and even goats sometimes, from the daily downpours. Once the rain stopped, people lived out of doors, cooking, washing, marketing, gossiping. The work was done in social gatherings; women flattened their freshly washed wraparounds with wooden paddles. Men beat time on stumps while making labor deals or haggling over a trade in goats.

I liked the S'lon women. They were dignified and strong. They laughed easily. They worked together as they did their tasks, while the children played happily. I saw no competitive sibling squabbling. "Unnecessary, with so many people to turn to for attention," Emily commented. The women sang about their work as they tended boiling pots of material being tie-dyed. They sang carrying water, carrying wood for a fire, carrying bags of rice. They carried their babies on their backs as they danced. A nine-month-old baby, taken off her mother's back and set down on her feet, immediately began the rhythmic dance she had felt through her mother's back since birth.

James, our host, took us out on the town. His favorite bar, where all the men knew him, was a tin shack open on one side. A woman in a colorful turban sold homemade beer, served from a huge gourd, while a juke box played.

The men joked together, arms around each other, unashamed to show affection. Some danced rhythmic African style, opposite or arm in arm, unselfconsciously, as no doubt their forefathers had danced for centuries.

In answer to my questions, James told me there was no homosexuality or rape in his country. Almost no divorce either. "Our marriage is not like yours," he said. He and his friends laughed when they talked about those oddities, American and British married couples who touristed Sierra Leon arm in arm, or hand in hand, "as if they are afraid to let go of each other."

These bars were clearly for men, but occasionally a woman would enter, stand back until she caught James's eye, then he would step outside with her for a moment. These were his "corner-corner" girls, he explained with pride. He was sending them away because he had American visitors.

Emily told me, "The men in the smaller villages, in the bush, are quite different. They are dignified and quiet. There is responsibility that goes along with having many wives. The chiefs carry a strong sense of authority, coming from the trust and respect of their people. I like them better."

We got home late. James' wife, or at least the mother of his children, let us in matter-of-factly, and went back to bed, we assumed with James. The next morning, she seemed quite content, gossiping with a dozen other women as they prepared a meal for themselves, for their two guests, a dozen or so children, and a few assorted relatives.

I noticed on many occasions that women in Africa didn't seem upset by their men's gallivanting. "Perhaps because polygamy has always been accepted, women don't expect anything different?" I asked Emily, "Or perhaps because no man limits himself to one woman, no woman feels it is any particular disgrace or threat to be one of several."

"Or perhaps," Emily said, "the women enjoy one another more than they enjoy the men anyway."

When word came that I would definitely be going to Port Loko, Emily worked to get herself reassigned there. To my immense relief, the reassignment came on the day before I was to leave. After our trunks were packed and loaded on a big open truck called a lorry, Emily confessed she had an additional reason for going: a priest she knew from her last stint was now serving in the church there.

"I thought priests were supposed to be celibate," I teased, as I hung on to the side of the truck.

"Did I say he wasn't?" Emily retorted. "Besides, we might not even like each other any more. It's been years. I was a gorgeous twenty-one when I was here last."

Our lorry moved out of the city through plains of grass taller than our heads, through villages of thatch-covered huts, through dense growth that threatened to cut off the road at times. Hours of jolting dirt roads later, we arrived at our new location.

How Port Loko got its name we didn't know. There were no ports, unless one counted the little wharf on the river, with half a dozen rotting rowboats, one with a dismantled engine that looked like it hadn't worked in months. It was a small inland town, with one long cement sidewalk, a foot off the ground. On this was strung a series of shops, dark inside, with high wide wooden doors left open all day. Some of them were a kind of hardware-grocery store combination, where one could mail letters or buy stamps or fill a five gallon gasoline drum. In another, I could see an old-fashioned switchboard, but I never saw a telephone. Shopkeepers leaned in the doorways, only their long white gowns showing, their black faces consumed by the cool dark interior. On one end of town was a cement block school and a small dormitory, built by the British some years earlier, simple but well constructed. On the opposite end of the street was a two-story stucco building with a bell steeple; the front of this was the church; the back, a sign indicated, was a clinic. Both looked quite abandoned.

There were a few cement block houses scattered along the dirt road, and many more nearly invisible, back in the bush. Goats and chickens roamed freely in and out of houses and stores. Children followed us from the lorry, even peering in the windows of our Spartan dorm room, as if we were strange museum specimens, especially me, with my sunless white skin and straight pale hair.

Emily was assigned to teach English to small boys. Girls were not sent to school. The principal told me I would be working with the oldest students, 18 to 20 years old, in the most advanced class, the eighth grade. Emily explained that education was not free. Students could take months or years off to earn enough money to continue. I had never taught elementary classes, but I was sure I could do better than what I had seen teachers doing in Freetown.

Their history as a British Colony was only briefly behind them, and though their schools were run by blacks, those teachers too had been schooled in an oppressive colonial system. They had been whipped and caned, and that's what they handed on to their students.

My students were well disciplined, sat straight in their desks and called me "ma'am." I sensed a smoldering anger behind their good manners. When the principal pointed out the five-foot cane in the corner of the classroom, I told him I wouldn't be using it. He gave me a contemptuous look.

That day and each day following, I took into the classroom the lesson plan they assigned to me, and the administrators would watch through a window as I taught the class. The materials hardly seemed appropriate to the needs of students who came from the bush and would be trying to make their way in Freetown. But the British had taught Shakespeare's *Midsummer Night's Dream* in the eighth grade, it would be on these students' graduation examination, therefore these six-foot black Africans would memorize *Midsummer Night's Dream*. The Elizabethan verses must have made as little sense to them as a Zulu masked ritual would make to me.

Each day I would teach the materials assigned, then I would spend a few minutes with what I thought would be more useful, writing about their history, writing letters. I would give quizzes afterward to show my evaluators that successful learning did not depend on punishment.

The principal and the senior teachers, all wearing ties and white shirts, would make a circle with their backs to me, examining the few errors on the quizzes, talking among themselves.

Then the principal would point out my flaws. "But you see you failed to establish respect. Did you not notice the boy in the back row, leaning on his elbow? That is a sign of disrespect. You should not allow it. Now he will think he can do anything in the classroom. And what did you mean, talking to them about writing letters to students in America? That was not on the lesson plan, they are paying money to be ready for their exams, and that will not be on the exam. Besides, they have no money for stamps and foolishness. They were laughing at you behind your back."

I told them, "I have seen no evidence that punishment motivates learning."

The principal stood tall and proud. "In our country, a teacher is a respected and honored member of the village. He is, to use the American word, a great success. And we learned this way. How can you tell us it is not a good way?"

One day, walking across the open courtyard between classrooms, I saw a big African standing with a desk balanced on his head, punishment for some minor infraction, I was sure. When I left my classroom an hour later, he was still there, passively accepting his humiliation, though crumpling with the heat and humidity.

I went to the principal and suggested that perhaps someone had forgotten the man. "Surely no one would intentionally leave him there! That would hardly be civilized." The principal glanced up from his papers. He looked at his watch. "All right. But you tell him if it happens again, he will stand all day."

The student eased the heavy desk off his head, carried it to the shade, and sank down on it, saying nothing to me. He was a handsome six-footer, his shining blue-black skin marred by three matching pink cuts across each cheek. I asked him what tribe the marks indicated. His eyes flamed with anger. "I don't know. They were given me at birth. If ever I find the man who marked me, I will kill him."

I was shocked by his rage. It seemed clearly displaced. To be angry with his tribe after what the school was doing to him. Emily explained to me that the highest success was to be recognized as a Freetowner. "Those tribal marks will forever mark him as a bushman, no matter how well he recites British law or Shakespeare."

After our work was done, Emily and I would sometimes join the village women, who sat in groups under the trees, braiding one another's hair into marvelous creative sculptures, or sewing cowry shells on their bright wraparounds.

They sang always, blending their voices with skill and grace:

"Akba woman do you buy an ok bo ro." (Lazy woman, go buy a gourd) They were busy and resourceful women, but their work and pleasure were joined.

I bought some lengths of tie-dyed material, wrapped it as the women had taught me, around my torso and head. Emily laughed. "Well, honey, you just 'bout got that washin' done?" I laughed, too, as I unwound my turban. Their beauty was their own, created for them, earned. "This pale blonde honkey ain't got it."

One day as I sat visiting, a woman set her little girl in my lap. The child had skin than shone like licorice, deep brown eyes with curled lashes. "She's beautiful." I said. The mother was not especially surprised at that; all little girls are considered beautiful there. "Take her back to United States with you," she said.

"You would not really let her go!"

The mother proudly arranged the shining black braids, not one whit sentimental. She said, "She'll have a good life in America, cars, pretty dresses and movies."

The line between their lives and the spirit world wasn't clearly drawn. It was common for a woman to report that a stick that she had seen in the path had changed to a snake before her eyes, or that a snake had changed into a stick. Children were given names meaning "I don't want you" so they would not be taken by spirits to punish their parents. No one swam in the river because an evil spirit lived there.

One day a body was found in the bush, a black man in the kind of two-piece khaki suit politicians often wore. A woman told us that the death came from a voodoo curse. Voodoo was not just an amusing superstition; people there feared it as Americans fear cancer. I asked the woman, who had complained of the President's oppressive policies, why someone didn't simply put a hex on him. She explained patiently that of course any one with that much power would have protected himself from curses and hexes with the proper medicines and rituals.

One of the more experienced Peace Corps men told me a story that showed the power of beliefs. Dan had been assigned farther back in the bush, where the only dwellings were huts, and where the natives spoke only their own tribal language. To keep himself in touch with his world, he had purchased a treasured shortwave radio, which he kept in his hut. One day it was gone. The only person who knew he had it, and could have gone into his hut without arousing suspicion, was his houseboy. The chief agreed the houseboy was suspect, but being a wise elder, he said there was still another possibility. The Peace Corpsman himself may have been lying; something else had happened to the radio and he wanted the village to make restitution, or make trouble for the houseboy.

The chief set up the rules the tribe had followed since time immemorial. Some oil would be heated to a certain temperature. Both suspects would put their hands into the oil. The guilty one would be burned; the innocent would not.

My friend was, of course, skeptical and frightened. The chief assured him that in his entire life of fifty long years, the test had never failed. The guilty, marked by the hot oil, always confessed. The innocent was never burned. Desperate to get his shortwave radio back, my friend agreed to the ceremony. The kettle of oil was heated over a fire by the chief himself, who seemed to know exactly when to ask them to put in their arms, up to the elbow.

"My houseboy screamed and pulled out his blistered arm. My arm was not burned," Dan told me, his amazement still showing in the telling. "Only when he showed the chief where the radio was hidden did the chief apply compresses to take the pain away." He shook his head. "I know. If I hadn't seen it myself, I wouldn't have believed it."

"Maybe it's like our lie detector test," I suggested. "The guilt creates a physical response."

"I don't know. But I could tell you a lot of stories like that."

Another PC, a tall, raw boned woman who had served three years, took me in her Land Rover to visit her encampment further back in the jungles. We drove half a day along dirt roads, skirting mud holes and cows and small children herding goats. Wanda was housed in the top floor of a two-story garage that had been built many years earlier by the British, probably to house their trucks. It was the only structure of that kind for miles around.

The moon was full, and the monkeys chattered in the trees all the night long; I went to sleep listening to them, a chorus of happy egos, shrill and somehow ghostly.

In the middle of the night I was awakened by rhythmic pounding and banging, and women's voices, hypnotic repeated chants. It was the most purely African sound I had ever heard. Going to the window, I saw in the moonlight forty or so women, parading in a rather ragtag group down the dirt road below. I hurried downstairs, wanting to follow them, see where they were going, and why.

Wanda caught my sleeve. "The price of watching this ritual, if you are caught, is high. Death by stoning." She explained that it was the full moon, the time to prepare the virgins for marriage. They would go into the bush with the older women. There they would be ritually prepared to be given to husbands on their return. They would be taught the sexual expectations of womanhood. Their faces would be marked, their bodies would be altered.

"Clitorectomy?" I asked, horrified at the thought of the young girls being neutered by a sharp rock or a tin can lid.

Wanda shrugged. "Anyway, they are taught everything they need to be good wives, and in three days, they will come back and be given to the husbands the chief has chosen."

"How old are they?" I asked.

"Twelve probably. Maybe thirteen." I thought, no wonder James's wife didn't care when he came back from town so late. No wonder the women, even the corner-corner girls, seemed content to live among themselves.

Wanda accepted and respected the traditions of the people. She was there to be with them, she said, to help where they wanted help, not to change them.

She had what most of the experienced Peace Corps people had in common, a kind of unruffled maturity, a confidence that came from spending two years in a place that constantly challenged them, emotionally, culturally, and physically. Some had permanent discolorations from fungi, some had bad scars from cuts that had not healed, some had gone through the bone-crushing pain of malaria. There was an air about them— "I have done this, I can do anything." There was also an independence about them, a sense that they did not need reassurance from others as much as most people did. Very aware of my own need for reassurance, I envied that.

Mail from the States finally caught up with us. I had several letters from Joe telling me how much he missed me, how unhappy he was, how he was isolating himself. It was painful for me to read them.

Emily was spending more and more of her evenings with her priest, working at the church hospital. That left me alone with too much time to brood, too much time to reread Joe's unhappy letters, too much time in the small room in the damp block building. I walked the dirt roads around the village, seeking the solace of beauty. My surroundings were spectacular, sunsets that flamed across the sky, flowers of all kinds blooming along the paths, streams meandering through the jungle growth, falling into small quiet pools. It didn't help.

Even though I took quinine regularly against malaria, I had flashes of fever. At night, I tossed in the prickly humidity, jerking awake if a mosquito got under my netting. More and more often, I woke in the morning deeply depressed, almost unable to get out of bed. The work I did at the school seemed a travesty. As Joe wrote of his longing and loneliness, I kept my fragile connection with him and others by talking letters onto a tape recorder, which became part of a very disturbing dream: *I discover my brother Johnny making off in a car with all my valuables, including my tape recorder. He just keeps smiling suavely, and pulls me into the car too. Later, with some others, we are held captive by a woman in a big house. I finally succeed in getting her down and tied up, then begin to hit her because she was going to get loose and get us again, but she is covered with padding or something; she doesn't seem to feel any of the blows, just keeps telling us this and that, and trying to get us. So I go looking for a gun to shoot her.*

When I woke, I felt like I was the one beaten all over. It occurred to me that Johnny usually smiled, no matter what was going on; he even smiled and said things were "just fine" when his business was going bankrupt. He cut his real feelings off from himself and others. Clearly the dream was telling me I tried to keep smiling above all my painful feelings, my loneliness, anger, fear, and I was beating myself up about it.

One rainy day, tired of the inevitable rice and tomato sauce served at the dorm, I walked to the marketplace for some eggplant, some bananas, and some of the little green oranges that looked inedible but were sweet and ripe inside. On the way back, I stepped aside to avoid a loaded lorry, and scratched my ankle on a broken stick. It left a small but deep cut, and I had to splash my way back through water contaminated by human filth. I immediately treated the cut with disinfectant, knowing in that climate, a sore could open to the bones in only a day. One of the PC's had to wait for 24 hours for the Peace Corps to pick him up after he got malaria, and the local hospital, I had seen for myself, was not a place you wanted to go, sick or well. Used bandages, washed and unwashed, hung on racks, flies buzzed around unwashed bedding.

A telegram came from Joe telling me a college had called to offer me a position. "Come home." I wanted to call him, but I didn't know where to find a phone on Sunday or how to handle the payment.

I argued with myself. I should stick it out. I had a commitment. If I would just stick it out, I would achieve the kind of stature I'd seen in the veterans. I was just copping out. How could I go back and face my friends? "The big adventurer is a wimp."

That night Emily, the priest, and I went to a big send off party for a PC who was returning home after two years, taking back with him a S'lon woman, Mamoona. They offered me a ride to Freetown if I wanted it.

I sat on the verandah overlooking the river, with the moon shining and the monkeys chattering. A Peace Corpsman, a little drunk, sat on the steps, repeating various forms of "S'lon is so fucked up...." Inside, people were smoking dope and listening to American Rock'n Roll.

My cut ankle was not healing. My principal would be glad to see me go. I decided to go back to Freetown and talk to the Peace Corps office. Perhaps with this offer in hand, they would try harder to find a more appropriate assignment. And in Freetown, I could call Joe.

Whatever happened, I would not be coming back to Port Loko. Emily helped me pack my few things, we vowed to find each other again "someday, somewhere," and the PC honked from the Land Rover. After a stop for hot rice chop at Mamoona's, whose mother prayed and sang Christian hymns over our heads, we started down the long wet road.

The Peace Corps Director in Freetown put me at ease about going back; apologized for offering an assignment that they could not provide, assured me I had done my best. She sent me to a nurse for a new quinine prescription and to have my ugly sore taken care of: another day might have created serious problems.

It would take the Peace Corps about ten days to get me out. Meantime, they gave me a room in a small hotel, plush for S'lon. It had a small cot, a mosquito net with only a few holes, a fan, and a "bathroom" with a bucket and a shower head.

While I waited, I explored the beaches, some of the most beautiful I had ever seen, green and azure coves, white sand, sheltering trees. The water was warm and safe, yet almost no one else was there, since most Africans had been taught there was an evil spirit living in the water. I would bring my towel and my book, swim, and spend the time reading. I wondered, "Am I progressing, going home to Joe, going forward into a relationship, or regressing, running away from the difficulties of Africa?"

On the beach, I met Frank Schmidt, at 60, the oldest Peace Corpsman in the country. A retired rancher, he had come to show them how to turn their jungle swamps into rice paddies. Before Frank came, it was either feast or famine for S'lons, because their mainstays were plantain and eggplant, neither of which could be preserved. Rice could, and it grew well there. He was a local hero, awarded national recognition by the President.

Frank took me down to help pull in the nets with the fishermen and the villagers. With my feet planted firmly in the wet sand, I tugged on long narrow nets heavy with thousands of flopping, gleaming fish.

I taught a black woman friend how to swim. Meldina's whole family came out daily to watch. Meldina was first to show her tribe that the evil spirit could not take the one who knows how to ride the water. In return, she gave me an intricate bracelet that she had made herself, of leather and cowry shells.

One day, lying on the beach in my bikini, I became aware I was being watched by a man in a Mercedes. As I walked to a water fountain, he got out of the car and approached me. A handsome, well-dressed man, looking more Mediterranean than African, he introduced himself as Mahel, but "You call me Maurice." He was Lebanese. He knew a little English. I knew no Lebanese. He had to be direct. "He is such a small man," he said, casting a look at my Peace Corps companion. "You come my house."

I didn't, but the next day he was back. He took me to see his fine white stucco house, where a servant brought dinner on the patio. I found him charming, particularly the almost childlike simplicity made necessary by our limited vocabulary. One moment he mourned frankly the new "wife" he left in Las Vegas. The next moment she was forgotten. He came to see my room, which he found "most ugly for you." He opened my closet, picked out a long slinky dinner dress I'd brought, just in case something like this should happen, and said, "Tomorrow wear."

The next night, he took me to an elegant casino on the beach. He took my arm possessively as he escorted me through the gleaming mirrors and chandeliers, wearing the shimmering dress, my hair pinned up fetchingly. I'd gone from a female Albert Schweitzer to Marilyn Monroe overnight. In the expensive Lebanese quarter of Freetown, I was the coveted American blonde.

Every day after that, Maurice-Mahel took me to the beach, then to his home where I lounged in luxury, waited on by his maids, while he went out somewhere. Late, we went out to dinner at some luxury oceanside hotel, usually with his friends. On a rooftop overlooking the ocean, we would spend hours over a meal, each course a chance to talk and linger and savor the slow movement of African time.

Then he took me to the casinos, where he told the corner-corner girls I was his American wife. He enjoyed gambling, especially blackjack and roulette. I would get bored, and find an American newspaper to read while I waited. One night when he was ready to leave, he snapped his fingers for me as he walked past. I was furious. "Don't you ever do that again," I hissed at him. "That is a gesture reserved for dogs."

He looked around the room, embarrassed. "Shh. Don't be loud at me." One was not chastened by a woman.

Maurice-Mahel, to my surprise, accompanied me on the ferry trip to the airport. He gazed into the water with exaggerated sorrow. "I miss you," he said. "I do not even go to the casinos tonight from missing you." I couldn't help but smile. From Maurice, that was a great tribute. And a fine farewell to Africa.

Scott picked me up at the airport. Away this short time, I saw my son more clearly. He had always been very sensitive, but his painful early childhood had confused his understanding of himself, his value, his place in the world. I saw him working to overcome a habitual low-grade anger, trying to sort out his confusion about himself. Always more generous with others than with himself, he was quite accepting of me, especially my decision not to stay in Africa. He was much more accepting than I was about that.

As I made the long drive to Southern California, I realized I wasn't as anxiety ridden as I usually was, wasn't rehearsing what to say to Joe. Perhaps I had learned something in Sierra Leon besides what my limits were. I hoped so.

Joe was working on the Blazer when I pulled in the driveway. He went right on working on it while I got out of the car. The man who wrote those passionate longing letters was nowhere in sight. The man under the hood gave me a brief hug and kiss, and went back to what he was doing. My perspective had changed too; he seemed shorter, more awkward, not quite the romanticized man of his photos.

The following day I found out that the job I had come home for was gone. "You were by far the best qualified," the Department Chair said, "But we couldn't be sure you were coming."

Forgiving myself for copping out on the Peace Corps was hard, finding out I had done it without a guarantee of a job was harder. Joe said I was beating myself up about it. "It must be like having a hand over your shoulder all the time. Everytime you do what you want it's whip whip whip."

I was reminded of the dream I'd had in Port Loko: *We are held captive by a woman in a big house. I finally succeed in getting her down and tied up, then begin to hit her because she was going to get loose again, but she is covered with padding and she doesn't seem to feel any of the blows.*

I went to the clinic to clear up traces of malaria and check on the ankle sores. The doctor, checking me over, asked "How old are you?" I told him. He said "You're the second beautiful 44-year-old I've seen today." Once more I was reminded that who is beautiful depends on the mind of the culture, especially the male mind, and how vulnerable I was to that shifting ideal.

Joe was divided about me being there, felt responsible for me coming home. I said, "Joe, I am a grown woman, responsible for my own decisions."

We made a contract: he would support me for a few weeks while I looked for a job, and in return, I would cowrite with him a book he'd always wanted to do.

We went back to enjoying each other. We picked wild elderberries and made pies. We picked fresh oranges in the orchards, climbing the ladders and filling the bags with the marvelous round fruits. We picnicked on the beach. We drove up in the hills and watched the sunsets. We read poetry together. We made love.

I began to wake up eager, ready to go each morning. I continued to see a slight shift in our relationship; I didn't idolize him anymore. He was fine. Also human and sometimes very funny.

Soon, a temporary position opened up at the college. I was doing the kind of teaching I wanted to do, I enjoyed my classes. But I was new, nervous, and I made mistakes, after which I would agonize for hours. I dreamed: *I am teaching my class at City College. We are on a field trip, climbing up a steep hill. I can barely make it. I tell my students that and they are lively and supportive; they gather around me and help me up the hill.*

It was a positive dream: I could admit my mistakes and ask my students for help. When I thought a class wasn't going right, they could tell me what was wrong. When I followed their suggestions, things always improved.

I took a part-time position; filling in for another teacher without preparation created more stress, but I needed the money. The pay for part-timers, all women, was patently unfair, not even close to what full-time teachers made, and there were no benefits. I joined other part-time faculty and organized for fair wages. I went to the first Women's Caucus at the college. I wrote in my journal, *"Realizing I'm not good yet at going to bat for things, get defensive and weepy when I meet opposition."* But I didn't quit.

I spent hours at home, planning classes and grading papers. I walked off the stress on the beaches, watching the bareback riders, listening to the gulls. I jogged up the coast road until I was too tired to worry about my classes or my relationship.

My dreams showed I was beginning to confront the dark fears and anxieties that poisoned my life: *I am in the cab of a big truck, the passenger side, not steering. There is a man in the driver's seat and he pulls a knife. I meet his eyes, eye to eye. I do not reach for the knife, but apply an invisible force against his using it. My gaze is not pleading but a statement. He is very big and dark and mean.*

I took a class in Reevaluation Counseling, and joined the co-counseling group that came out of it. Its purpose was to give people a safe and inexpensive way to talk about their lives in the company of a trained listener. "The most effective counseling is not directive. It has to do with listening supportively, noticing and pointing out "hot spots," giving feedback, not advice." I soon found that co-counseling offered a community of dynamic people who could trade one-hour listening sessions with one another as often as they liked. I made some of my best friends in that class, and we continued to counsel each other after it was over.

During this full and rewarding time, I had a disturbing and powerful dream: *I'm in our house with my mother and my sister Beverly. The sun is shining, and I am sitting on the kitchen floor with the cat. For some reason that makes sense to us, I'm cutting bits of the cat's feet off. Then I cut off too much, a whole paw. Oh mother, I wail, what shall I do? Shall I kill her or shall I put it back on and try again? The cat has hardly noticed I've done this, but now begins to try and walk and when she starts to step down there are great gobs of blood. Mother quick, tell me. She's bleeding! I'm in despair now, wringing at my face. Earlier, cutting the cat, I'd been quite calm, thinking she'll never be the same now anyway, might as well kill her.*

I woke crying, with a deep deep pain in my chest, and soft feelings for my mother who was sometimes soft and gentle. It was good to feel that I must have once loved her. In the dream, I was cutting off the softness, yet I wanted, longed for, the softness.

I took the dream to a co-counseling session, and talking about it led me again to the cat I'd killed when I was two or three.

"How do you feel about it now?" my partner asked.

"People who kill cats can't be good. Under all this striving to be good is a basic feeling that I'm bad."

"All I see there is good, even killing the cat," she said. "The child who wants softness from her mother and gets it from the cat, can't kill her mother for pulling away, but she can kill the cat." Her words reverberated through me, as the truth always does.

Joe and I drove up to the cabin for a ski weekend, and to see my son Mike, who was living there now. Mike would alternately treat me like he didn't want me there, criticizing me or ignoring me, which I took very hard, then complain that I did not give him enough time or attention. I wrote in my journal, *"Double message stuff; he did/didn't want us there but still wants be the favorite son. Scott says I let Mike push me around out of my need to hang on to his love for me."*

I knew this was the normal and necessary mother-son separation process, probably more difficult because Mike and I had always been so close. Too close, since Mike for so many years filled in for my husband's emotional absence. But the conflict left me with a deep sense of loss.

My dreams showed guilt and anxiety about my kids, confusion over their roles in my own sexual life. One dream showed metal plates under Mike's shoes, suggesting there is something under his floor he did not want to feel. Gangsters pursued my sons and I in a shopping mall, representing some unacknowledged fear pursuing us though the mall of life. In another, there is some confusion about a bathtub. "Obviously there is a lot of cleaning up to do," I wrote, "Separating sons from lovers."

Joe was often gone on biology cruises for weeks at a time, which made it difficult to rebuild the relationship we lost when I left for Africa. He still was not committed for the long term. As the weeks passed, we slid back into the old patterns: I was bringing home far too many anxieties about money and part-time work, he was feeding into my insecurities by spending time with other women and reminiscing about his ex-wife.

Our sex life soured. I would give in to Joe's desires to play sex games; sometimes playing the dominant partner, pushing Joe around, calling him belittling names, treating his genitals and his masculinity with contempt. Afterward I could not climax, despite how turned on Joe was. Or I would play the passive role, and though I would find sexual satisfaction, I would end up resenting him for his dominance and withdrawing afterward.

There is more than one kind of Dark Continent, I thought. Africa or Long Beach, I was faced with it. The sexual games we were playing again caused great anxiety, greater than my job or our relationship. We were coming too close to exposing a past that I did not want to see.

Joe found my anxieties difficult to cope with. He gradually divorced himself from my conflicts by burying himself in his work, fighting off my pleas for attention and reassurance by concentrating on what he could master: scientific pursuits, skiing, bicycling.

Despite my professed desire for commitment, a part of myself wanted to get out of there. My dreams showed I was afraid of breaking through a protective surface to something consuming:

I am riding my horse in the country and I am happy. I am just walking the horse and there is a feeling that I always just walk it, never run it. Then I come around a bend in the road and realize that I must go back. Off to one side I see that I am in an area where there is just a thin surface of high raised earth, a crust of earth; one could easily break through and sink, so I set out at a gallop off to the left to get back to where I came from, riding light and fast to keep from breaking through. The area seems bleak and lonely, though there are houses in the distance, built on this same surface crust. My thoughts are: it's ok, I can get back by running my horse so light and fast he won't break through the crust.

I wrote in my journal: *"A downer. It's like that mud is in me and I don't want to look at it, I'm afraid I'll get caught in it."* This was followed by heavy black confused scribbles.

Another journal entry: *"I dream a lot; all I remember of one is I am screaming and screaming, wailing from way down deep. I have never cried like that before."*

The nightmares increased as the situation with Joe worsened : *Thugs, all in black clothes, in a black car, pull over to see what we're doing. We give them some story and they go on. We sneak around and between some buildings and look in a window at a beautiful woman being held captive. We are going to free her and the thugs want to stop us, this other person and I. The feeling is good. We are strong. We are outwitting the thugs.*

But I wasn't outwitting the thugs. My morning depression worsened. I wrote in my journal:

Feeling really low, so tired of trying, trying not to feel low, trying to get a job together, trying to write, trying to get something together with Joe, trying to make myself a hopeful, happy person, trying trying trying. I've no faith that life is ever going to give me what I want, no faith in myself to get what I want, or even to know what I want. Even fantasized this morning the ultimate end of trying, swimming out to sea so far I can't get back. I know I wouldn't really do that. Sometimes I just want to quit, just let the goddamn world take care of me for a change.

One night I woke Joe. "I need to talk."

"Ummm."

"I need to know, where do you see us going with this?"

"What do you mean?"

"Do you want me here when my job's up?"

"Well, I want you to stay as long as things are good with us."

"Well, they're not so good with us. What now?"

"I don't know." He struggled to wake up.

"I'm pretty wrapped up about the grant proposal right now."

"Do you want me to wait around or what?

"I guess so."

"So you want me here next summer?"

"I guess so. I never think about summer but I think about us together next summer," he said, in a defensive swallowed voice.

He rolled away. I wanted to pound him. I lay there warring between hating myself and hating him. I got up and read until morning, furious with myself for getting hysterical and making a big deal of it. I felt hopeless about ever getting past my anger with men.

I had a dream about my father. I was cornering him with my anger and resentment and he was confused, perplexed and defensive. Now I was cornering Joe with my anger toward my Dad, and Joe was confused, perplexed and defensive.

My arrogant, who-needs-you woman moved in then to take over. I started putting out job applications in other states. I had a liaison with another man.

I told Joe I was angry that he wouldn't say what he wanted. He said, "All the women I've ever known don't ask for what they want, then hit me over the head if I don't give it to them." He gave me a shrug of his shoulders and eyebrows.

I thought that was his way of showing I couldn't get to him. I said, "That's your pattern, you toad," and laughed.

Dream: *A woman has come to visit Joe and me. I'm trying not to be anxious or jealous but they know I am. She is a big blonde with short hair, as big as Joe, and they are leaning together and I know something's going on. She is very cocky and self assured and scornful of me. Joe says to her, c'mon, let's get out of here. I am furious with him and hit him and hit him, but never with much strength.*

That dream was followed by a connecting dream: *Talking to another woman about shock therapy. She is big and blonde and buxom and young. She believes just a little electricity is good for you. We all (there are several of us) go downstairs into a gray basement with cracked leaky cement walls. The woman confidently places herself in a place (she's done it before) where she will get a small amount of electric shock. (I'm not aware of any wires or connections, she's just standing in a certain place.) For some reason there's too much and she is electrocuted before our eyes. We watch her die in agony.*

I am later telling another woman about it in her fine safe home upstairs. She is an admirably calm woman, like Mary at the 8-Mile House and Erika all in one. She calmly takes me into the living room for tea and asks me to describe the electrocution. She laughs, Oh, she's like me, eh? But she wasn't. They are very different women.

I wrote in the journal:

The big dumb blonde, sexual, voluptuous body but not much self-worth, represents the part of me that doesn't take care of itself in love affairs, the part that says a little jolt or shock is good for you. She wants to feel, I guess, but she overdoes it. I hurt so much that at last that part of me can't take anymore and goes dead. All the painful but unwise sexual situations, where I was too easily sexual and then rejected, all together are too much. My system shorted out. The woman upstairs, my higher self, is humorous and intelligent. She laughs and says "You thought it was me," meaning I might think I had killed that part of myself that is valuable, confident, admirable, intelligent and has high self value but that I hadn't. But I have been emotionally overloaded and can't deal with anything more right now.

Reading that entry twenty years later, I saw the accuracy of that analysis, but I saw another layer still under that dream. I thought of my experience under hypnosis; the child went into the damp cracked basement with her father. For no reason other than how she happened to be standing, the child is given a larger dose of electricity (sexuality) than she can handle. She blanks out, while the other parts of myself watch in agony.

But the dream says the electrocution is repeated. What could that possibly mean?

The older "I" is both disturbed and excited by what I am discovering. In many different ways, the journals are confirming what the hypnosis uncovered: the problems with my mother were severe, but whatever had gone on with my father was the underpinnings, the basement, of my whole personal life.

I have another, contrasting dream: *I am running a nursery school somewhere in a dark wooded place. I am walking down the front stairs with someone who is asking me about how long I've done this and I say, Oh, I have always taken care of the children, off and on, and feel very competent and comfortable about it.*

Twenty years later, I am intrigued by these dreams. They seem to be suggesting that there was a part of myself that had always been taking care of the child, even while the cocky self-assured woman and her opposite, the needy woman, played out their conflicts in my life.

The college notified me that there would be no position for me in the fall. That meant that I had to decide: stay with Joe and look for any work I can get or look for a full-time job elsewhere. Returning from a ski trip, I told Joe. "It looks like time for us to split anyway."

He kept his attention on the long narrow road, crowded with returning L.A. skiers. "Yeah. It does seem like things have kind of petered out."

I crawled in the back of the Blazer to sleep. I had a dream about a phone booth with no phone, about missiles, broken off skis. I was investigating illicit use of University funds.

The next day, my co-counselor asked, "What links those images?"

"Explosive, cut off, self righteous," I said.

"We are all just repeating our childhood patterns," she said. "The child tries to get attention from the parent, and failing, tries to get power. Failing, the child tries to get revenge, failing, withdraws."

That night I curled up in a chair with Joe, feeling childlike, vulnerable. "I'm sorry I have to leave, but I need to be alone. I'm happier alone. People hurt me too much, I can't cope with people."

He touched the tears on my cheek. "It sounds like you're saying you can't take anymore."

"That feels right. Can't take any more emotional overload or hurtful rejections. I don't want to meet other men, don't want to be involved with anyone."

In August of 1975, I left Long Beach for a community college in Texas. I had returned from Africa thinking I was ready to settle down, ready to quit running. Now I didn't know if I was going forward to greater independence, or fleeing, but I left my lifetime home, California, my friends, my family, to teach at a new college in El Paso, on the Mexico border. In my open car, I sang with the radio.

"Here I go once again with my suitcase in my hand.

I'm running away down River Road.

And I swear once again that I'm never coming home.

I'm chasing my dreams down River Road."

8

The
Border Years

Border: boundary, frontier, a place where two cultures meet, or the line that separates them. A cross over place or a line of demarcation. *(Webster's dictionary)*

El Paso Del Norte, the pass to the North from Mexico. As I drove my blue Triumph, top down, through the rocky hills west of the city, I felt as though I were landing on another planet. The slopes around me sank into rough-edged depressions like craters blasted out by asteroids. On the hills above me, amid spare sharp-leafed agaves and cactus, sleek stucco condominiums with red tile roofs imitated the adobes of old Mexico.

I drove past ASARCO, American Steel and Aluminum Refining. Black smoke drifted down across the valley of the Rio Grande, shrouding the tumbled tin shacks and scattered adobe huts of the Mexican poor.

El Paso sprawled at the foot of Mount Franklin, a barren rock outcropping topped with radio and television towers, its lower slopes dotted with homes and apartment houses.

The city itself, the fastest growing in the nation, I'd been told, was a conglomeration of railroad yards, truck terminals, a tawdry downtown area that served the Border bargain hunters. On higher ground were spacious "Anglo" shopping centers amid neighborhoods beautifully kept by Mexican gardeners and housekeepers. Everything showed the scarcity of water. Even the Rio Grande was a pathetic muddy stream walled with concrete. The entire town was built of stone, concrete, clay, or brick, with a few cactus and agave gardens, all that could survive the fierce afternoon sun.

I stopped at the University of Texas, with its looming and oddly appropriate Byzantine architecture. A man, teeth flashing in his classically handsome Spanish face, directed me east of the mountain.

Winding across the summit road, I could see a narrow strip of green where the last dregs of the Rio Grande wound through the Lower Valley. I could see the glint of sun off the windshields of cars waiting at the check point to cross the bridge to the United States. I could see neatly officious Border Patrol buildings on each side of the concrete banks.

Dropping back down, I headed north through a stretch of high desert reaching as far as the eye could see. Out there lay the long wooden barracks of a U.S. Army training post, surrounded by cyclone fencing and barbed wire. This was the temporary campus of El Paso Community College. Beyond that, a lumbering tank looked as anachronistic as a dinosaur. Fort Bliss. I smiled at the irony.

When I had flown in for an interview, the department chair had met me and driven me to the "campus." Rather than facing the usual interviewing panel, I was sent to each faculty member separately, a process that required repeating the same information and answering the same questions over and over. "How would you deal with remedial students? Would you be willing to learn Spanish? How would you motivate Mexican Americans to read and to write in English?"

By the time I got to the last member of the department, I felt like a badly recorded song on a phonograph that was running down. Sweaty from trudging between sun-scorched buildings, blistered from walking gravel paths in high heeled shoes, I arrived at David Henry's office. I took one look at his open, welcoming face, and dropped into a chair, completely letting go of my professional air.

"How about a nice cool glass of water?" he asked, in a soft, gentlemanly, Oklahoma drawl. He did not interview me. He listened to me tell him how frustrated I was with their exhausting procedure, and how doubtful I was about working in such a place if they did offer me the job. I was horrified with myself, jeopardizing an opportunity so thoughtlessly and unprofessionally. Still, something about David made me feel he was an old friend.

He smiled at me from under a shaggy head of unkempt hair. "I knew as soon as I saw your application letter that you were the one we wanted. The only one that didn't sound like it was copied down from a text book. Now I'm even more positive."

David Henry was to become the first man I ever had a genuine, non-sexual friendship with, something I was taught as a child, could not exist.

He had recommended to me some hacienda-style apartments not too far from the college. I found them, high on the side of the mountain. They had balconies overlooking the desert, and a welcome swimming pool gleaming with blue Mexican tile. Fortunately they had a vacancy. Every crevice of my open car was stuffed with my most treasured possessions; typewriter, guitar, my most treasured books, manuscripts and journals, my favorite pictures and the beautiful hangings Joe had brought from Thailand. I had packed one suitcase with my favorite clothes; bell-bottomed jeans and silky shirts, long cotton dresses and Birkenstock sandals, an embroidered sheepskin coat from Afghanistan. I unpacked the car, blew up an air mattress, and started housekeeping.

As I sat by the pool that afternoon, preparing for my classes, a ten-year-old boy came up to me. "Are you a man or a woman?" he asked.

I was surprised. "A woman. Why?"

"You look like a woman on the top but a man on the bottom," he said, eyeing the fluffy golden hair on my slim and otherwise feminine legs. I knew then I had some cultural adjusting to do.

I would be a border dweller in many ways: a Californian in a Texas/ Mexico culture, a single woman in a married community, a woman on a campus where all of the administrators were men, a pacifist on a military base, a mountain woman on a waterless desert.

It would be a week before classes started. I went to a nightclub where David said the faculty sometimes went. I saw him sitting with a woman, waved to let him know I was there. He didn't acknowledge me in any way, and I noticed there were no other women there alone. I wondered if I'd made a fool of myself, and went home feeling vaguely guilty, arguing with myself: This isn't California, you know. "Decent" women don't go out alone. Look, you only waved to let him know you were there. That's a healthy reaching out and you don't know why he didn't acknowledge you.

I threw myself into my work, which I enjoyed. I looked for new ways to bring the Mexican culture into the Anglo curriculum. In my Literature class, I substituted Lorca for Shakespeare. The students enjoyed acting out the dramatic roles, so much like their own melodramatic soap operas, their own passionate romantic lives. I shared with my basic English classes my struggles learning Spanish, so they would not feel so "dumb" struggling with English.

A week or two after classes started, a young woman came to my office to ask about an assignment. I took the opportunity to ask her, a Mexican-American, how she thought the class was going. Angelina looked uncomfortable, and finally said, "Some of the girls think you are being seductive." I saw myself by then as a "women's libber," dressing in jeans, with straight hair and little makeup. I was taken aback. I asked in what way I was behaving seductively. The student said, "You don't wear a bra."

Gesturing toward my small breasts, I said, "Obviously, I don't need a bra."

Angelina said, "Here in El Paso, the only reason a woman wouldn't wear a bra is to be seductive."

I was amazed. "I thought being seductive was the reason women wear those pointy contraptions that exaggerate their breasts."

During a discussion after a campus theater production, I asked why the men in the play were all so passive. "Emasculated," a Chicano actor said, "The women did it to them."

"I can't accept that," I said. "Those men had some responsibility for letting themselves be walked on."

"That's Women's Lib stuff," another man said. He and the actor gave each other knowing looks and walked away.

I was feeling an alienation almost as dark as that I felt in Africa. I went into the walk-in closet, closed the door, and cried, not wanting to be heard through the thin walls. I joked in letters about being a closet crier, but the journals show I was fighting severe depression.

At every opportunity, even a four-day weekend, I made the twenty-four hour drive back to California, drinking it in like the thirsty desert dweller I was, returning to sandy, rocky El Paso feeling like a Hebrew exiled from the promised land.

One morning, lying in bed, refusing to get up and face the lonely day, I got a telephone call from a woman who taught Psychology at the college. "I saw you walking across the campus today, and you looked so sad. Are you all right? Would you like to play a game of tennis?" Thus began a friendship with Nedra, a blue-eyed, black-haired Texas Liz Taylor, bright, challenging and funny. She played tennis as indifferently as I did, which left time to talk. She was a cynical, sophisticated and talented poet. After the game, we sat on Nedra's balcony and drank wine, read poetry, and talked about what was wrong with men.

"I could do this for hours," I said, as the sun sank through the haze.

"Yes, it would take hours to cover what's wrong with men," Nedra laughed mischievously, deliberately misconstruing my remark.

By the next weekend, we were going across the border to Mexico, singing and drinking and dancing in the elegant restaurants where one could dine in splendor for less than the price of fast-food in El Paso. Nedra, a native Texan who spoke fluent Spanish, introduced me to the rich culture in Juarez, the folk arts museum, the Sunday concerts.

At a faculty meeting, I met another strong woman, Tracy, who was raising her children by herself after divorcing her alcoholic and abusive husband. Her teenagers were still confused and angry about the divorce, and Tracy was trying valiantly to maintain the expected social responsibilities of a good Texas lawyer's wife on half the salary. She had a jaw of steel, developed from smiling brightly as she walked the tight wire of a lower administrative position at a campus run entirely by men.

With all that stress, Tracy was quick to show interest in co-counseling. She learned the basic techniques quickly, and our weekly sessions gave both of us a place to let off the pressures of our lives.

David, it turned out, was so near-sighted he simply hadn't seen me in the club that night I'd gone looking for him. He asked to join us, bringing two or three others for training, and soon we had formed El Paso's first Co-Counseling organization. I was feeling a little more at home; I had brought something of California to El Paso.

I was invited to read with a group of local poets, the only woman and the only Anglo. My poetry was personal, sometimes explicitly sexual. Afterward a man said, "I envy your husband." He was flustered when I said I didn't have one, that the poems had been written for several different men.

With David and a group of male faculty, I hiked 17 miles into the Soledad Canyon, a rugged all-day trek. "Pretty good for a woman," one of the men said. "Pretty good period," I said.

By the end of the semester my students brought me presents and told me how much they'd learned. They invited me to their parties. My teaching evaluations were so good that David, kidding, said I'd forged them.

I started AWARE, the college's first organization for women students and faculty. Though it was 1975, male counselors were still advising women into low paid secretarial and clerical jobs, while the men were counseled into electronics, mathematics and pre-professional studies. The vast majority of all scholarships went to men. One psychology instructor taught from his own notes, which included biased and unsupported beliefs that women were unreliable and undependable because they had children and went through menopause.

I joined the Faculty Senate and took strong political positions. I headed the Title IX Committee, whose job it was to make sure the campus was living up to Federal requirements regarding equality for women. Although a few of the lower positions in administration were held by women, the top 33 administrators were males. Statistics in hand, I called in the President. Confidently, I said, "Unless we start placing more women in top administrative positions, we are going to lose our Federal funding."

The President looked me straight in the eye. "I don't think you understand the law," he said, waving a copy under my nose. "The law only says we have to show intent." The smug expression that accompanied that deliberate perversion of the law lit a fire under me.

By the end of the day, I had gathered seven of the most progressive and intelligent women faculty and staff. Within three weeks we had organized and carried off El Paso's first Women's Day. For twenty-four hours women lined up at an outdoor microphone, with television cameras going, telling our stories, listing the facts. Top administrators were invited to speak, but their blustering double-talk was greeted with jeers by women who had heard it too long.

That night, we seven instigators watched the events on three different news channels and read articles in four major newspapers. I was jubilant. "It is the first time in my entire life I have felt what men must feel in the locker room after their team wins a major game. We're a team! And we did it!"

I had a dream:

I am an older woman, staff in hand, herding a pack of wolves through a canyon. A young man is walking with me, talking. I am his teacher. The wolves are magnificent, streaming through the canyon. There is a disturbing thought: are they going to a canning factory?

The wild power of a pack, followed so effortlessly by the Guru woman, was mitigated by an unacknowledged concern: where were the wolves, the wild energy, going? Would they be canned? Like dog food? Domesticated?

The changes that were made on campus were not revolutionary—promotion of two women to higher administrative positions, awareness training for male counselors, the psych instructor advised to replace his biased notes with a factual textbook—but things would never be the same again, and everyone knew it.

David called me his dragon guru, told me I was the bravest person he'd ever known, with the courage to do and say what I like without fear of other people's reactions. The courage to live "differently." I was doing and being what I always wanted to be and I didn't even realize it. I dreamed

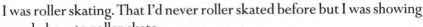

I was roller skating. That I'd never roller skated before but I was showing people how to roller skate.

Soon after that, Gloria Steinem, lifelong spokesperson of feminism, visited the campus. One of several at dinner with her, I was impressed with the gentle, respectful friendliness of this powerful woman. At her lecture, I watched how, with a few pleasantly spoken words, Steinem could stop the hecklers in the back row and still keep the rest of the room's entire attention without raising her voice. Steinem, my own age, even bearing some resemblance to me, became for me the model of a feminist, strong in a distinctly female way, with respect for the opposition.

I myself did not feel such respect and tolerance. In fact, I was becoming increasingly intolerant of women's conditioning to be passive and subservient, to put up with the domination of men. On dates, I could no longer just be the supportive listening ear while a man tried to impress me. I could not play dumb and let him tell me how I should do things, or support his assumptions that he was infinitely more interesting and competent than I was. I decided I'd rather be home alone than catering to such men.

A movie that came out that year, *Hustler*, filled me with anger and disgust for days. In the film, women were beaten, shot, hit, slapped, raped. Rich men used money to tempt a teenage girl, then called her a tramp. Gross dialog, "Look at that whore ... that sweet Chinese ass ... is her slit sideways?" was not new to me, but I was more sensitive to it. I seethed with anger at the men in the film, and at the women who tolerated them.

Nedra thought my reaction extreme. "You need to contact the Rape Crisis Center, work it out. Put it in a positive place somewhere."

I said, "'I've never been raped so why do I need a rape crisis center? Besides, how can that kind of stuff ever be put in a positive place?"

Another movie, *Sibyl*, disturbed me too, for reasons I didn't yet understand. In my journal, I wrote:

Because of early childhood horrors, the woman has split herself off into different personalities that she doesn't remember as herself. That's not so foreign to me, mine are just more aware, conscious. I am seductive and flirtatious at times, sexually manipulative, sometimes charming and in charge, sometimes frightened and insecure, sometimes feel like a dud. Sometimes I feel I'm not in charge of when these personalities take over. Sibyl climbs under the piano, speaking gibberish. I climbed under a chair at a workshop, crying, I won't look." My mother was not a monster, as Sibyl's was, yet I know there was something back there I won't look at. Joanne Woodward, the doctor, is warm and loving and caring, the best movie shrink I ever saw. Love hurts, Sibyl says. Love heals, the doctor says.

Hustler, *Sibyl.* I was walking very very close to an underground minefield. Still, I did not recognize that. Instead, I backed clear off and returned to my usual source of comfort and distraction. Men.

I had several love affairs those years in El Paso, some pleasant but short lived. I met Dana, an Austin college professor, at a conference, and after a short, passionate, correspondence, invited him for a weekend. When he first arrived, I curled up in his arms like a grateful child. He said, "I see the suffering in your eyes." I felt acknowledged, cared for. I enjoyed sex with him at first. But he didn't. "You don't want to let me inside of you. You just went off to your own world and left me."

The next morning in bed, I felt an overpowering conflict. I wanted to pull him closer, and at the same time, to push him away and hit him. After he left, I cleaned out every trace of him, put everything back the way it was before he came, threw away everything he gave to me. It was hard to even remember how good it had been earlier, I felt so much repulsion.

Roberto was a sensitive, sophisticated, Mexico City artist that I met at a concert in Juarez. Several times I noticed that after making love, lying against Roberto, dropping off to sleep, my breathing became panicky, and I couldn't stop the fear of suffocation. I knew it was extreme anxiety over closeness. One morning when I was driving toward Juarez and crossing the border to meet him, a tightening, hard edge, started in my stomach. It was familiar. With growing attraction came fear and pain, like leeches on the artery of joy. Not long after, I became mistrustful and guarded, and finally "turned off" to him entirely.

I dreamed: *A family, rather dumb, like the Bumsteads, are in this house, telling themselves it is good but it is dark and shabby. Their daughter, a teenager, had shot a man (who wanted to be shot) and some insurance money was coming. The owner of the house is a brash sure-of-herself woman who says you can buy anything you want just by asking them to carry it awhile for you.*

The dream was about shabby bargaining, killing people for insurance, for safety. Taking what you want and paying for it later. I thought it was time I investigated my pattern of cutting people off when they got too close.

Dr. Fosworth was a cold, glassy-eyed man with thinning hair and puffy skin. The way he slumped down in his chair and gazed across the desk at me made me feel like a bug under a microscope. But he was reputed to be the best psychotherapist in El Paso, and he probably was at that time.

Going into my first session cool and guarded, I amazed myself by crying over everything I thought were dead issues—my parents, the death of Cap's wife. "No wonder you have so much terror," Fosworth said, "with your mother's sex fears and your father's rape fantasies and then the experience with Cap."

"Lucretia Borgia," he said, after I told him how I was attracted to men until they moved in, then I backed off.

His comment made me laugh at first, then I cried. Was I really just a mean and vicious person?

Freudian stuff, he said. I want to castrate men. With Joe, wanting commitment but not giving it. Always the one who leaves. If Joe made himself vulnerable, would I then turn off the good stuff, castrate him? I felt powerful when I swallowed my father's genitals in fantasy. When I told boys no as a teenager. But I feel vulnerable when I'm saying yes, helpless, underneath, then resent them for it.

"Why would I do that?" I asked him. "Why would I go back to Joe three times when I'm the one who gets hurt?"

Fosworth said it looked like I had to have control. "As long as a man is backing off, you're safe, but if he moves in you've got to cut him off. People only have to be that much in control if there's a vast amount of terror underneath." I felt my eyes get wide at the word terror.

"We're all afraid of the same things and we all want the same things," he said. "That's what makes psychotherapy so easy. The only things we're afraid of are the things at the subconscious level; we've got to relive them."

"But everything I told you, it's all conscious, I've relived it in counseling, and it's still there." I cried tears of discouragement.

At the end of the session, he asked me if I was going to be all right. "I mean, you're not so discouraged that you'd just pull the plug on yourself, are you?"

I gathered myself together, straightened my shoulders, wiped a Kleenex under my eyes. "No. There's always a floor under me," I told him. "I can always do it ... I'm very healthy."

He said, "Call me if you need me."

I smiled through my tears to reassure him, "I'm fine, I can make it." As I drove home I remembered my mother's brave little smile while she lay dying. "I'm fine. I'm getting better."

In the next session I mentioned the sickly smile. "My brother John always says 'I'm fine,' too, no matter what's going on. Dad put him down constantly, and John would turn around and put me down."

"John and you both learned the lesson: Never give anybody anything they could criticize you with, therefore, needs," Fosworth said, jotting down notes as he talked. I remembered my dream in Africa, when John showed up as a communication shut-downer, a communication stealer, taking my tape recorder.

I told Fosworth how much I had admired my father. "No matter what happened, he always had it all-together. He was always the master of ceremonies, the local mayor. People looked up to him."

I told him how mortified I was when my father got up and left in the middle of the senior play, when I had a starring role. "I thought I was finally going to show him I was special too, and he walked out. I was an embarrassment to him."

"He was not admitting his own needs," Fosworth said, "and teaching you to deny yours by putting you down for them.

"Your whole childhood you were being told you don't really have needs. If you show needs, you're just lazy, dramatic, silly, emotional. You still feel that whatever happens, you can't be needy. If your needs show, you run."

I talked about Dick and Dad and their similarities. "When Dad died, I said to Dick, 'You're alike, you both let me down when I need you.'"

Going home, I heard a popular song in my head. *Corey, you're a mean ol' Daddy but I love you.* That's what they had in common, I realized, Dick and Dad. He was an old bastard but I loved him.

I told Fosworth I had a lot of toilet dreams. "In one, I'm at a party. Very crowded, no place to use toilets. I yell, 'Isn't there one damn empty toilet in this whole place?' They're all full of men. A man gets out and gives me his." I had to laugh. "It's true. The toilets are all full of men."

"What did you want to get rid of, flush away?" Fosworth asked.

"I don't know." I told him how I'd crawl like a dog to my father after he'd punished me. "It was humiliating, but I wanted him to love me so badly. He would laugh, embarrassed." I told Fosworth about doing S & M with Joe. "I stopped without really understanding why."

"It was not a game anymore, getting too close to real feelings," Fosworth said, "Dark feelings, feelings you want to kill someone." I started to cry.

"What's the image?" he asked.

My body went into a twisted, defensive position. I couldn't speak, only whimper.

"Somebody's hurting you and you can't fight back," Fosworth said, reading my body. "You're helpless. What's happening?"

"I'm scared," I said, getting my breath back, coming out of it.

"What happened? What scared you?"

"I can't remember," I said, "I was about 4 or 5, we lived in Richmond. I'm scared."

The appointment hour was up. I was wide-eyed, like a frightened child, as I fumbled for my purse. When I left I said again, "I'm scared."

When I got home I kept crying for about twenty minutes, until a headache came and I stopped. My left foot turned up at an odd angle. I had a flash of my father with an erection, my father at the foot of the bed. Bumbly, something about sex, no clothes on. I went blank."

Reading the journal twenty years later, I stopped, excited. There I was, right on the brink of it! Twenty years ago, I had written it in my journal! I circled that section, put big exclamation points by it. I had blocked it from my mind all those years, did not remember ever writing this! I could barely contain myself. Like a crowd cheering from the sidelines, I read on, rooting for that younger woman. "Don't stop now. Don't give up. Keep going! You're almost there!" But to my amazement, when I read the next journaled therapy session, there was no more about my father. Instead, I had switched to my mother. Undoubtedly the father issue was too terrifying to pursue.

Over the next few weeks I told Fosworth how my mother had put her hand over my mouth to stop my crying at night. How I'd strangled the cat.

"Men and cats and mother," he said. "You want to pull them close and you want to kill them at the same time."

"I understand how that would be for mother and cats. The softness, all mixed up with how she whipped me and shamed me. But why *men*?"

I had a powerful dream: *Fit into the wall there is a toilet, very modern and sleek, with a line that runs to the sink. I notice sparks coming from poorly insulated places. Later blood comes from some place. The water tank is tilted over crazily but it will still flush. I call for Dad to come but a younger man comes in. I show him the blood and ask if he sees it too. He does, so I'm not crazy.*

After that dream, I clearly remembered my mother coming up behind me when I was four or so and slamming me into the toilet because I was "playing with myself." I saw the long filament of bloody spit from my mouth to the toilet tank. I saw my brother John seeing this from the bedroom door. I had written: "Seeing him seeing this was very important to me; it proved to me I was not making it up. I was not crazy."

I told Fosworth how my mother would threaten to cut off my hands for masturbating. "I never masturbated after that, and even now, I often wake with my right hand going numb and painful, my left hand holding it back."

I told the dream of the glassed-in child who must be gotten out, but the people in the main building make her put her arms through the glass key hole. "She can't get out 'til she cuts off her own hands," I told him, crying. "We called for the uniformed man to come, but he's stupid and bumbly, and comes too late."

Telling it, I had gone back into the dream, sobbing for the child. "I wrap the arms up with the child, in butcher paper, and wail for what's happened to her." I was as demolished as a woman who has lost her own daughter.

"The uniformed man, stupid and bumbly, didn't know what to do," Fosworth said, "He is your father's sexual embarrassment. Your mother is in the guard house with you, guarding against your sexuality. You don't care if she sees the cut off arms, she'll be horrified, you want her to be. You make her throw them to you. The part of you that's your mother won't see your needs. You punish yourself for strong feelings with headaches. You do what you want, then punish yourself."

The rage and fear of exposure that therapy stirred up was terrifying to me. I dreamed of fleeing on a train with permission to "board now and pay later." *My blouse is falling open, but I just pull my coat over it and get on anyway, determined. Later we are fired on and have to clear an inspection station for bombs before we can cross a bridge. I have a feeling the bridge will blow up behind me, after I walk away. Lots of soldiers, underground. There's a Robert Redford kind of guy with me. (Fosworth's office is near Radford street.) A helicopter off in the distance explodes, things all falling out of it, fires on buildings too, the world begins to shake and move. It's the end of the world. We all run. But it turns out it's not.*

The exploding helicopter and threatened bridge are the free-floating anger in me, Fosworth said, reminding me that my poems also show anger and vindictiveness toward men.

"Who cares?" I said, angry, kicking the chair as I left. "All this stuff has come up in co-counseling a thousand times. So what? It's going nowhere!"

I can scarcely make out the black angry scribbles in the journal.

Came home and kicked the door damned near off its hinges. I'm not going back. I hate all this stuff. This is dumb, stupid, useless. I feel toward Fosworth like I feel toward men before I leave them. You can't help me. I don't give a damn for you. What do you know?

"It's the same pattern played over and over," Fosworth said. " Men aren't going to help you, won't meet your needs, and you're sure's hell not going to meet theirs."

I told him I could not afford many more sessions.

On my last visit, Fosworth summed up what he saw: "We all have these monster needs, unmet child needs that can never be met. Sometimes we think we've found somebody who can meet them or they find us. Either way we're overwhelmed by our own monster needs or overwhelmed by his and have to get out. Even if we could get this need met, we wouldn't like it, it's too much. We're totally ensnared in it all, left holding this huge mass of murk."

He suggested I pay attention to when I lock up or back off and remember just what the other person was doing when it started. "This is the point at which the acceptability level is reached and we just back off and leave the person alone. We are separate. We don't need to meet these child needs. Wouldn't like it if we did."

I decided that was the best I was going to do. Just get back out there and do the best I could to stay conscious of what was going on.

Dream: *My therapist invites me to a party at his place. He tries to pull my hand up a slit in his pants to his balls. I say no, and take my hand away. He says why not? I say, why? Others are starting to show up, a guy with a funny plaster head mask, pulls it off, we kiss. He says people come and do things there, Monday whippings, Tuesday chains, and I reply, gee, you ought to get some little dishtowels embroidered, with kittens. Monday whips, Tuesday irons, Wednesday ... etc.*

The embroidered dishtowels were an emerging clue to what will show up in a memory later. They were what my mother tied me with. The subconscious was continuing to work past my denial, past my resistance, throwing up small fragments of an emerging puzzle, nothing large enough to frighten me away.

Nanci called, dynamic and caring, supporting my decision to leave therapy. "You've got to decide some day you're all right the way you are. You're just alone and lonely, anybody would be. You miss and need your family and friends and they need you. Come back to California where you belong. I don't think I could ever do what you've done, I couldn't even exist, going from man to man. It's too painful."

I started an intense and obsessive love affair with a man who was in El Paso for a year to work on his Medical Degree in Juarez. He was bright, attractive, straightforward, athletic, in his forties. When we met at a party, we were immediately attracted to one another. He told me he was married, and would be returning to his wife after he finished medical school. I told him I wasn't looking for a husband, so it didn't matter. I believed that we could have a wonderful year together.

The journal began with rhapsodies:

We skied at Río Doso, walked the mountains of Cloudcroft, went to concerts and films at UTEP. We talked and talked and talked. We took baths in my big old-fashioned bathtub together, listening to favorite records. We cooked in my little kitchen. He listened to my lectures on literature, took me to Juarez to see the blackened lungs of a cadaver.

But despite my determination to keep my needs limited, within weeks I was wheedling him to tell me he loved me. It was as if, if I had that, I could stand what I was doing to myself.

"I told you at the beginning, I love my wife. Much as I care about you, that's not going to change."

"You can love us both, can't you?" I argued.

On long holidays he would fly back to the East Coast to be with his wife. Alone, I agonized. For months, I went though all the pain of separations and reconciliations, all the drama of "the other woman." We tried to break up; after a day or two would fall back into each other's arms.

The day he finished his studies and left for good, I could not even go to work. I cried myself to sleep night after night. I began to have thoughts about not going on, somehow ending it so I wouldn't have to keep on wanting and trying and losing. I called Tracy and asked her to come on her lunch hour. "I can't stand the pain," I told her, "but I don't want to kill myself."

"Well, I'm glad of that anyway," Tracy said, trying to hold back a little smile at my melodrama.

Little by little I recovered. I told my suicide fantasies to Nedra, who was in a painful long-term affair with an alcoholic, and we made up tragic fantasies. I would hang myself. "He would find me dangling from a noose. 'Take that grizzly sight, you bastard.'" Nedra pictured herself languishing beautifully, dying of an overdose. "How beautiful she was," they would say, and wish they had treated her better.

A black friend was more practical; "You went in the barn with a dog that had fleas so now you're going to have to scratch." If I mooned around, he'd say, "Get that tiger back out. You're the one who's got it caged up."

I returned to Dr. Fosworth for help. "Your man friend got scared and closed off as soon as you moved in on him, and you were doing your rush into Daddy's arms only to be disappointed," he said. "How many times have you done that, run to be disappointed?"

"About a hundred," I said. "So foolish, so silly."

"Only to daddies who don't know what to do with it," he said. "The reverse role takes on your father's contempt for weakness and turns it on others when they're vulnerable. You play peekaboo—Here I am, I'm everything; now I'm gone. The thing to do is just stay in there and work it out, rather than try to find someone less flawed or wait till you're less flawed."

I was quiet for awhile. "I don't want to do that anymore, it's foolish."

"What's foolish?"

"To keep hoping."

He said, "We all have to keep hoping, don't we?"

In another session he told me the problem was sexual. "You're angry with men because they get off, they get what they want from you. You don't always get orgasms, do you? You don't tell a man when you're not satisfied, do you? You don't finish those feelings in sex," he said. "You finish them outside of sex."

That session left me furious. I drove home with images of smashing things, flailing wildly. That night I dreamed I looked in the mirror and saw a death's head under the surface of my reflection. I woke up frightened, with my hands so locked between my knees the circulation was cut off.

I felt like someone was prying my legs open, but there was no feeling at all in my whole torso, except feelings of terror, sexual twinges. When it reached the point of breaking through to tears, a painful headache stopped it, followed by relief and sleep.

In the next session I told Fosworth about the death's head dream.

"The dream means that sex goes over the surface of all the cut-off feelings," he said.

I said, "I can't help it, it's that or nothing. They wouldn't give me anything. They wouldn't let me have it."

"Who's they?" he asked.

"I don't know!"

Now, reading the journal, I wanted to reach back there in time and tell her: It's not penis envy, it's not an all encompassing need for Daddy's attention. Don't you see? It's a child who has had her body used by her father and is punished for her own sexual feelings by her mother. One has taken her sex for himself, over her fear and terror, the other has whipped sex out of her. They won't let her have it. That's who *they* is, Fosworth. Listen to her!

In the journal, childlike scrawls:

I felt so frustrated, I kicked the chair when I left. I can't get past this, the wires just shut down and keep me from remembering. I'm stuck. Afraid of getting hysterical, I went into the restroom there and felt like tearing the partitions down, like beating on the tiles until they cracked.

I cried softly as I read it. How badly that child wanted out of her invisible glass booth. How hard she was fighting. And how afraid she was of what she would do if she ever got out.

In my next session, I was depressed. Silent. "Afraid of letting go," Fosworth said. "You're afraid you'll destroy someone."

"All I can destroy is me, that's all I've got," I said.

At home after the session, the memory trying to emerge finally broke through: *My head hurts really bad. I want to pull the wires off. I want to be free. I feel like someone's got me tied up and I want to be free. I want out! Leave me alone! I hurt! I want to cry and throw up. I want to stop all this hurt but I want to know what happened. I see wire clothes hangers, I saw them after the session today. I think wire clothes hangers and I start to wail and twist but I don't remember anything like that. She wouldn't have done that. She couldn't have, she was too good. When she died they all came and said she was so good and I always knew she wasn't.*

I'm crying and I'm not breathing. I don't know how much is true and how much I'm just doing this. I wail even as I write this like some mad woman sitting on my bed wailing, and my forehead hurts so bad I want to stop and go to sleep. I want to tear at my face and my eyes, my clothes. I'm trembling. I'm cold. It can't be cold; it's 70 outside. I put on my robe. The hammer is in the next room, it upsets me. I want to go put it out of sight.

Back and forth the mental battle raged. I was so ill I threw up, shaking and confused, sick with guilt for having such a memory about my mother.

I was very tired. I told Fosworth, "This is all old, I've seen it before. I can't go back further, I don't want to. I want someone to pound on me so I'll feel it, so I'll know what I did to make her do that to me."

In a far away voice I said, "She is kind then and good then, after it's all over, she's kind and good, like Joe afterward. I could feel soft again after it was all over."

I sat in silence while Fosworth waited. "I feel dizzy now. It comes in waves. This couldn't have happened. She couldn't have done that. I'm making all this up to blame her, aren't I? Did I make up horrible things because I wanted to take daddy away from mommy?

I looked at Fosworth for an answer. "Well, did you?" he asked.

The tears were gone now. I was breathing high in my chest. "Probably what she did wasn't so bad and I made it terrible to get her in trouble. There. I feel better now."

Years later, reading that, I wanted to reach back in time and tell him: The reason she feels better now, is she has denied the whole thing. She's a good girl. Mommy and Daddy are happy now. It can all go away.

"It doesn't really matter whether it's true or not," Fosworth said. " It comes to the same thing."

"But it does matter," I had written in the journal. "You're not supposed to lie, especially about your mother. Whether a person is a liar or not does matter." Then in big firm writing— "She tied my hands with dishtowels. They had embroidery on them, kittens, saying Monday, washing, Tuesday, ironing, Wednesday ...

I remembered the earlier dream: *Monday whips. Tuesday irons, Wednesday...* It all made sense now.

By the time I went to my next session with Fosworth, I had won the battle. The doubt was gone. "Yes, I remember even the little details. She tied me to a brown metal bed frame with embroidered dishtowels. Those big ones they used to have, twisted into ropes to go around my wrists. She whipped my genitals with a bent wire hanger. Because I was bad. I don't remember what I did that was bad. I knew if I just forgot about it everything would be all right." I needed help to comprehend it. "How could my mother do that to me when she was so good?" I asked Fosworth.

"Nobody's that good without it coming out someplace," Fosworth said. "You didn't want to remember how bad it was because she was the only mother you had, and she had all the good stuff too, the soft stuff, the warmth. The cat is your mother; the part you cut off because you wanted the softness. But it is also the part that has claws."

That summer, I went to the cabin at Tahoe, where Scott was now living. We sat on the porch under the towering pines and I told him that my mother had tied me up and whipped my genitals when I was a child. It was the first time I had ever told anyone other than a therapist. I was breaking the silence of an entire lifetime.

That night I had a terrifying dream: *I see her—shimmering, translucent, ephemeral—hovering by my bed. The ghost of my mother comes to punish me for telling lies about her.*

I screamed in my sleep, waking Scott, downstairs. He tried to calm me, but I was even paranoid about him. Did he know about the spook world too? An owl hooted outside the window and I started. "That's her, the owl." I was trembling, terrified to lie back down. "She'll take my life, take my breath, if I go back to sleep."

Scott brought hot chocolate, spoke calmly. "Mom, she is in you, and you can face her there. If you put her outside you, you are powerless." Somehow, I slept.

A lot more anger started coming out. I got angry at a summer institute that didn't go the way I wanted. I was furious with Ruth for bringing a man to the cabin when I wanted time alone with her. I was angry that the cabin needed so much work.

By the time I returned to El Paso, I had seen an old picture in a new mirror, and I was not sure I liked it. As my anger surfaced, I reminded myself of my explosive father. I was beginning to trust Fosworth. My father had not believed that my mother whipped me, but Fosworth did. Our sessions continued, sometimes going nowhere, sometimes building to almost unendurable terror of something still not named.

I wrote in my journal one day: "I think we're almost to the bottom of it. I got dizzy and hysterical today, stopped myself from going on with it. They'll hear me screaming,"

I kept seeing images of penises, large penises, penises up close, swollen, full of blood. Fosworth said, "It's you and men. You want to castrate them. You want to kill them."

"No, I don't." I said. "I want to kill me, but it would feel good to want to kill them instead."

In the next session, I went, unknowingly, into a trance state. *I'm like a child and sitting on the kitchen floor, my mother is at the stove, her back to me. I see a door just over my right shoulder and whatever is behind it is terrifying. There is a table down in the basement. Don't put me down on the table in the basement...*Fosworth's phone rang. He answered it.

I held my arms out in front of me, looking at them curiously. "I can't ever remember feeling so much power in my arms before."

From twenty years in the future, I cheered her on. "You're close, you're close! Before the basement you had arms. You're getting your arms back!"

But in the journal, I had written: "Fosworth's session left me feeling really schizoid. Whatever was behind that door, whatever was happening in that basement, was at the base, the bottom, of it all. Yet Fosworth did not pursue it. He didn't seem to think it was very important."

Fosworth was a Freudian, trained in Freud's ideas of penis envy. He believed women had an insatiable and demanding desire for their fathers, or daddy figures. "Sometimes I think he's just sitting there chalking up another of these castrating women," I wrote. "There's more to this than that."

Fosworth said, "When you want to go after a closed man with claws and hammer, it's like the child, going after her mother and father with claw hammer because they won't include her."

But there was no resonance, no "That's it!" No piece locking into place. He did not pursue the recurring images, the toilet associated with something threatening that I wanted to flush away, the closed door with something frightening in the basement, the powerless glassed-in child, the terror that stopped my breathing in sexually close situations. We had gotten to the worst of my mother stuff, but that was as far as his Freudian training could take him.

Again I focused on my work, my home. I hoped that by putting everything I had into El Paso, letting go of my ties to California, I might be able to settle down and be happy. The college, growing rapidly, had moved to a large modern campus, and I was making more money. I decided to buy a house near the campus. I would have to sell the cabin, which was painful for my sons, who had grown up there, and for me; it had provided a center from my wanderings. My new home was a New Mexico style adobe, with log supported ceilings, adobe fireplace and walled patios. A block from the campus, I made it a regular stopping place for faculty get-togethers.

Nedra and I made a long-planned trip to Southern Europe, touring Greece, laughing and crying together over our constant misadventures. Greece, with all its Goddess history, intrigued me. When I roamed the hills, always in the shadow of Athena, I felt strangely at home.

In a museum among towering and magnificent marble statues, all male, I asked the docent, "Where are the women?" He showed me a few small figures, some broken fragments of larger ones, several heads with the noses broken off, and torsos with no arms, always no arms. I learned later they had been deliberately and maliciously destroyed, hundreds of years ago. To break off the nose of the Goddess meant she could be discredited. To break off her arms was to rob her of her power. When I stood at the site where the Goddess had been worshiped, I felt my own small prayer forming; "Come back to us, Athena. We need you."

Back in El Paso, I took writing classes at the University. Ray Carver, the modern master of short story, was there as a visiting professor, with his wife, the poet Tess Gallagher. Ray was a gentle man. He did not critique my work like a professor—you need to do this or that, here it fails, here it succeeds—but went into my fictional reality with me. "There is so much love in this story." He helped me to get *Roadside Trinity* published.

A classmate, Carolyn, and I would go across the border to Juarez, female Hemingways. Sitting in a cantina with goats bleating from a pen in the back, and goats roasting on a barbecue in the front, we would read our manuscripts to each other.

My life was full and rich. Despite my occasional vows to give up men, they showed up like dandelions in a lawn. Charley loved to ride horses and go dancing at the big out-of-town Western roadhouses. I told him the truth about what I'd learned in therapy: "I get close, get scared and angry, then back off."

One night when Charley and I playfully wrestled on the floor by the fire, Charley asked, "What do I have to do to get you?"

I said, "Why does anyone have to get me?"

I felt the gate come down, felt myself turn cold. I said, "Too much gushy love stuff," went into the kitchen and started doing the dishes. He asked, "What's the matter?"

I said, "I just want to do the dishes," but I wouldn't look at him. He kept after me. "When I need to distance, just let me," I said.

"Okay, but I want to know exactly what happened, when it first started. Let's trace the triggers."

"Charley, back off. I just want to do the dishes."

Charley put his big gentle hands on both sides of my head and tried to make me look at him.

I felt a rage come up through me like wildfire. "Goddammit Charley, let go of me!" I flung myself away from him, glaring hate. Startled, he drew back, and I started to cry. "Oh Charley, you don't know…when you did that, I wanted to kill you!" Charley put his arm around me.

"Can you tell me what happens?"

I shook my head, still crying. Finally, I said, "I keep having images of strangling and flashes of a terrible killing rage. Oh, Charley, I'm so afraid I'll hurt you…."

Charley, a strong, muscular man, laughed gently. "Hon, you ain't gonna hurt me."

"You just don't know what it's like."

Charley stuck around and tried to love me, but I wouldn't let him. He said I never really let anyone close, even friends and family. "You control who moves in and how far, and if anybody comes in without being pulled on a string, you shove them back out." He took hold of my shoulders, looked me in the eyes. "You punish yourself for every little bit of happiness you get but, Babe, no matter what you've done, you've done enough time for it."

I had a dream: *I have a big beautiful white horse. It has gotten away and I have gone looking for it. At night I hear this noise, like something rubbing and turning those old clothesline pulleys outside the house and I know he has done that on purpose to let me know he is back and I am so happy. I bring him in the house and want to breast feed him so do it symbolically, first with a bowl of water, then a bucket of water. It is a happy dream.* My sexual relationship with Charley was that big white horse.

I couldn't break through the surface with Charley, so he broke up with me. I didn't blame him. A friend of his laughed and said, "Charley thought he had a little old garter snake, and it was a cobra."

There were more men. I had a glorious romantic fling with a charming bright man who was sexy and attractive, a man who took me to sexual heights, who razzle-dazzled me as I razzle-dazzled him. He was married, "getting a divorce."

Another dream: *I'm running a parade. I've read the names of all the people supposed to be in each group but many are missing. When the parade's ready to move out, I'm angry because there are still gaps and I tell the people, "You should have gotten someone to fill those gaps."*

The dream was telling me how I avoided the gaps between men, tried to fill all of them with a show, a parade, so I wouldn't feel lonely or unwanted. I wrote a telling line in my journal: "The problem with falling in love, you've got to be like a junkie, an addict, got to get that fix." Later I was to learn that's exactly what I was, and why.

As I looked back on that last affair though, I could see some progress in my development. This time when my lover promised to divorce and marry me, I continued with plans for my own life. When months had passed with no divorce plans, I confronted him, making clear my own needs and my own terms, without tears and pleading. Faced with direct honest conditions, he withdrew. I did not go into a depression, but accepted the truth. "I'm grateful that I had not been drawn any further into our fantasies." I came out of it feeling stronger.

For a writing class, I started a screenplay based on the life of Jeannette Rankin, America's first Congresswoman. I had discovered that almost no one knew who Rankin was, yet the more I learned of her, the more I admired her, a gutsy turn-of-the-century reformer and pacifist. I was indignant that I had never learned of such women in my history classes.

My professor told me about a creative Ph.D. program in Ohio where I could finish my screenplay as a dissertation, as long as I met their other requirements. A few months later, I got a letter from Ohio University, "The committee was especially enthusiastic about your work."

An artist friend at the college, Phil Behymer, told me, "You're always running away from pain, that's why you're so full of pain." He said it casually, while sketching. It hit me like something coming from the side, got to me before I could defend against it. He gave me an enormous portrait of myself as a going-away present. It was not flattering; it showed a complex woman, in large and therefore looming perspective. The eyes look out from the side, elusive, the smile twists cynically , the deep furrow in the brow seems to hold something back. Phil said, "I painted what's there when you're not covering."

In May of 1980, I wrote in the journal:

Excited about what's next. Scared to death too. Mike thinks Im making a mistake, should stay in my nice house and keep my good job. He may be right. Tomorrow I will be 50 years old. Half a century. Makes me sad to see all the years gone by, all the people lost, and about to lose some more.

I left El Paso in June. The song that kept running through my head this time was from the Sons of the Pioneers:

> Keep 'em movin' Dan
>> don't you listen to 'em Dan
> he's a Devil not a man
>> and he spreads the burnin' sand with water—
>> Cool—clear—water.

Minnesota, 1992. I had been going through journals since early that morning. I stretched, got a cup of tea, and watched the sun set over the lake. The ice was still holding. It would be weeks before it broke up, freeing the river to flow its winding way south.

As I made a small salad, put a burrito in the microwave, I thought about the dynamic, courageous woman I had been reading about. I picked up a snapshot from the photo album. A tall, confident looking woman in jeans, a scarf tied through a mass of permed hair, stands on a rock overlooking a bluff. Her hiking boots are planted firmly apart as she smiles frankly at the man taking the picture. She does not look like a woman who would say "I do" at an altar. She does not look like a woman who would give herself away, as I had a few months earlier.

9

Fifty,

Refocus

For thirty years my writing had tugged at my sleeve like a neglected child. When I was twenty, taking care of two small babies, dealing with an angry husband, I had somehow found time to write, though my painfully typed manuscripts rarely left the dresser drawer. When I started college, a play I wrote for a class assignment was chosen to be performed by the theater department. Over the years I had written and published a few short stories, but I had never given myself the opportunity to take my writing seriously.

After years of giving it only scraps of time, I was now giving myself two years to study writing, finish my screenplay, and get a Ph.D. in the process.

My Rankin synopsis won a scholarship at the Squaw Valley Screenwriters Workshop in California. I went to Lake Tahoe, joining a dozen fledgling writers. For a month, we worked with a professional screen director, producing a small section of each of our scripts.

I had never been happier or more comfortable in my work. We got up early, read each other's scripts, and after a personal conference with the director, rewrote for production. The Rankin Story was very ambitious, covering large expanses of time and geography, a large cast. The director chose to do one of the intimate family scenes. "I was impressed to see what a talented sensitive director could do to make my work come alive," I wrote my family. "He makes it touch the hearts as well as the minds of the viewer. My play was the favorite when all twelve were shown at our final Academy Awards."

I drove to Missoula, Montana, to do more research on Jeannette Rankin, and to meet those few people left who knew her personally. I camped in a mossy green valley by a slowly flowing stream, went to interviews looking like a professional nevertheless. I saw for myself the site of the lumber mill where she had once worked, skirts tucked up, helping her father get the boards cut for the new sidewalks in town.

I left for Ohio University with my typewriter and my screenplay in a box behind the front seat of an overloaded Datsun 240Z, hopeful that with some more work, I would one day sell it and enter the world of professional writers.

Ohio University lay in a pleasant valley isolated in the Appalachian Hills close to the border of West Virginia. I drove into a cobblestoned village called Athens, out of the founders' admiration for the early Greeks. The oldest land grant university in the Midwest, it had all the charm of a Christmas card: steepled brick buildings, ivy covered arches, even bells that rang out across the campus, *We Love the Halls of Ivy, We're Poor Lost Sheep Who have Lost our Way.*

I drove the winding streets into the hills, found the more ramshackle housing where the older students lived, balloons and colored parachutes turning them from ramshackle to quaint.

I found a little downstairs apartment, linoleum floors, gas heater, but windows overlooking an oak-studded canyon. I spent my evenings there, mostly bent over a huge electric typewriter on a makeshift table in the middle of the small living area, "Like a shrine," a friend commented. I typed research reports and literary criticism, I typed short stories, take-home exams. I typed syllabi and exams for my freshmen classes.

My goal was to finish the Ph.D. program in two years and get back to California. It meant there was little time except for teaching and studies. I knew no one, and was a good ten years older than even the oldest of the other graduate students. I put my nose to the typewriter or the books. I struggled with an all-male faculty that often did not understand, or want to understand, what I, a woman, had to say about my favorite women writers, Eudora Welty or Flannery O'Connor or Joyce Carol Oates. They demanded proof that I could conform to their own masculine perspectives.

I would have to master the usual requirements—The Language of Old English, The Structure of Postmodern Works, Post-Sauserrean Language Theory, The Semantics of Barth—but though they were demanding, they were a minor part of my program. I was writing, writing, writing.

In a theory class I hypothesized that women writers produce form differently than male writers, corresponding to sexual differences: males impose meaning, I believed, while females take in meaning, process it, and return it in forms different than those of males. The one feminist who was on the faculty, Dr. Edwards, invited me to dinner. "I am uneasy with your desire to look for patterns in what is distinctly female in writing. Don't you think that feeds into old anatomy-is-destiny stereotypes?"

With no feminist theory classes yet, I felt a bit intimidated. "I know the abuses have been great. Still, I believe we must know what those differences are, and I think they are distinct differences, if we are to cherish and defend them."

I observed, "You seem quite angry."

She said, "I am angry. I am tokenized by the faculty males, sabotaged by the women who work for me, and unsupported by other women." I was disturbed by her anger, and left feeling unsupported by her as well.

I had a screenwriting professor who did not like anything I wrote; he was looking for sitcoms, which I had never been interested in, and when I tried to write them, I wrote badly. I resented spending time on Old English, a language I would never use, and did not do well at it. I didn't find my Freshman English students, mostly eighteen-year-olds financed by their parents, nearly as interesting as my community college students, who had fought their way into college and had some adult experience. Probably most difficult was the personal isolation, working, working, working, to get finished and out as quickly as I could. I completely forgot Fosworth's cautions—problems come from going too far into relationships or staying too far out.

Ohio was reasonably close to Michigan, where my sister Beverly now lived. I had almost lost touch with her over the years. I would write to her, but she never answered my letters. I would call, but our conversations were perfunctory—How are you? I'm fine. How're the kids? I had never quite given up getting past that cautious superficiality.

On winter break, I headed north to upstate Michigan, with vaguely disturbing questions about the past, and an undefined disquietude. I wrote a story about that visit.

Winter Sisters

It snowed the last hundred miles from Grand Rapids to Travis City. The car had chains in the trunk, Helen made sure of that. She could put them on if she had to, but she was almost to her sister's now. The 240Z slipped and fishtailed around a sharp curve, but she remembered not to fight the wheel, and recovered. She passed an isolated gas station and garage, dark, closed. Well, she'd lain on her back under a car before. She didn't like it, but she could do it if she had to. She felt that way about a lot of things in her life; going to parties alone, turning fifty, driving all this way to see her sister.

She didn't like being the one who always had to maintain the relationship with Beverly, if there was going to be one. For years she had written her sister long letters, never receiving any answer, not even a card. She had even tried sending stamped, self-addressed envelopes. Even their phone conversations were perfunctory. "I'm fine. Debbie's graduating you know, and Brick is working in Martin's tire shop now after school."

It had been thirty years since she'd seen her older sister, thirty years since Beverly left California with her charming and scandalous second husband, Martin. Since then, they'd both been busy with families and jobs. Besides, they had never been close. Beverly was quiet, introverted, always had been. When they were young, Beverly had been the dark silent beauty; Helen the popular outgoing one.

How much our lives are created by the accident of our bodies, she thought. Not as pretty as her sister, she'd had to develop other assets. Helen glanced in the mirror, ran a hand through her own well cut hair, still blonde, though darker now. She looked forward to appearing at her sister's house as the successful younger sister, in designer sports togs and new white Nikes, California youthful without being silly. She had never been able to get away with feminine frilliness anyway; she was too tall for that.

She touched a strong stubborn jawline in a face otherwise worn soft, somewhat professionally kindly, by decades of teaching.

Marriage gone, children gone, their brother off in Saudi Arabia, this was her only bond with the last of her original family, a bond strengthened in some way she couldn't quite understand, just by the weight of years. Well, she was here now, but she was not going to have any expectations of sharing sisterly truths and memories. She would accept her sister exactly the way she was. No expectations. She could do that. A jawline muscle twitched.

The snow was starting to build an inch or so on the road, around the little two story frame houses, closer together now, square as Monopoly hotels. Pines were taking on delicate white skirts. Snow had been plowed into fresh heaps on the sidewalks. Passing the city limits sign, she turned off the car radio, pulled the folded towel from behind the small of her back. Martin had said they would wait for her at his tire shop. She checked the address again.

By the time she pulled up to the green and white frame building, it was past ten. The closed sign was hanging in the glass door, a metal

Goodrich sign creaked in the wind. A light from a back room shone onto a snow mantled tow truck. Her neck stiff from the strain of the drive, she checked her makeup, practiced a bright smile, then with a brisk youthful step, went around the side of the building to the door marked "office" with a brisk, youthful step.

A tiny woman wearing a man's shirt over a print blouse looked up from her desk, an inquiring brow raised, as if for a late customer. As recognition dawned, her face brightened, and she rose from her chair. Helen opened her arms and took in the small body that came only to her shoulder. "Let me look at you." Her gray hair pulled into a barrette on the back of her neck, Beverly looked like one of Helen's students done up as an old person for the college play. Under the exaggerated lines from nose to mouth, the two vertical lines across the forehead, under the heavy glasses, was her teenaged sister's perfect oval face, the gull wing brows, the straight elegant nose.

A heavy man with a great wave of white hair came in from the stock room. "Martin" was embroidered over the pocket of a well pressed cotton work shirt. "Well, if it ain't Helen, still as good lookin' as ever. Guess it runs in the family." Martin's gallantry had hardened into a kind of burlesque, a caricature of charm.

They left her car at the tire shop, since Martin said it would never make the unplowed grade by their house, and took his truck. Beverly sat in the middle of the big cab, matched set with the man with the great beer paunch and the loud voice. The C.B. radio crackled and mangled distant voices. Comfortable. Country.

They arrived at an isolated farm house. Behind it, headlights framed dark rows of cornstalks collapsing into the snow. Martin, first out of the truck, leaned into the door between garage and house, and whistled.

He turned to his wife. "Where's Skipper?"

"I don't know. Why didn't you close his dog door when you left?"

"You said you were gong to do it."

"No, I didn't," Beverly said defensively. "I said...."

"Goddammit, now we'll never find him!"

They plunged into the house. Helen could hear them searching from room to room, yelling at each other. "Why didn't you...you told me...by now he's out on the highway...." They spilled out again, Martin going one way, Beverly the other, their heavy fur-lined boots sounding hollow on the pavement. "Here Skipper, c'mon boy." Helen stood by the truck with her luggage, seeing the pattern of this marriage, "why didn't you...but you said...now he won't eve...well, why did you...."

A small black Scotty mix emerged from the woods across the road. "Is that him?" Helen shouted, pointing.

"Don't scare him! Stay where you are, he doesn't know you." Both rushed from opposite directions, while the dog stood looking from one to the other. Martin got there first, scooped the dog up in his arms and stormed into the house, pointedly ignoring the women responsible for the near tragedy.

"That dog is pretty important to him," Beverly apologized as they dragged the luggage through the door behind Martin. They passed through an addition off the kitchen, a long narrow room with a tall wood stove, an easy chair on each side, a wooden-handled sewing bag lying open. There was a stack of Golden Oldie records, a collection of clowns which had once contained whiskey, and a set of bound Readers Digest Best Stories from 1971. The piano and guitar Martin no longer played, Beverly said. Beyond the kitchen was a darkened parlor, light falling across heavy damask curtains.

"It's late and I know you're tired," Beverly said, showing her upstairs to a room that had once been her daughter's. Posters of kittens and horses and rock stars still waited on the walls, glass and plastic animals on the shelves, though Debbie had been gone for years. After her turn in the downstairs bathroom, Helen sank gratefully onto the soft sagging bed, and turned out the ruffled bedside lamp.

Lying in this teenager's room, upstairs in her sister's house, she thought of their own upstairs room as teenagers, their twin beds side by side. Even in that small dormered room, her sister had never talked to her. She remembered how silently Beverly would go through her forty-minute bedtime ritual, forcing thick hair into rows of tiny pincurls while Helen, a mere eighth grader, watched in admiration.

When Beverly had been in high school only a few weeks a handsome senior named Keith had asked her out. He was captain of the baseball team too. Helen knew it was an honor for a senior to notice a freshman, but Beverly showed nothing on her smooth, impassive face, just went on twining her dark hair into little spirals, opening hairpins with her straight white teeth, piercing, clamping, the tight coils.

Helen had been out riding when Beverly left on her date the next night. Though she tried to stay awake as long as she could, she had fallen asleep before Beverly got home.

The next day, when Helen came home from school, their mother was carrying on and Beverly was chastised.

For months Beverly had not gone out with anybody, not even girlfriends, just stayed home after school, cleaned house, and did her homework, and never said a word to Helen about what happened that night. Helen decided that Beverly must have been in love with

Keith, had passionate sex with him out of that love, then he had abandoned her. She knew that Beverly had never seen him again. A romantic teenager, she had admired her noble sister, mourning the loss of the love of her life.

After high school, Beverly had married a man who was well thought of in town, had a good job at Western Auto, and was from a good family, a cut above their own. Helen had imagined them quite happy together, in their perfect little two bedroom bungalow just outside of town. But there were some jarring moments. One night, Helen and her new boyfriend had gone to the movies with Beverly and Hal. Some celebrating servicemen passed by them in front of the theater. When they saw Beverly, her mass of curls piled high on her head, her trim legs in high heeled shoes, her knee length plaid skirt and matching sweater, they whistled.

"Lucky guy," they said to Hal. That was the kind of attention Beverly always got. Most men would be proud.

Hal replied sarcastically, "That's what you think, Buddy."

Helen was shocked at his cynicism, but Beverly's face showed nothing. In time Helen saw that Hal never gave his wife a word of appreciation; in fact, he constantly disparaged the fidelity of women in general. "Too late to keep the barn doors locked on that one," he once remarked of a radiant new bride. He wrote, "Sucker!" on the groom's car. His friends laughed.

Shortly after, Helen herself had married, a miserable time of poverty and mutual resentment. Then she'd straightened out her life, remarried well, finished college, got a good job. Helen remembered feeling rather smug, actually.

During those years Beverly had become more and more resigned to Hal's derogatory attitude. Then one day she came by herself to see Helen. Through tears of shame and guilt, she said she was in love with Martin, a fun-loving repairman at the body shop where she kept the books. Martin, a charming man by nature, showered her with appreciation and adoration. He wanted to get a divorce and marry her. Such things were not taken lightly then, especially in a small town.

"I guess Hal was right after all," Beverly said, a self-disparaging half laugh through her tears.

"Nonsense," Helen said. "He made this almost inevitable."

During their divorces, the town made Beverly and Martin so uncomfortable, they left the state and began life anew in his home state, Michigan.

When Helen's children were gone, she went through her second divorce, and a series of men followed that. She had adjusted to the single life, she said in her letters to Beverly. She could give more time to her work now, to the students. She had more time for reading—at last time for the classics—for writing, for traveling. And she had her friends. She did not mention the struggle with loneliness, with faltering relationships, her therapy; she would get through it.

A bar of light fell across the posters of colts, kittens, puppies, her niece's favorite figurines, ruffled dolls, lamp shades. A lifetime behind her, she lay stiff and cold above Martin and Beverly's room, feeling her solitude more in the radius of their union, flawed though it was.

The snow fell all night, covering the rounded fields, bringing the neighboring woods into black contrast.

The next morning, Martin was going into Travis City on business. When Helen came downstairs, there was much discussion going on about road conditions. Beverly packed his lunch while, on the side, she watched a pan of fried potatoes and eggs. He sat stroking the dog. "Don't want nothin' to happen to you, do we, Skipper?" he pouted, giving his wife sly abused glances. "Wouldn't have nobody left to pet, would we?" Beverly ignored him, her lips set in a prudish line. She jabbed the spatula under the potatoes, scraped hard as she turned them over, flattened them against the grill.

When Martin left, the house seemed to settle down around them, breathing easier. Helen helped Beverly with the dishes, talked about her work, her studies, about her sons and their families. Beverly brought Helen up to date on her daughter's unexpected child, her son's new business. Helen determined not to push as she always had; no questions like, how are you and Martin really doing?

Beverly worked on some bookkeeping from the shop while Helen sat by the stove and read a Best of Readers Digest. After lunch, Beverly washed her hair, then said tentatively she might give herself a permanent. "Let me do it," Helen begged, "Like we used to, remember?" Beverly deferred out of politeness at first, then brought to the kitchen the shoe box of colored perm rods, the cotton, the box with the picture of a young woman with a perfect wave. Beverly prepared bowls for the chemical solutions, then sat, stiffly docile, under her sister's competent hands. As Helen wound the long gray hair on countless blue rods, dabbing on the acrid chemicals, she found herself complaining about teaching.

"Students can be piranhas, you know? Just eat you up, they need help and attention so badly. And grading papers, stacks of them. It is endless. You're never through."

"I'd think teaching would be such a rewarding job," Beverly ventured.

"Oh, it is. In spite of all that, there's nothing I'd rather do."

Martin called to say he was back in town but he'd decided not to try to get back up the hill. "Well, it will be plowed by tomorrow, I'm sure," Beverly said on the phone. "You going to sleep at the shop?" Turban wrapped, she turned from the phone with that self-deprecating twist to her lip. "That means after the bar closes."

Helen held her eyes a moment, and Beverly said no more.

As they started fixing dinner, Helen said, "Remember how we would argue about whose turn it was to do dishes?"

"Yes. You always won."

"I did not!" They laughed.

It was good to reach for the copper bottomed pans that had been their mother's, to use the same old white Mixmaster on its heavy black stand. Helen had wanted none of their mother's things; Beverly had kept it all, the pieces of quilts, the hoops of embroidery, the unfinished crocheted squares. Beverly showed Helen how to stoke the stove so that it would burn long and slowly. While they ate mashed potatoes and gravy, fried pork chops with homemade apple sauce, Helen told about her travels to Africa, to Southern Europe, Greece and Rome.

Beverly disappeared into another room and returned with a globe as big as her arms could hold. Proudly, she showed Helen how to look up the longitude and latitude of a city or country in an accompanying book, set the numbers on a dial on the base of the globe so a light would come on at that place. This woman had made only one trip in her life, the one to Michigan from California. Helen was awed. "I had no idea you ever wanted to travel."

"Martin doesn't know I bought it, " Beverly said. "It cost over a hundred dollars. I keep it in the sewing closet upstairs." She made little lights go on in Mexico, England, Ireland. "I know with Martin's health and the money and all, we'll never do it," she said in that flat self-effacing tone that had crept into her voice over the years. Helen tried to tell her they could do it but Beverly had made up her mind.

"You were the one who did things, even when we were kids. You were always the smartest."

Helen was amazed. "Why Beverly, you were always the smartest. Don't you remember? You memorized everybody's license plates, even strangers'. You knew by heart all the radio station numbers and the times for all the programs. You always got your math homework done long before I did."

Beverly looked bemused. "I did?"

"Yes! Really. You were always the pretty one too so I had to work really hard to find something to be best at, drama, yearbook, glee club, all that "

Helen watched Beverly adjust her thinking, sorting the incongruous messages. "But you're the one who went to college," she said conclusively.

They sat in silence. Helen fingered the crocheted doily under the wreathed candle centerpiece The fire made warm cracking sounds against the snow-stilled night.

"Beverly, why didn't you ever write me? Why didn't you ever answer any of my letters?"

"I never could think of anything to say." She looked down at her hands, as if finding them forever empty. "You read a lot of books I never heard of, you've been places..."

"But that doesn't mean anything. You could tell me about your life, about the deer in the corn and about the people at work..." But she knew it did, knew she had played up the trips, the promotions, the gilt-edged Tolstoy.

Beverly left the room, returned with a shallow cardboard box and dumped its contents on the kitchen counter. Cards. Forty or fifty of them. Birthday cards, Christmas cards, all unsigned, unused. At first Helen was confused. "To my dear sister at Thanksgiving" one read. Another, "Will you be my Valentine, Sis?" Year after year she'd picked out these cards for her. Helen swallowed hard as she traced the outlines of a fat yellow bunny offering a purple Easter egg, "Sister Dear, Wishing you the joys of Easter." Beverly stood smiling somewhat wistfully, hands at her sides.

"But why didn't you ever send them?"

"I don't know. I just never got around to it...."

Helen looked at her doubtfully.

Beverly said, "You didn't send cards. You sent letters. Interesting letters. I thought you might think Hallmark cards were dumb; you said once people should be more creative, speak for themselves."

"I did? Yes, I probably did, but that was years ago...." Helen reached to put an arm around her sister. Beverly stiffened. Helen backed off.

They loaded the dishwasher, cleaned up the kitchen, sat a while on either side of the stove, Beverly embroidering a pillow case with swooping bows and knotted flowers, Helen pretending to read. She was feeling something that she thought might be humility. It was not painful, she discovered, quite comforting really.

"I've been in therapy," Helen said. "But I'm not sure that it's made any difference."

The century clock from the darkened parlor struck nine times. "Sometimes when I am shopping downtown, I feel guilty," Beverly said, knotting her thread with one hand and picking up a new skein,

"I feel like people are looking at me. I feel guilty, like they think I've done something wrong."

"My God, Beverly, you've done less to feel guilty for than anyone I know."

Helen waited for her to say more, but Beverly seemed to be watching the snow piling up against the corners of the windows. Helen felt herself wanting something from her sister, wanting her to remember something, she didn't know what, something that would make a difference in her life.

"Do you think my hair is dry yet?" Beverly asked. They moved into the kitchen.

Helen unwound the fat pink curlers. Long gray hair fell in springy curls around the solemn lined face, looking absurdly girlish. "Have you ever tried it short?"

Beverly exaggerated a turned-down mouth. "Instead of looking like a little old lady I looked like a little old man."

"Well, let's dampen it. That will loosen the curl a little." Helen put the brush under the faucet in the kitchen sink.

"Beverly, do you remember Aunt Ruth? I don't really remember her, except in pictures. She looks so alive. Mom always said I was like our Aunt Ruth. She was tall, I guess, and a little wild. She committed suicide, didn't she?"

"I don't remember anything from those days in Richmond, anything before I was five," Beverly said, looking uncomfortable, handing her a hair pin.

Helen switched to a later time.

"I remember once coming home from school when I was in the eighth grade and you were supposed to be in school, but you stayed home. Mom was banging things around in the kitchen. Remember? What was that all about?"

"Well, I suppose that could have been a lot of things. Maybe I was sick or she kept me home for some reason...."

"No," Helen said, wondering why something she remembered so clearly, her sister didn't remember at all.

"It had something to do with that guy you went out with the night before, Keith his name was. I remember Mom saying something about your getting into trouble."

"Oh, yes." She handed Helen another hairpin to clip down her burgeoning curls. "Was that his name, Keith?"

"You don't remember? You must have been really in love with him, you mourned him for weeks."

Beverly looked mildly surprised. "Oh no, it was not like that at all."

She was silent a long while, as if thinking about that strange interpretation. "No. Not at all. It was my first date ever, you remember, and he was a senior and I didn't know what to expect, how I was supposed to act... you remember, nobody ever told us anything. I was just a brand new freshman. Anyway we went out with another couple, and after the show, Jack parked, and he and Patty sort of...slid down on the front seat. Keith and I were in the back seat, and he...pushed me down.

"I didn't know what to do, I didn't think I could do anything. They were doing it in the front seat. Anyway he...did it."

Her veined fingers rifled through a tray of hairpins and clips, picked a wide metal barrette and handed it to Helen.

"I didn't cry or fight or anything...I bled all over so he brought me home. Mom was waiting up, you know how she was, I couldn't hide my skirt...Anyway the next day Mother took me to the doctor, and for the next month..." She stopped.

There was silence for a long time as Helen fussed with her hair, taking in what she was saying.

"I wasn't mourning, I worried every day that I could be pregnant." Her tone was flat, her expression unchanged.

"My God, Beverly, you were raped!"

Beverly took back the hair clip, pulled her hair into a tight bunch and fastened it at the back of her neck.

"Well, I never thought of it like that." Her voice never changed from that self-effacing slur.

"Mother said I never should have let them park and I never should have gotten in the back seat with Keith. She said I was ruined. No man would ever have me. You know how it was then. I had to tell Hal I wasn't a virgin, right before we got married. It was too late to call off the wedding, he said. He never let me forget it." She went back to her chair by the stove, busied herself finding her needle, and the place where her stitches stopped.

"So that was why Hal acted the way he did. That bastard. And that's why all this time ...Have you told Martin?"

"Heavens no. He's got enough things he thinks are wrong with me." The stitches resumed, tiny, even, across the pillow case. Helen saw the years all circling back, the present growing up out of the past like petals stitched on a stem.

"My big sister, my beautiful little big sister."

They sat on each side of the tall black stove, one of them behind a book, the other impassively watched the stitches, knots and loops form a pattern in her embroidery. The snow fell softly all night.

On the two-day drive home from my sister's, I had lots of time to think about how little I had known her back then, how little I knew her even now, how little she knew me. I thought about how little most people really know about one another, even people who grow up in the same house, live in the same room.

How little we know even about ourselves, with the gaps and crevices and distortions of memory, with the defensive shaping of ourselves around the wounds of our past.

I knew now I was like my sister: there was no one I could show myself to, no one I would trust not to reject me if they really knew the truth about me, including myself.

I wondered as I drove: Would Beverly ever be willing to look at those six years that were a blank to her? Beverly had all our mother's things, had taken her persona even. Where was our father in all that?

Was I, like my sister, still controlled by the past? Did I too suppress my own vitality, my own sexuality, to serve the needs of men?

In January of my first year in Athens, I wrote down a dreamlike experience: *...fleeting images of someone inside me, hammering and screaming and breaking things, furious, wanting out, breaking walls, windows. "I want out! Let me out, goddamn it, let me out!"*

You'll kill me or ruin me if I let you out.

"I'll kill you if you don't."

You'll run away if I let you out.

"Damn right. Anywhere but here. Jeezus, a bar's better than this blackness you keep me in. Jail, a regular jail. I hate you for keeping me here."

If I let you out I'd be ruined. You'd run amuck, spend all my money, fly to Jamaica and find a lover, any kind of lover, and when the money was all gone, you'd be a disgraceful wreck and drink yourself to death and shack up with transients.

"Let me out. Let me out! You can't keep me here."

I was to find out years later, it was the voice of Sneaky Snake. And she wasn't going to be kept down much longer.

10

Fast Forward,
Rewind

I was working late at night, waking depressed in the mornings, haunted by nightmares. I went to the campus counselor. He listened to me cry for an hour, then reassured me. I just made large demands on myself. I knew what I was doing in the professional area, while sometimes forgetting to take care of the soft personal part of myself. "That part is mad and unhappy."

When he said that, I remembered the strange writing in my journal. "Let me out, goddammit!" But I didn't tell him about that.

In time, I met some women grad students in their thirties and forties. We would sometimes gossip over lunch. "I had dinner with your screenwriting prof the other night," MaryAnn said. "He said he finds you damned attractive, but there's something about you he can't put his finger on."

"Well, that's good," I said, making a joke of it. "I sure don't want his fingers anyplace on me."

MaryAnn continued. "I told him, you want to know what it is? She doesn't want to be taken care of so you're not her type of man."

I laughed. "Thanks, but I'm not sure that's wholly accurate."

The second year in Athens, I met an art professor from Ohio State University who became a warm supportive friend and lover. John worked with me on my video production, *Night Dreams*, a twenty-minute script about a young girl whose fear of men is traced, through cuts giving the effects of flashbacks, to her mother's sexual hysteria. John acted in that project, helped the production crews. Then he worked with me on my video art project, where we projected slides on to my body, painted white, to demonstrate the effects of psychological projection on the self. He worked hours with me on the tricky editing, the synchronization of the sound. Those were exciting times; I was overworked, tense, difficult, stressed, and totally happy. John put up with it all.

That year both of my productions won awards in local competitions, my finished Rankin manuscript was accepted as my dissertation, and I passed two sets of orals, one in English, one in Communications. "Brilliantly," I was told by my Major Professor, though like many women, I did not take that word seriously. I finished my Ph.D. by spring. "Less than two years!" the Department Chair said. "How did you do it?"

"Easy," I said, dismissing the whole thing. "I didn't know anybody here, so I had nothing else to do."

"There you go again," John said. John was an observant lover: he caught me when I minimized my accomplishments, when I equated being emotional with looking dumb, or workless as worthless.

We took the People's Express to New York City, where he showed me the art exhibits, and let me learn, just by standing there with him, what an artist sees, how an artist looks at art.

We went to the best theater in Columbus. He taught me to ride a bicycle, and encouraged me in my writing. We flirted with the idea of marriage; he was a supportive and generous man, and had more in common with me than any man previously. He found my company delightful; I was fresh, alive, and challenging.

But dark mafia-types still haunted my dreams. *In a N.Y. gallery a man makes a nasty crack. At first I try to ignore it, or rephrase it, but then I see him coming toward me with a sadistic smile on his face and I know he meant it. I grab his arm, furious, and start out the door. OK You're going to tell me and I'm going to hear it. But outside, I start down some steps looking for a rest room. A strange man says he'll show me but I know he is up to something, so I get away from him, sit in a dark theater and cry.*

Years later, in my house by the lake, I read that dream over a second time. The images were more clear now, repeating themselves again and again in different ways. The dark figure that stalked my dreams was jeering at me; I could enjoy my time in the art galleries, but he was threatening me with something that he knew and I didn't want known, like a blackmailer. I tried to find the toilet, to expel, to flush away something, but I was unsuccessful. Accosted by still another threatening figure, I finally gave up in frustration and "sit in the dark theater" of my life, crying.

What was it the dark man threatened me with? What was it I was going to make him tell me? Was it the knowledge of what had happened in the basement? Was there something else that happened in the bathroom? Was there some dark secret that, even as I swore to make him tell, I tried to flush away?

As I got closer to John, I got tense, started finding fault, creating problems. The dreams cracked down harder: *I'm in a big department store, wandering from section to section. One very elegant section with all good rich stuff in it is being held up by bandits who have all the employees lined up outside. I slip back to the other section and tell other employees what's going on. Then, I slip out, and just as I'm passing under a big truck and trailer, they see me. I've got a boy child by the hand, he wanders off, the road dead ends. I realize I can't get through and go back to the department store, and go down in the basement because they keep a woman down there. I'm not sure whether she's dangerous, she's back in the shadows. She tells me it was cruel and thoughtless to play with the child where she could see me, because she can't enjoy things like that.*

Another guilt dream. By this time, very familiar. The department store, my life and all its opportunities, is held up by bandits, the child I enjoy disappears, the road dead ends, the innocent joy is turned into a guilt trip by the woman in the basement. Gangsters, dark men from the past, and guilt from my mother, combine to keep me from getting the best out of my life. Over and over again, my dreams try to tell me; you've got to deal with what's in the basement, under the supporting structures of your life.

I told John I was going back to California. My screenplay was finished now, I had a brand new Ph.D., and I wanted to see what I could do with it. I had been exiled from my home state, my friends and family, long enough, I said. Maybe he could join me later. Bewildered, he watched me withdraw from him as if he had meant nothing to me. I loaded up my little silver Datsun 240Z, with its long shiny hood and big powerful engine, and headed west for Los Angeles, City of the Angels.

After wholesome Ohio, driving into Los Angeles was like entering a war zone: freeways were torn up, smog blanketed the nearby hills with a sinister haze, like that over a bombed out city. In the Black, Spanish and Vietnamese neighborhoods, angry graffiti exploded from every concrete surface, and everything was concrete—concrete freeways, concrete walls, buildings like bunkers. Drivers of Jeeps, vans, pickups and trucks, frustrated with the crawling traffic, jockeyed aggressively, threatening one another with curses and lewd gestures.

The Hollywood area was no longer the glamorous oasis for the glittering famous; streets were prowling with prostitutes and destitutes and pushers. Even the billboards with their dominating twenty-foot icons were sinister and violent. It was like a city that started out scaring itself for fun, and then it got out of hand.

The friends I was staying with laughed as they recounted stories: the hand that reached through the kitchen door in broad daylight and lifted a purse off the table while they watched in amazement. The beautician who had one arm in a sling; a losing encounter with a purse snatcher. I felt as if the ever present eyes of the predatory down-and-out were just waiting for me to make a mistake, give them an edge.

I did. As I made calls from a telephone booth in a tawdry gas station, looking for an apartment I could afford, my wallet was stolen. It contained all my identification, credit cards, cashier's checks for my entire savings, and all my cash. I was shaken to my core, forced to realize how much of my security I carried around in one little folded leather packet. I felt as though my "identification," literally my identity, was gone. My confidence in myself to survive in that environment was seriously undermined.

Fortunately, I had good friends. They put money in my hand, and helped me begin the long process of claiming my lost assets. House hunting again, ads for low-cost housing led me to neighborhoods with the trashy appearance of drug dens, or hang outs for prostitutes. The apartments I could afford had shabby brown carpets stained with cigarette burns and grease.

I finally found a place in the Hollywood hills, a garage a screenwriter had remodeled to help him make his mortgage payments. I had swimming pool rights, and in return for baby sitting his daughter occasionally, he gave me leads to people who might be willing to read my screenplay. The world was looking better.

I enrolled in a screenwriting class at U.C.L.A., met a woman I enjoyed, only to find when we went out one night, she was on drugs most of the time. I spent hours on the phone, trying to get past secretaries to people who made decisions. I spent hours sitting in offices after I got appointments, only to find the person I was waiting to see had already gone home. I learned that the world of Hollywood works by connections: if you know somebody who knows somebody, that's a start. After that you're on your own, and you've got to be aggressive.

My landlord was publishing a Sunday supplement, and gave me interviewing and writing jobs, which gave me an inside track to people who would read my Jeannette Rankin script. Over and over I heard the bad news. "It's an intellectual piece." The kiss of death. As I waited for agents to return my calls, I turned my attention to writing a new novel, an escapist fantasy about dolphins that I thought would make a good film. I estimated my savings would last another four months, then I would have to take a job.

John, believing our problems stemmed from his rather closed personality, came to stay with me while he went to a personal growth workshop. He suggested we do an intimacy exercise he'd learned there: "Twelve hours isolated with each other, no diversions. The only conversations allowed have to be about ourselves and each other." In an hour, we could find nothing more to say to each other, and ended up waiting it out silently, like a vigil.

But John did not give up. The next day, we did communications exercises: "Just listen, and repeat what you hear." He began talking about himself, his desire to be more aware of his feelings, how he felt about me. I experienced how freeing it was to simply listen, not to barge in and control, advise or criticize. I also experienced how hard it was to simply repeat what a person said, without altering the meaning or interpreting it.

Those attempts to restore closeness brought the sinister man, whose description fit my father, back into my dreams: *I am in a department store, tired and careless. I leave with a new dress but realize I haven't paid for it. I'm relieved I didn't get caught and go back and return it. Then I'm with this rather shady man, attractive, masculine and controlling, dark with a little gray in his hair, but there is something shoddy and sleazy about him and his friends. We have gotten a bed, like the one I've got now, a trundle, where one part fits under the other. It's loaded on a packed truck while we go away. When I come back, the bed has been stolen. My companion says he'll get me another one. He disappears in an arched doorway made of railway beams, where a road leads to a shabby rural neighborhood. He and his friends are all shady, survivors all, but on a level I feel is beneath me.*

When I come back again, there is a big black Naugahyde couch on the truck, the kind in cartoons about therapy, with curved back and arms, but the cushions are sliding off and the seams are splitting. I don't want it. It's huge and ugly. He keeps telling me it will serve the purpose and he got it for me and I'll take it. He starts walking toward me, as I yell, "I don't want it, I won't take it," and as he comes closer, I see he has the power and I'll probably end up taking it. He's not going to hit me, I just know he's got the control.

I woke from that dream exhausted and shaken. I knew the couch represented therapy, therapy that I needed for some deep-seated trauma concerning my father. But I had been in therapy, I told John as we lay in bed together. It did not help.

I said, "Something terrible must have happened to me as a child. I have so much hate and anger. I have flashes of wanting to kick the hell out of some man's genitals. No memory of who or why."

"Go into that anger, go back to the child," John said.

I refused. "I'm afraid I'll find out my father raped me or something."

John suggested a technique he'd learned in his workshop: "If you are afraid to delve into the threatening dream, you could take a trusted friend with you." I agreed to try it. In my imagination, I created Mary, who used to work in the Eight Mile House. I told Mary I was afraid that I might remember something about my father at the little house in Richmond.

I wrote the rest in my journal:

I was about two. He came home from work, picked me up. I was happy. I liked to be held against his chest. He got an erection and Mom was coming so he dumped me back in the crib, acting like I was bad. His erect penis was right at eye level, and I understood the penis was the reason I was bad and being dumped. I don't know if he hit me or only just dumped me like a terrible dirty thing. I was furious. I wanted to kick the penis with both feet, and scream and yell. But I didn't. I didn't dare."

Reading, I thought, that's not so bad. Just an embarrassed father and a child who took his embarrassment to be her fault. Could that create all these problems? Was Fosworth right, I wanted that penis?

I came out of those fantasies feeling drained, disconnected. John was comforting, but I felt very distant all the rest of his stay. Ghostlike.

When John sent the rest of my few things from Ohio, he confessed he had read all my journals before packing them. He saw in them constant repeated frustration: "It's like watching a director do the same play, over and over, trying to get past the frustrating ending."

At a party I met Stephanie, healthy, humorous, down to earth, solid. She had lived in Los Angeles all her life, had raised her two sons alone, even made a reputation as the best piano tuner in West L.A. She already had plenty of friends, but she was a generous woman. She made time for one more, listened to me talk about my confusion and my guilt over John.

Stephanie just took it for granted that any relationship with a man would have a half life of about six months, since that was her history.

"That's the history of almost everyone I know." This was a new perspective for me: in this social environment, my history with men, which I saw as failure ridden, was normal!

Those were the pre-AIDS years and this was the home of glitz and spectator sex. Stephanie and I swam at nude beaches, sunned in the paradisiacal Eden of Elysium. There were men everywhere. I flung myself into the singles scene with all the abandon of a drunk at the Last Chance Saloon. Unitarian Singles, the Sierra Club, Booklovers, dance clubs. I went out three or four times a week.

I began to develop the ability to observe myself. I noticed that the more attractive a man was to me, the more nervous I was. I dealt with that by "turning on," becoming coquettish, charming. My body made all kinds of unnecessary moves, emphasizing its curves.

"Even my voice gets curvy," I told Steph. I named that part of myself Marilyn Monroe. I had always felt an affinity for her, felt I understood perfectly why the real Marilyn behaved as she did.

Within weeks I was having sex with two different men, and each of them knew about the other. One of them, Richard, insisted on complete honesty. "That's the only way that we're going to get past all the bullshit," he said.

Richard was thirty-eight, experienced and articulate; he talked frankly about his active sex life, his fears, his anxieties, his inability to make much money or to stick with one woman. He was good looking, dark, with a broody sensitive face and a shock of perpetually unkempt hair. He was seeing several women.

I confessed to Richard I wasn't as honest. For example, I'd been seeing another man even after I wanted to break it off. "He calls, and I say yes because I don't want to hurt him."

Richard said, "You've got to take care of yourself or you'll do him more harm. Let him know how you feel without putting him down or cutting him off."

"I shouldn't get so involved with people so soon," I said. "I should hold back until I know I want something more permanent with them."

"Would that be taking care of yourself? Then you can push us all away and work on a book and in three months you'll have it all to do over again. Or you can take care of yourself with us. Give and get what you want and need, no more, no less."

One night when Richard and I were making love, playful and affectionate as always, I got hysterical, pushed him away and pulled him to me at the same time. I wanted to hurt him. I started to cry, cried the whole time we were making love, but didn't want him to stop.

He said, "You've been raped."

I said no, I hadn't, but there didn't seem to be any reason for so much terror.

Shortly after that, I broke up with him. Stephanie said all her friends were like that, no matter what age. "They both do and don't want a permanent relationship. I've learned to tell a man right away; here's what I'll do. I'll fall in love with you, I'll be everything to you, lose myself, and in three months it will be over." She laughed, put on her coat and left for her dance class.

I started noticing how much money there was in that part of the country; million dollar homes all around my neighborhood, harbors studded with million dollar yachts, Rodeo Drive where a simple dress or sweater might easily cost $800. It seemed to me if there were so many people with so much money, I might as well meet some of them. Within weeks I had met a handsome dynamic vice president of a computer sales company, and he was teaching me to sail his thirty-foot boat.

We sailed to Catalina Island. I took the tiller while he slept off a hangover below deck. When we moored on the island, I impressed him by diving under to check the set of the anchor. I lost myself in the rocking of the boat at night in the harbor, studied the way the water moved like slow heavy mercury in the moonlight. I leaned into the foam, exhilarated, as we caught a gust heading home.

He was impressed. "Most of the broads I meet don't want to lift anything heavier than a cocktail glass. I have to hold their hands just getting them on the damned boat."

We went dancing, wild and free on the crowded pulsing dance floors of the beachside clubs. I wore low cut dresses with high heeled shoes, because he liked them. I wore a tiny bikini when we sat around his pool.

I could run five miles on the beach, and I could tell him, "Leave me alone, I'm writing." I was proud of my ability to keep my balance with such a powerful man, I told Stephanie. "I can keep his boat on course when he's below deck, sleeping off his martinis. I can fend off his sexist chauvinist jokes and go him one better. I can play poker with his friends. He thinks I'm the greatest thing since sloe gin, and I'm getting a chance to see how people with a lot of money live."

I called him Captain Beastie and he called me Superbroad. I gave up my garage and moved in with him. We played with the idea of marriage. I rented an office where I could work and fought to keep at least six hours a day clear.

I wrote:

> *Captain Beastie and I go through the vows and broken promises common with heavy drinking. I am learning to care a great deal for him, but even with the help of Alanon, I have trouble with the blunting effects of that much drinking. Our sex life is deteriorating. I stopped having climaxes, I'm no longer sure I ever had one. I asked him to slow down, but he says he's a jet pilot, likes to move fast. He laughed. I can soar, you just flap along and can't get off the ground."*

My son Mike was getting married. He and Jean had lived together for years; it was time to make it official. I was invited to the wedding, they told me, but Captain Beastie was not. "He's loud, crude, dominating, and insensitive," Mike told me. I said I would not go without him. He got invited. My friends wondered what I was doing with a man whose tie had little pigs and MCP's on it.

A few months later, I completed *Dolphin Girl*. The story had come to me simple and clear: a girl is raised in captivity with a dolphin as her only companion. When the scientist takes the dolphin away, the girl must either get to the ocean and join him or die. There is a well meaning couple who want to make her normal; a twisted and warped doctor who wants to keep her the way she is. Nobody liked the story, not my family, not my friends, not the agents I worked so hard to get it to.

There was some of my glassed-in child in the *Dolphin Girl*, and its rejection hurt at a very deep level. The day I came home with a last devastating critique from an agent, Captain Beastie was on the telephone, drink in one hand, ordering seats for an Army-Navy game. When I showed him the rejection letter he said, "Yeah. Well, how's three rows back? Okay?" I walked out, finishing one more cycle of expectation, hope, disappointment, and despair about my relationships with men.

I moved into my office in Long Beach. I ran on the beach each morning, swam each afternoon, showered in the yacht harbor restrooms. At night I brooded about how it might have been different with Captain Beastie.

My window faced the corner of Pine and Ocean. Across the street was an eight-story brick building, its arched windows boarded closed. A rickety wooden roof had been built over the ground floor storefronts, making it look like the setting for some kind of redevelopment Western.

I was already past fifty, and the high school dreams, dimly imagined and constantly changing—writer, adventurer, teacher, wife of a Great Man— were growing distant. I slumped in the swivel desk chair, looking at the heaps of newspapers, crumpled up job applications, overflowing wastebasket, thinking I ought to take my glasses back off. What kind of a home was this?

Rummaging behind the mattress for my one towel, I found my overnight case under my shoes, let myself out into the marble floored halls, making sure nobody was around. You're not supposed to live in these offices. It's against the codes.

On the way to the women's room, I noticed another suite was boarded off, a lot of them were now. The floor below was mostly artists, studio space, but all the floors were gradually being shut down as people vacated. The building was to be razed soon, its white-tiled parapets replaced with a multi-storied hotel complex. Meantime, it was cheap rent and the manager could still make a few bucks as long as I would pretend not to be living there.

In the women's room, more gray and black veined marble, a mausoleum, I pushed open the paint-coated window so I could see across the parking lot to the harbor where the Queen Mary loomed, magnificently and permanently beached. From there I could see tiny tourists trailing along her decks, gazing up at huge pictures of the movie stars who used to play shuffleboard all the way to Europe. Behind her was another monument to size: Howard Hughes' Spruce Goose, the largest wooden airplane ever built. The white dome which housed the plane rose on the bay like a great stalled moon.

I'd seen the tourist videos of the Spruce Goose story. People had said it would never fly. In one grand fling of bravado, Hughes had taken her up; she roared over the ocean, her pontoons barely clearing the waves, for a tenuous and noisy mile, and sank back down. "There, she flies," Hughes had reportedly said, and never took her up again. I identified with the Spruce Goose. I could never quite get off the ground either. I identified with Howard Hughes too, especially his later life, when he became an eccentric hermit.

When my granddaughter Elizabeth was born, I was not asked to be present at the home birth. When I drove up to see her, I loved her immediately, such a strong spirit, calm, sure of herself and her wants and needs. Mike acted as though he wasn't sure he wanted his mother there, acting so grandmotherly. "She's ours, not yours," he reminded me. I knew he was going through a lot of confusion, rejecting much of what I represented while he built a strong and stable family of his own. He needed to do it, but it hurt.

I wrote in my journal:

Mike says I drove off his real father by being over protective of him, Mike, rather than let them work it out. As if a four-year-old can work it out with an abusive father. He hates being a man, being expected to take charge, he says, when his mother and his wife have so much anger about men. I never realized before what all my man-stuff has meant to him. Scott becomes ever more gentle. He told me he loves me, and I can quit being anxious about him. I cried.

I went to work finishing some of my stories, stacked up in boxes around my office. I thought of the years of writing involved, with very little money from it. I tried to remember that John Gardener carried boxes of manuscripts around with him for years before he began to publish regularly. I sold three short stories. I sent out the two novels I had written years ago, and the new fantasy novel. Eventually, a management company optioned my screenplay. There wasn't much money involved, but there would be much more if it got produced.

I knew I could not stand up under the anxiety of living poor, so that fall I took a full-time temporary teaching job at the City College. I moved in with Stephanie, vowed six months of celibacy, and threw myself into teaching, knowing I had to have good evaluations and recommendations if I wanted a permanent contract.

That was the end of my writing for a long while. But not the end of the nightmares: *I have a white camper truck. I've asked some men to load a body for me, and when I get in the cab, they've put it up front, in the passenger seat, sitting up. I can only see an arm and shoulder through the heavy canvas. I say I can't drive with that there, it will fall over on me, and it's too heavy for me to move by myself. I tell the men to put it in the back.*

I woke up at 4 a.m., tossing and turning, feeling as though my whole body was made of fear, as though I were dragging my father's dead body around with me. The dream was telling me that I had been trying to get men to help me with my father's body, help me to deal with his effects on my life. Now I wasn't seeing any men, so I wanted it loaded in the back of the truck, out of sight. I could see pieces of it, a shoulder and an arm. I was in the driver's seat, but that old dead body was still there, ready to fall over on me as soon as I rounded a curve, and that would be a terrifying experience.

As my six months of celibacy came to an end, I found myself already looking around for the next man. Steph laughed about it in the kitchen. "Love addiction is like alcohol," she said. "I get yearnings and cravings, each time is the last time, each time it's hangover and low self esteem and family destruction, each time it's compulsive, can't stop till the binge is over, each time there's nothing I'd rather do than get high on love."

We said we should found Loveaholics Anonymous. For the first time I understood what Captain Beastie said a year ago when the doctor asked him what got in the way of realizing he had a problem with alcohol. "If I realized it, I'd have to give it up."

Some changes were happening at a deep level though. The journal recorded a significant dream:

A woman friend and I take Marilyn Monroe out in a rowboat. I am in the bow, Marilyn in the middle, and someone else in the back. In the middle of the river, Marilyn falls in. I never see it happen, never see her down in the water. I keep wondering why neither of us goes in after her; it seems to be because she is just gone. The woman in back of the boat, on the tiller, knows more about it than I do. We aren't too upset. Later, we go to Marilyn's place by the river, such a funny little riverside shack. We try on fashions she had designed. She was a good designer.

I cried after that dream. I had always loved my beautiful, childlike, smart, little grandstander. She turned men on, and they turned her on. Even though she couldn't go past that, she took what she could. Her life, her funny little shack, was built of temporary partitions, not very solid, but she couldn't build anything stronger or better than that for herself. Her designs were for better places though. She died grandstanding, standing up in the middle of the boat, and very unhappy. Now, my own Marilyn Monroe was gone.

As my friends John, Stephanie, Richard, and even Captain Beastie, made me feel safe and accepted exactly as I was, positive dreams came to support my progress:

I am climbing a rope ladder, old and ragged, up to a wooden platform in a big solid oak. I am doubtful about it but want to do it. A young man holds the ropes for me at first, and boosts me by the seat of my pants over a part where the limbs are broken. I am scared and insecure. He stands below, encouraging me, telling me he'd done it and he was scared too, but it was worth it because he'd never had to be so afraid again. I find a good solid hold, wrap my arms and legs around the tree, and hang on to it for dear life, waiting for the next surge of strength to pull me over the top, confident that I will make it.

Reading the dream years later, I cheered her on. She's found her arms! She's hanging on for dear life!

11

Winding Down,
Winding Up

After finishing a temporary teaching contract in Los Angeles, I took a position in Bishop, a small community east of the Sierras, about half way between Reno and Los Angeles, where I was to run a training program for Paiute Indians. The director was a powerful, well educated businessman who had returned to his reservation. He was determined to help his people find better lives without giving up what they had—their land, their extended families, their Indian pride. The job was out of my field, but it was challenging and I knew it would be rewarding. I would be back home in my calming Sierras, hiking along the rivers, picnicking by the clear lakes, skiing the long sweeping trails of Mammoth Mountain.

Because the program had been failing, Al put me in full charge. "You say you can pull it out, now do it."

It was a modern version of the old one-room school. Twenty students came into the computer lab each morning and spent most of the day there, leaving only to go to on-the-job training sites.

I had an assistant to handle personnel and find job sites, and another to handle the computers. I would teach Business Writing, English, Job Readiness, and Math. I had to learn accounting and business practices fast enough to keep a lesson ahead of the students.

The students, mostly Paiute women, were already defensive and angry about the way their previous program manager had treated them. She once trailed them outside, shouting when they tried to leave. With histories of disrespect from "whites," with lives of poverty and prejudice, they thought they were failures and were fearful of more humiliation.

Their absentee rate was high. Their dropout rate disastrous, their job placement poor.

I searched for ways to connect with them, to foster self esteem and pride. Some of the older women were respected as elders in their tribes and did not want to be thought of as students. I asked their advice, I listened closely, and paid attention to their needs and their suggestions. I found ways for students to express their tribal histories and identities in their class projects, to bring their leadership skills into the classroom. I respected them and showed it. I brought in speakers from the white business community, so that they could learn to respect one another.

It turned out that one of my white speakers was Al's political enemy. Tribal reservations, like white bureaucracies, have their own inner politics, which I was not part of. I was beginning to learn how little he trusted me. Often, just doing my job, I would bring down the wrath of someone on the "res." Two students that I suspended for cheating were related to powerful tribal rivals who came stomping into my office, accusing me of taking sides.

I dropped an arrogant young man from the program because he seldom showed up. Because he was the son of one of the leading elders, Al demanded that I reinstate him. He said we needed to show the funding agency we could keep our students. I explained why I could not reinstate the student: "One reason for the poor attendance is that word is out that it doesn't matter. I can't bring absenteeism down unless there are consequences." When Al insisted, I reminded him, "You hired me to run this program." Reluctantly, he conceded, with warnings about dropping any more students.

I knew the program was worth saving. I worked long hours doing paperwork, attending meetings on the res, meeting with students, learning new skills. Gradually, attendance steadied, retention rose.

Al called me on the carpet again. I had advised two students who were complaining to me about each other, to work it out for themselves. They did. They had a hair pulling fight in the classroom. "You're not strict enough with them," Al said.

"They're not children," I said. "They can learn to deal with one another rather than run to me, learn better ways of dealing with conflict."

"You don't know Indians," he said.

I wavered. I went to a sweat lodge and talked to a well respected elder of the tribe who said, "If you run it his way and it doesn't work, you will have doubly failed. You will never know if your way will succeed unless you do it your way."

I struggled to maintain my integrity in a tribal administration where people were suspicious of one another and of the white lady academic who wanted to do things her way. As the program continued to keep its students, to place them in jobs, to prove itself trustworthy, it was still hard for Al to trust me. He feared I might take too much credit for the success of the program. He would stay out of it entirely for weeks at a time, then he would interfere, reverse some decision I'd made without telling me.

Finally, he drew up an organization chart with the personnel assistant between him and me. I faced him across the table. "You hired me to run this program, reporting only to you. If you want him to run the program, you are breaking your word. Why? Haven't I kept my end of the bargain?"

"Are you saying you won't work for him? That you would quit first?"

"I am," I said. We eyed each other across the table.

"That chart doesn't mean anything," he said.

"It does," I said. "Both to him and to me."

Our eyes held. He reached for the chart and said he would change it. He never did, but at least it disappeared.

The program grew. The program prospered. My students, bright and experienced, learned the basic accounting and computer tasks quickly. They began to trust me.

Graduations were a time of joy and tears, as cousins, parents, grandparents, uncles and aunts gathered to celebrate what was often the family's first step out of poverty. Graduates of the program were now among the few in the community trained to manage a modern computerized office. They did well on their jobs, and broke through the atmosphere of prejudice in the community. The program won national recognition for its success, for the numbers of students that were graduating, and for the numbers placed in jobs.

My album shows me at fifty-two, backpacking in the Sierras or planting a tree before my rough sided mountain house, 7,000 feet above sea level. They show sunsets across the high desert, the elegant smooth contours of the great sandy sweep of Death Valley. They show me wandering through ancient bristle cone forests that had been standing since before the time of Christ. They show me laughing in front of a classroom, or handing out diplomas to proud Paiute women with straight shining hair.

I started seeing Lyle, a City Councilman. He reminded me of the men I had known as a girl, the kind who hung out around the 8-Mile House.

He wore plaid shirts, khakis, and western boots. He combed his wavy hair straight back and kept it short at the sides. He was sure of himself and his leadership ability, his skill at guiding the City Council, his political skills with the people. I suppose he could have been called a "good old boy." He enjoyed taking me out in his Cadillac, slipping into my mountain house to spend the night. I enjoyed his paternalistic, masculine companionship.

I had a dream: *A woman takes me to a house that I am going to be living in for awhile. It is a beautiful old estate, made of river rock. The woman who owns it is away for a year or so. She is evidently a recluse. The roof leaks everywhere. I am told it can't be fixed. That doesn't seem to be a problem. It has a fireplace but it can't be used; there are a couple of big iron stoves pushed together in the center of the house. The dining room table has a big planting box full of dirt on it, and I'll have to put a board over that to eat. There is a children's room with lots of built in compartments, I think children may still be there. Then I am left alone.*

I know I have been brought here to be executed. I am not frightened about this, just accepting. But before they do this, there is entertainment, a string of dancing girls, about ten of them, young, awkward and wholesome, wearing bright flowered dresses of silky material, knee length. They all remind me of my mother, some very girlish and others older, all small with short brown hair. They have a good time dancing and go out the French doors as I watch calmly, knowing that next I'll be shot with a black revolver. I hear crying, the wrenching heart broken sobbing of a deeply hurt child.

The dream was about my new relationship with Lyle. The recluse who controlled my life was going to be gone for awhile. I would be free for a year to do my mother's dancing girl routine with a man from my mother's time. I could nourish myself but there would be nothing planted that would grow. The recluse's house did have a fireplace, a hearth, the heart of a home, but it was cold. Two makeshift stoves were pushed together instead. My love affair with Lyle would be makeshift. The child part of myself may be still alive; there are compartments in the back, I am not sure anyone is there. The part of myself who has done this before knows that in the end, the same execution will occur, the revolver, the cycle, will go around again. I am numb to it. The child, who feels the pain, cries out from the back room.

Reading the dream makes me very sad. I have come to understand now that the house is always my inner life. I can still hear the child crying from some distant room.

As the dream predicted, the revolver spun again, and a year later the recluse was back. When my work got demanding, Lyle helped me at first, then feeling upstaged and neglected, shifted his attention to more appreciative women. I had to hear it from my friends.

A Course in Miracles, which I had studied with a group in Los Angeles, became the steadying influence of my life. A text on spiritual psychotherapy, the course was very simple. Over and over it taught that whatever is happening, the most important goal is peace, inner peace. That inner peace came from trust and acceptance in Holy Spirit, who always knows more than the ego. I would come home from a nine or ten-hour day exhausted, having dealt with an argument in the classroom, or a verbal attack by a competitive staff member, or an encounter with Al, storming in at the last minute to push through an important grant proposal.

I would open the Course and read: *I am here only to be truly helpful. I am here to represent Him who sent me. I don't have to worry about what to do or what to say, because he who sent me will direct me. I will be healed as I let him teach me to heal.* The words always calmed me.

I led a weekly *Course In Miracles* group of ten or fifteen people. Their trust in me sustained me when my trust in myself was weak. The photo album shows us, arms linked, at a summer retreat in the mountains.

Now pictures in the album show a strong athletic looking man, Les, a high school teacher and athlete. One picture shows us with backpacks, standing on rocky peaks above a glistening chain of lakes. Another shows us picnicking by the stream near my house. A few pages later, we are sitting on the deck of his house in town. We look happy in the pictures, a solid, good looking couple.

I remember how excited I had been about meeting Les. He was sensitive and caring, healthy in both mind and body. We enjoyed the same things, had the same values. This was not going to be a one year fling. I was ready to choose a good man and fight against the patterns that interfered with a good relationship.

When I could not work some problem through with him, I would study the course: *Our task is not to seek for love, but merely to seek and find all of the barriers within yourself that you have built against it. It is not necessary to seek for what is true, but it is necessary to seek for what is false. Every illusion is one of fear, whatever form it takes. If you seek love outside yourself you can be certain that you perceive hatred within, and are afraid of it.*

I told him when I was angry. He didn't believe anger was a part of a good relationship. When I was afraid, he would hold me tight in his strong, muscular arms. I told him I loved him. He called me GaGa.

When my patterns or expectations would make trouble with Les, I would study the course: ... *Teach only love, for that is what you are. ... Love is letting go of fear. ... Attack is a call for love.* Almost always, from blaming or anger, I could return to a state of inner peace, and our lives continued to braid themselves together. After a year, I rented out my house, and moved in with him. I said I wanted to get married. He said he wasn't ready yet.

In some ways, Les was like my father; he assumed a dominance that was easily threatened. That came out in a kind of resentful undercurrent. He was defensive about my somewhat more prestigious position. He had a way of laughing uncomfortably at my female characteristics, my woman's body. Like most men his age, he assumed sexual rights, and was angry if I "cut him off."

My dreams continued to push me to acknowledge the poisoning influence of the past: *Les and I are making love. I hear my father come in, he doesn't even knock, just walks right in, goes through the room to get something from the closet. Then he sits at the foot of the bed. I am furious and tell him to get out; we have a right to be left alone. He makes snide, sneering comments to Les about sex and not being married.*

Although I felt the Course made our relationship possible, Les resented my strong connection to it. The night before Easter, I asked him to go to church with me the next day. He declined, "I can't stand all that grisly Easter stuff, the crucifixion and all that."

"The Course says the lesson of the crucifixion was that we cannot be crucified," I said. "We are all safe in the mind of God, so any crucifixion is only an illusion."

He gave me a scornful look. It was exactly the kind of preaching that Les hated.

The next morning, I had a kind of waking dream, a vision: *I am on Les's deck, wearing a white terry cloth robe, operating on a cactus, transplanting a core from another one, grafting a healthier center. Behind me a gardener stands, a young man with dark hair. He says to me in quiet humility, "You're the doctor." I hear the reverence in his voice, the kind I feel when I come upon some wonderful thing, like a deer in the woods. I say, "Yes, but I don't know anything about plants," though the transplant was obviously going to take. When I turn toward him, I feel a powerful sexual surge throughout my body and I realize my arms are around his neck, though our bodies aren't touching. I am embarrassed that people could see us. I feel guilty. He goes back down the path and we have an unspoken agreement that I will follow. But Les has gone the other way, and I start down that path to follow him instead, knowing I would not be unfaithful to Les. But I feel guilty anyway, as if I were going to meet the gardener later. I catch up with Les, who asks me to go for a walk. I say I couldn't go in my robe. I'd have to go all the way back to the bathroom in the house to change. There are then some wanderings and some crowded bathrooms before I change.*

The unconditional love I felt from the Jesus figure was more powerful than any I had ever known. That experience was so strong that years later, I could still be filled with love, just by remembering.

I am taken still by the power of the vision, the simplicity of its metaphors. The windows of Les's house had, in reality, been lined with potted cacti, a good sign that he didn't want anybody getting to his vulnerable center. In the dream, Les invites me for a walk, a short journey, which was what he was offering me at the time. But what most fascinated me about the dream years later, was the ending. I hadn't understood it earlier, but now I saw "going back to the bathroom at the house to change," as a suggestion that I would have to go way back to the bathroom of an earlier house before I could change. Something in that bathroom would precede change for me. The long wanderings and crowded bathrooms—that was what had been happening the past few years.

I felt exhilarated. Was there hope then that after all the crowded bathrooms, I would finally emerge able to follow the path of love? Not romantic love, but the kind of unconditional love represented by the Jesus figure, the gardener, in the dream? Was he perhaps my own inner male? As Jung would say, my *animus*?

The training program in Bishop was running well after three years of hard work, but it was still dependent on "soft money," grants from the Federal government. Al and I had to constantly prove its effectiveness to receive operating money for the following year. I was confident we could do that indefinitely. The number of students coming to the program increased, and they stayed to graduate. Job placement was better all the time. On the Reservation, former students were moving into leadership positions, taking new human relations skills with them, improving things. But Al continued to be somewhat mysterious and erratic, staying away for weeks at a time, then storming in and out daily.

A dream emerged to warn me to be aware: *I'm sitting on Dick's lap at the cabin in a chair like my grandfather's. He is trying to show me what the symbols mean in one of my stories I still don't understand. Others come in, gentle Indians. I say, see, just because our men raped their women, doesn't mean they rape ours.*

What I saw in that dream later was the connection between Dick, an abuser, and my grandfather; Dick's sitting in my grandfather's chair, taking his place. Dick once demonstrated to me, to make a point, how quickly a man can rape a woman, even a strong woman like me. He had me down in seconds. In the dream he's trying to show me something in my stories, my past—had my grandfather been one of my abusers?

The dream was about denial. In the dream I still don't see it; nice people don't rape or exploit women or girls. In my grandfather's lap I was being shown what I still didn't understand. Even a grandfather can exploit innocence. Yes, even the gentle Indians can too.

Shortly after that dream, Al was charged with embezzlement; of siphoning money off our grants in order to support his drug habit. I should have been able to see it, his erratic behavior, his mood swings, his angry frantic highs followed by unexplained disappearances. I had been naive. I believed that my hard work was appreciated, that Les would protect my position. With our financial credibility destroyed, there would be no more grant money.

Another dream: *My boss and I are married, and we're in bed together. Suddenly he gets up and nails our child, a girl, to the wall with a big spike through her head, and I'm helpless to do anything about it, for some cultural reason. It is too awful to look. When he gets back in bed, there's blood on his hand and I scream at him, "I hate you." There is a sense that there's been no murder, and I feel where the illusory stake has gone through my own head.*

He had indeed put a spike through the head of our child, the program. I was powerless to save it, to take over the program, for cultural reasons. I was not a Paiute. I was not of his blood.

After the funding collapsed, the local Community College picked the training program up for a few months, then I was out of a job again, I was out of my field, and I was four years older.

I applied for every opening that came up in the state, driving ten or twelve hours to Los Angeles or Sacramento or Mendocino. I came out in the top contenders again and again, but couldn't get past second or third in the final interviews. "They can't say so, but they are looking for young blood," my friends in the college system told me.

The situation put a strain on my relationship with Les. I tried to handle it sensitively. I invited him to sit down on the couch and took his hand. "I can stay in Bishop if we're committed to each other. If we aren't, I can't afford to pass up an opportunity elsewhere, no matter how far away."

He crossed his arms. "Women have leaned on me too much. I've only recently made up for what I lost in my divorce, and I'm about to retire."

I reminded him that I had never leaned on him, quite the opposite; I carried more than my share of our expenses. He remained noncommittal.

I sent applications out of state. Time was passing, and the long drives, the exhausting search process was wearing on me.

Brighton University invited me for an interview. They were good solid people with little of the intellectual chest thumping common at some universities. I swung into my most dynamic performance for a teaching demonstration and they offered me the job.

It would be hard to leave California again. It would be hard to leave my family and friends. But it was an opportunity to get back into my own field, an opportunity to build a retirement fund I desperately needed, and perhaps it was time to break through the impasse between Les and me. I loaded my car, now a conservative Audi, and headed East.

To my astonishment, Les went on ahead, checked the place out, and liked it so much he arranged a place for the two of us. I took that as a strong sign of commitment.

I set about my new tasks: I was teaching in a University for the first time in years, responding to the demands a nontenured professor must face; to prove myself as a teacher, as an academic intellectual, and as a writer. At the same time I was learning that Minnesotans don't easily accept strangers into their mostly family circles. Without Les's confidence in me and his companionship, it would have been even more difficult.

In return, I was expected to accept his terms. I would come home from a nine hour day and do my share of the housework or painting or wallpapering, although he had been doing as he liked all day. And I had to agree it was only fair to share fifty-fifty. The same was true for money. Bills were shared fifty-fifty, though my living expenses were far less than his, and his retirement income greater than my starting salary.

A dream: *I get in my car to drive somewhere, but there is a bumping sound under it. I stop, and see there is a body under the car. I go and get Les to help; he gets in and drives faster and faster, even with the body bumping along, while I try to make him stop. He only laughs, until finally, my father's skull-like gray head pops through the floorboards.*

My dead father was coming closer to the surface, closer to breaking through to consciousness as I turned over the wheel to a man very like him.

For two more years I lived with Les, until plans to build a house together forced a decision. One night when we had guests, he laid out house plans for a place on the river. I was taken by surprise; it was a big house, with space for tenants and a big shop. I could scarcely wait until the friends left. "Les,

I don't want to share a house with tenants. And I'm not sure I want all the noise and dust from a shop in the same building."

His face hardened as he rolled up the plans. "I know more about these things than you do. Have you ever built a house?"

I was speechless.

"Well I have. Don't you think I know what I'm doing?"

"Of course you know what you're doing, but don't I have anything to say about it?

His arms were crossed. He went silent. I knew there was no point in saying any more.

We were on a camping trip on the Canadian border when I had to tell him what I had known for several weeks. "Les, I'm sorry, but I just can't make such a heavy financial investment without a commitment."

He stopped what he was doing, set the campstove down on the table. His expression showed he was deeply disappointed. I tried to soften what I had said. "I can't find myself alone out in the woods somewhere in a half finished house and my retirement funds all tied up in it. It would be different if we were married; we would be sharing the risk…"

When he crossed his arms, it seemed to me they expanded, and his chest as well. "I'm not ready yet to get married, if that's what you mean."

"Les, you've known me for four years! If you're not ready now, when would you be?"

His face was tight. "I've told you before, you're too independent. And you're too controlling."

At first I was furious. "*I'm* controlling!" I stomped off down the dirt road though it was a pitch black night. Then something broke in me. When I came back an hour later, I crawled into the back of the van and cried like a child, hour after hour. The next morning I walked, still crying, under the tall pines, which seemed at the moment like the only comfort I had ever had. I knew my overwhelming grief was not just about Les: it was about the terrible losses in the past as well. And it was about some kind of terrible hopelessness.

We tried to be good to each other after that, but our relationship never recovered. I bought my own place and moved out.

I was at first relieved, happy to be alone, out from under the pressure of Les's demands that I conform to his expectations, out from under the long cold chill we had lived in since I decided to buy my own house.

Summer in my lakeside home was a delight. Eagles perched in the trees almost daily, otters and beavers played in the waters, Canada geese brought their fuzzy goslings, demanding food. I canoed the Mississippi River, I planted trees and flower bulbs, and got ready for a long cold winter, alone on the snow drifted shores of an ice bound lake.

Les was soon involved with another woman. I was hurt that he could recover so quickly, while night after night, I brooded over our four years. What had happened? Where did I go wrong? Why did I have relationships when they left me feeling terrible afterward, inadequate, unlovable?

An image surfaced: *My self separated out and used by another body. I am a baby. My father is diddling my genitals, which at first makes me laugh, then becomes too intense, like being tickled, out of control, tortured even. Then he plunges his finger, or thumb, in my vagina and his swollen penis into my mouth. The fear, choking, suffocating, rage are all one. We are wedded in this secret: he needs my body and I need his love. We make trades. He puts his shame off on me and rejects me. I am enraged but needy for his love, separated, try to get it back, play it out over and over. I hear the question in my mind, a raped baby? How could anyone rape a baby?*

I came out of that feeling weak, staggering, like someone who's fought round after round. Then I slept for hours and did not want to wake up.

When I got up, I found a picture of my father, saw in it my own downturned mouth and deep frown lines. I couldn't remember exactly, only vaguely, the sexual abuse, but I remembered my terror, my vulnerability to male genitals.

I wrote in my journal:

> *When he took my sexuality, I took on his power and identity since my own was gone, my powerlessness too terrifying. Males have the power, except when I rebel and make them eat their own genitals. I'm angry and lonely. I think of all the men I've been involved with, all the love and pain and fighting and caring and making up. What more could hell be? How I hate it all. Aunty Mame is maimed.*

I played the piano, I wrote, I worked, I rode my bicycle, I had parties for my women friends, I had small suppers for colleagues. I went to church and joined its committees, did its endless work. Gradually, I felt strong and humorous and competent again. I was older and wiser, and even more fiercely independent.

I fought for a decent salary and fair promotions, published some stories. Eventually, I won tenure, and felt at home with my department's faculty. That part of my life, the professional life, I was handling well.

I had done something else I had never done before: I had made a commitment to a man and fought for commitment in return. I had stayed in there when it was hard and not turned off. Les and I had four years of telling one another the truth, as closely as we could come to it. Because he looked after his own interests so well, I had learned a lot about taking care of myself. My confidence was growing.

At that time, I had recorded a dream: *I get a call from my father. He's in Indiana and dying and I have to get there in time to meet my grandfather. My young lover can't go. I decide to call a travel agent, but can't find the phone book, can't find the number. I make strange connections, not sure what city, what day it is, when to return,. I'm giving and getting insufficient information. The travel agent is strange and flighty and flip and undependable. I finally take off in a small plane, with a woman pilot, but I'm not sure it's the right one and go back. And my young lover—how do I explain him to Dad?*

The dream perplexed me: My father was born in Indiana. His interference in my life was already clear. The flighty travel agent was how I'd been with Ken, my young (new) lover. But why must I meet my grandfather? I remember one grandfather well. The family called him the old bastard. His idea of fun was to give me what looked like Chiclets chewing gum, but was really laxatives.

When Ken and I broke up, I had another dream: *A young and sexy me is kidnapped by a dark aggressive foreigner as lover/captive. I escape but I am recaptured. I am ambivalent about it all. There are car crashes.*

The young sexy me, the part that loved Ken, was kidnapped by my father, who was dark, aggressive, and foreign (in the sense of strange, dark and sinister). We crashed.

I closed the last journal on the page where I decided to go to Larry Anderson for hypnosis, for confirmation of my memories. He helped me get to that one devastating experience. "It only happened once." Then I had gone into a marriage with Carl thinking I could now simply make things work right; I was "fixed."

I was convinced that the memory released by my body that day in Larry Anderson's office could be trusted. The journals had confirmed that. But I knew I was not healed from that experience. It was either more devastating than I thought, or—and this seemed most likely—there was much more.

Having steeped myself in the years of my past—laid out in my journals like a long long movie—I felt prepared, even eager, for the appointment with my new therapist, Glenda Parkinson. I didn't know I should have been packing, like the old legend of Demeter and Persephone, for a descent into the underworld, looking for a kidnapped child.

12

Sneaky Snake Meets
The Bitch Queen

The morning before I started therapy with Glenda, I recorded a dream showing that my subconscious was already doing its preparatory work.

We are visiting someone who has just bought a house. It is split level, simple and open. The woman is fixing a turkey in the kitchen. I don't know what the man is doing. I go upstairs and it has started to rain. At first I see only a damp spot on the wood floors, then I see that part of the house (the unused side) is leaking. I tell them it will go through to the rooms below and ruin the plaster. They come up and by now it is leaking badly, even coming in a small window under the roof. There is a stuffed bear that I have seen earlier—I fuss over it because it is so real; it moves and curls up. The leak is dripping right on it. We laugh.

I go downstairs and ask where the other woman is. A woman says, she's gone to check on a turkey. I think that strange, because she's been gone so long. Does she have another family elsewhere? I don't know any of these people very well.

I gestalted the dream: The house I am visiting is my own split-level self. The roof is leaking—cleansing rains, spiritual growth, will not be kept out much longer. The side that has been lived in, my conscious life, will get ruined too. The water is pouring in through a high window, which reminds me of the mind's intuitive side, but also of the basement window of my childhood. The stuffed bear is stuffed childhood feelings; I have been sleeping with a stuffed bear since the incest came out at Gary's.

The woman who has been gone a long time has something else cooking. Another turkey. Another man? As I struggled with my feelings about Carl's impotence, I had been fantasizing about other men. The dream was pleasant: the house was simple and open, the people friendly. I felt it boded well.

When Glenda Parkinson came out of her office, I was reading a magazine in the waiting room, trying to present a composed appearance. Glenda was attractive , fashionably dressed and groomed, businesslike, very professional, with an edge about her that made me feel safe; she was not going to be sloppy or intrusive. She no sooner made me comfortable in the office than I fell apart. With tears of panic I recounted my hypnosis the year before. "My incest stuff is ruining my marriage." I told about the accident. "A part of me is trying to get me killed!" I told her about my marriage. "Carl is wonderful. He's kind and generous and intelligent, but I am so short tempered! I have just turned off to him sexually."

Glenda listened, her face composed, her eyes lively, commenting briefly in her soft Texas accent.

I told her how I struggled against my growing aversion to Carl. "I'm living in his house, but I'm like a cat shut up with a dog. I don't know how long Carl can be expected to take it." Finally, my outpouring slowed, and I felt nothing but weariness. "I have been very tired lately, such an effort, holding back my demons."

"I don't think you need to panic," Glenda assured me. "When I started practice ten years ago, no one was trained to work with incest, but so many of my clients came in with the problem, I had to work out some methods for myself. Now, of course," she gestured to a case full of books, "a great deal has been done."

She asked a few questions about anger, how and when I expressed it, and sent me home with some tapes. I agreed to listen to them but didn't think it had much to do with me. "All I can express is anger!" I laughed through my tears. I knew there was something more destructive going on than expressing anger would fix.

Alone in my house, I listened to the tapes, I listened to Beethoven. I painted a picture of planting hands. I wrote: "I'm happy, sitting here in the sunroom, enjoying the early morning beauty of my home, the flowers, the trees and other plants, the green lawn and blue lake."

That night I had another house dream, vivid and explicit. I didn't know it at the time, but it was to become the central metaphor for my therapy: *Several of us have moved into the big family home of one of the men. He is taking care of me. I'm an adult, but some kind of patient. It is a big old house with many rooms, but we have to stay in two little crowded rooms off to one side with a closet-sized kitchen. I say, it's not so bad (it's awful). A door opens to a balcony where the previous tenant used to sit, a balcony cluttered with bed pans and old junk, but then I see this balcony doesn't go outside; it just overlooks the inside of the house.*

There is some confusion. We have to leave? We have to stay? There is unpacking and then some need to pack again in case we have to leave. The man, the caretaker, says he will find a way to change the phone systems so when we call in or out, other people in other rooms can (or can't?) pick up the phone and monitor, for safety against the bad people who live there. One is a lady, one her stupid son, one a child, strange and bandaged. There is a key to the doors I'm told, we're free to come and go, and even use the front door, though we haven't yet. We go in and out a side door. In one scene I'm lying down and the stupid groping son is pawing me, stroking me with soft hands. My caretaker seems to just allow this as harmless but it gives me the creeps. The little girl is about seven, with skinny legs. I try to relate to her, I feel safe with her, but she is strange too, withdrawn and silent.

Later it seems we may have to leave again (or may not) and I'm not packed. While I'm gone to work, changes may happen, my caretaker didn't ever unpack. He's now taken the old fire escapes and changed them around so they go under the windows. All this is rather secretive, though there's no sign of the people who own the house.

"It's a horrid place," I wrote in my journal. "My waking self detests it and all of its occupants except the little girl, and she's not my problem. I'm just the patient here, make no decisions for myself, just do what I'm told. This house reminds me of Carl's house, in that it has become a horrid place for me, a museum of his married life, and in some ways, he is like the caretaker. Another part of me says it's not so bad. It's big and roomy and luxurious. The confusion about leaving or staying is the struggle I am going through, constantly wanting to flee, to run, but I keep telling myself I could do this. This is a good thing. The fire escapes are even set under the windows in a way that I can't get out. The communication lines? The parts of myself I have to keep from communicating with each other. Keeping things both from myself and from Carl."

Although that dream was to be the key to my therapy, I did not share it with Glenda in my next session; I worked again on my marriage. "I don't know what's wrong with me, I'm always on such a short fuse, and Carl is so good to me. I can't bear any kind of sex with him anymore."

Glenda said, "You didn't really have much time to get to know each other, to become friends. You need to learn the other areas of intimacy before you deal with sex, which is about tenth on the list of importance. Maybe you'd be more willing to be close in other areas if you didn't think it had to lead to sex." Rather than trying to force things, she suggested Carl and I might try backing off. "You could begin with ten minutes of nonsexual touching."

That night when we got in bed, Carl was patient and gentle. He started stroking my wrists and arms. It took a great effort on my part to allow even that. I had to keep reminding myself that he was not my father. I felt my breathing tighten, go shallow, tried to deepen it. He was Carl again. Ten minutes seemed like an eternity. My entire body was pulling inward. Then he lay his head across my chest, and his hair brushed my face. I pulled back, pulled away as if I had been brushed by something loathsome. "The hair ... the hair ... I can't get it off." My hands pawed at my face. I began to cry hysterically.

"It's not you," I assured Carl as I cowered across the room from him. Then a headache shut it all down. Carl was calm as he left to sleep in the other room. "I'm concerned, but not worried." He believed in his ability to weather anything. I curled up with my teddy bear, exhausted.

I was afraid I was going crazy. Glenda assured me that I was behaving normally for someone healing from incest. "But that nightmarish episode? Hair in my face?"

"Helen, if you were forced to do oral sex, there was hair in your face!"

I continually worried about what I was doing to Carl. "How can I put him through all this?"

Glenda told me firmly that if Carl couldn't accept my need to heal and what it takes to do that, then there was something wrong. "Healing and intimacy involve learning trust," Glenda said. "Your healing, not your marriage, comes first."

The flashback brought on by his hair was so traumatic, I avoided Carl even more. I spent the evenings after work in his house, but on weekends I went to my own home, pleading for time alone. I wrote in my journal: "It's pretty awful, this incest stuff, worse than I thought. One voice says, it didn't happen to me, it happened to her, the child. I guess they are all the people in that creepy house that I dreamed."

For my next session, Glenda had asked me to bring pictures. I had seen nothing particularly conclusive in the few tiny snapshots I had of myself as a child. In one I am a chubby happy two-year-old, riding my tricycle. In another, I am sitting on my father's lap. My father's hand is curved down across my thigh under my dress, the other wrapped around my buttocks. Glenda was horrified by what she saw.

I said, "But if he was an abuser, would he do that in front of a camera?"

"They think they're not doing anything wrong," Glenda said. "Look at how you're perched there, feet turned in, barely alighted." The open trusting expression of the earlier photo was replaced by a shadowed anxiety.

"Something has happened," Glenda concluded.

That night I woke from troubled dreams. Unable to go back to sleep, I decided to talk to a tape recorder as I would talk to a trusted therapist. When I played the tape back, I heard at least six voices: a weeping child, a critical adult, an unscrupulous con-artist, a crying woman, a rational one, and behind it all, a calm presence saying, "Breathe now, breathe."

I destroyed the tape lest someone hear it and confirm my fear that I was crazy. Over and over, the next few weeks, Glenda would have to reassure me: "You are not crazy, you are healing."

Panic attacks came faster. Anything could bring them on, a smell, a touch. In the bathtub one day, the desire to touch my genitals created fierce anxiety. Pushing against all the old terrors, I fingered the soft labia and felt nothing. It was as if the flesh were dead. My breathing went shallow. I was shaking, remembering my mother breaking through the door. "Do I have to cut off your hands?"

Wrapped in a towel, I sat on the bed, rocking back and forth like an autistic, my right toe down, tapping rapidly, my left toe dug in as if to run, the heel up and rigid.

I spoke gently to myself, to the child in my past, "It's all right. You can feel that place or not feel it."

But the child keeps crying. "It's gone and it won't ever come back." I ask her what it felt like and she cries harder and says she can't remember. I tell her I'll put her down for a little nap with her teddy bear. She says no, she wants her gramma. I had wanted to say mamma, but she clearly said gramma, so I realize I am Gramma, I tell her Gramma will stay with her, or she can come with Gramma and sit close to her in church. Then I know the child felt the warmth of Gramma's love clear through her body.

In my sessions with Glenda, I began to defend my parents. About the incest with my father, I said, "It only happened once." He was charming, he was good.

Glenda said, "Incest victims often go to great lengths to protect their fathers. What about your relationship with your father all those later years?"

"It was normal," I said. "I always wanted to please him.... We were together when he died."

"You were your father's little sweetie."

"No, that's not really how it was. I wanted to be that, but I wasn't. He was critical, judgemental, treated me as if he were ashamed of me. I was always doing my pleasing dance."

Glenda asked, "What about your mother, after the whipping incident?"

"She whipped both my sister and I sometimes, but just on the legs. Things were pretty normal after those early years. All kids get whipped."

"Did your mother ever try to kill you?"

"She put her hand over my mouth when I was a baby and I couldn't breathe for a long time. I was terrified. I thought she was trying to kill me, but she was just trying to make me quit crying."

Glenda waited.

"She threatened to cut off my hands, and I really thought she would," I said. "But that was a common threat back then, when people thought kids shouldn't play with themselves. She took good care of us. She was a good mother."

"Good mothers don't whip their children and call them hellions," Glenda said, "There was something evil there."

"No," I said. "They were neurotic but not evil."

Glenda said they had taught me to associate pleasure with pain, but that it could be reversed. "How are you and Carl doing?"

I shook my head. "I'm like a person who is raw all over. Nothing Carl says or does is right. That makes him anxious, makes him say stupid things, which irritates me even more. 'How many potatoes should I fix?' Who cares how many potatoes? It's hard for me to remember when I wasn't this way. I can make all the resolutions I want, but I can't keep them. Maybe I'm just a bitch and that's all there is to it."

Hesitantly, I brought out of my purse a dialog I had written several weeks previously. "It wrote itself. I just took a pen and switched hands for each part." Embarrassed, I handed it to Glenda. "It's pretty gross. I just wrote whatever emerged."

HB: What's going on? I'm married to a fine person who loves me and will give me everything I want. He appreciates me and treats me well.

Hellion: He gives me the creeps. He's old.

HB: Well, I'm not young. I'm almost 62. My face is lined, I have varicose veins.

Hellion: I can't look at that saggy old body. How can you do it? He can't even fuck you. Just wants to get all worked up about it, then can't make it with you.

HB: I know you see it that way. I asked him not to undress in front of me or go around naked. As for the rest, I can go for years without sex. I don't care. I like oral sex and so does he.

Hellion: Yuck. I can't stand the idea of that wimpy penis in your mouth. It's gross.

HB: I've experienced some warmth and closeness, some glimpses of how nice it could be. Then you just moved in and took over. You like men who are controlling, so why don't we give up control with Carl? He'd love it.

Hellion: No. He'd want it back. Penis in the mouth stuff. Everybody wants something back—or he'll want you to jack him off. Hopeless job.

HB: So what are you going to do now? Just keep pushing him away until we split up and I'm alone again?

Hellion: Yeah. Why not? You don't need this guy.

HB: You sound really contemptuous of him.

Hellion: I *am* contemptuous of him.

I waited for the expected disgust or shocked reaction. Instead, Glenda said, "I like the one you called Hellion the best. She fights for what she wants and she knows what she wants."

"Really? I'd been afraid to show you that part, so gross and ugly."

Glenda said, "Helen, you forced yourself to have oral sex."

"It was either that or nothing! It didn't feel loathsome until later." I dropped my head in my hands. "It's all mixed up together," I said, feeling hopeless. "Love and hate, passion and loathing."

"It will clarify," Glenda said.

My trust grew. The next time, I took a detailed drawing of the house and all its inhabitants, exactly as it was in the dream. Glenda examined it respectfully and carefully. Then she looked closely at me. "The house dream represents a total passive victim mentality, the passive woman stretched out on a table, the child pressed against a wall, and in the shut off part of the house where the caretaker lives."

"The caretaker reminds me in some ways of my father," I said. "He always decides when we stay and when we leave, what gets talked about, and what doesn't." I told Glenda about my teenage years, when my father held forth at the dinner table, telling stories, being the important one, while everyone else silently listened. Then I told her about how he met my sister's date with a gun. "Dad and his gun and his flashlight." I smiled ironically.

"That's how abusive fathers act with their daughters," Glenda said. "The caretaker and the creepy crawly man are one and the same person, the two sides of your father."

"The passive woman reminds me in some ways of my mother, especially when she was dying," I said.

"He married a 16-year-old from an abusive situation," Glenda reminded me. "I don't think your mother is even in the picture."

Glenda looked closely at the figure of the child hunched against a wall. "How do you know the girl is seven?"

"I can see her ... I just know ... Maybe she told me."

"What's this on her legs?"

"Bandages."

"Why?"

"I don't know. Cuts. Glass." I told her about my dreams, shattering glass, losing my hands if I break through the glass.

"Where were your arms when your father abused you?"

"I don't remember. I remember he was tickling...." As I spoke, I felt my face and body twist, and suddenly I was experiencing it again, my flailing arms and legs, my terrified helplessness. I was crying. "I don't like to talk about this," I whimpered. "I only remembered it in hypnosis."

"All right. It's all right. We don't have to talk about it now." Glenda waited a moment for me to recover. "Who is the owner of the house you drew? Is it you?"

Head down, tearful, I said that I didn't know. "There are no communications with the rest of the house."

Glenda, looking at the way I was huddled in the chair, said, "You need to make friends with that little girl."

At home, I went into meditation to see if I could experience being the woman who owns the house. *I talk to everybody who lives there, the bandaged girl, the passive woman, the male caretaker, the creepy man, and a new person who comes out of the wall, Sneaky Snake, angry, spiteful, powerful. When the girl asks her if she knew about sex she disappears back into the wall, which makes the girl cry. I talk to the whole house then, tell them I am calling them all together; we are all needed because there is a badly hurt little girl. Then I realize there is another part of my mind, on the upper right side, that is still asleep. I tell her she is having a bad dream, she can take all these parts of herself back now. I tell her when she wakes up she will remember what she was before this happened, this split. Now I like the snake; she has lost everything, even her arms, to keep her spirit. Her fight. Her "self," her sexuality.*

When I came out of that meditation, I had one hand in the other hand, talking to it and kissing it with great tenderness. I felt an overwhelming love for Sneaky Snake, the one I had thought was my enemy.

"She and the Hellion are the same," Glenda said. "Your parents tried to break your spirit. Sneaky Snake has kept it alive. She fights for herself."

I told Glenda about the time when I was about five and the current in the river swept me under a fallen tree. "I didn't even struggle. Just waited for it to be over. Someone came and got me out or I would have drowned."

Glenda said, "The person who married Carl is the same one who floated under the fallen tree. You had nothing to live for."

Glenda showed me a check list of all the symptoms of early childhood abuse.

"Some fit me," I acknowledged. "Flashbacks, nightmares, inability to maintain intimate relationships, yes—but some I don't have—alcohol or drug abuse, insanity."

"I left one off for fear of frightening you," Glenda said, watching me closely. "Have you ever heard of multiple personality?"

I looked at her, frightened.

"It's nothing to be afraid of," Glenda said matter-of-factly. "It can be a very positive response to trauma. Only very creative people can do it. There's no need to use alcohol or go crazy if the multiples are handling things."

She suggested I continue to get in touch with all the various parts of myself. "That loathsome part had to be created, too. It has to be accepted and even appreciated. Different personalities are created to handle different tasks."

Tearfully I told my friend Susan at lunch my fears about the possibility of multiple personalities. "What if people find out?"

Susan reached over and touched my hand. Then, with a bit of mischief in her eyes, she said, "What makes you think everybody doesn't already know? Perhaps you'll be the last." I laughed through my tears. Putting our trays away, Susan said, "I'll be happy to see whichever one of you comes to lunch next time."

Carl thought it was important to keep things in balance, to keep acting in positive ways, to hang onto what was sane and orderly. He insisted on taking me dancing, which I usually enjoyed, but now I felt like an institution inmate out on leave. As we watched other couples in the graceful stylized motions of the waltz, I told Carl that I felt like someone with amnesia.

"I don't know who I am or who I was or who I will be. I can't make small talk or dance when I have so much anxiety." I could feel my lips trembling, an eye twitching, even as I talked to him. "Nothing is sure anymore. I feel myself disintegrating and I'm scared."

"I read in one of those incest books how important it is to believe you," he said.

I felt a chill. After the day, months ago, when I first told him about my incest hypnosis, it had never once occurred to me that he wouldn't believe me! After all he'd seen, I wondered, could he think I was faking all this?

That spring I somehow managed to get through my classes, then for three months, I stopped going anywhere, withdrew from all church work, and saw only one or two trusted women friends. To give me time, Carl went to stay with his family in California for awhile. I devoted my entire being to therapy, both formal, with a therapist, and informal, following my instincts.

Often terrified and exhausted, I faced fragments of the past that would no longer be held back. All of it—dreams, memories, therapy, my so-called real life—seemed disjointed, uncontrolled, surrealistic, at times, insane. I was developing faith that the wholeness of it, the perfect sense, the creative logic of the inner being, would emerge with time.

Mornings were hardest. I would wake from dreams of shattered glass and cracked tile. Exhausted, preoccupied, I'd wander the house, moody, sullen. The handwriting in the journal is harsh and erratic.

Don't like my teddy bear, its floppy arm reminds me of a penis. I have images of breaking through glass. Getting cut up if I do. Feel crazy, angry like there's too much here, too many years, too much stuff coming up for Glenda or anybody else to handle. Afraid of all this. What will I do when Carl gets back from California? I'm worse than ever about him. I don't ever want him in my bed.

I told Glenda, "I want to ask Carl for a marriage moratorium."
Glenda said, "Are you asking me for permission?"
I was but I said, "I just wanted to know if you thought it was wise."
Glenda said "It's not only wise but necessary. At least for the summer."
I felt a welling up of appreciation. I never had anyone so supportive of me. I told Glenda, "My mother would say, 'What about your father?' If she were alive, she'd say, 'What about poor Carl?' I always came last as a child."

"How are you doing, getting in touch with that child?" Glenda asked. I saw the connection, saw that I sometimes treated myself the same way.

"We need to get in touch with the bandaged little girl. What is the connection with fragments of glass?"

Glenda led me into a guided fantasy in which I met my child. She was wearing an elasticized plaid swimsuit that I remembered.

"Take her to your safe place now," Glenda said.

I wanted to take her into my house on the lake, but the child moved away from me, pulling against my hand.

"She won't go with me," I said, with closed eyes. "She doesn't trust me enough to go in any enclosed place with me." Then I knelt to her height and said to the child, in a gentler voice, "Okay, but I won't abandon you. I'll be back. I'll be here if you need me."

I came out of the guided fantasy aware of how frightened the child was. Glenda assured me that the memories themselves wouldn't be as bad as the terror of them. "You've been through the real thing and survived; these are just memories." I sat silently.

"All right," she said gently. " We'll start with Sneaky Snake then."

"She knows the bandaged child and protects her," I said, hearing my own childlike voice.

Glenda said, "But the passive woman has compassion for her."

I laughed scornfully. "Because they're both helpless. She can identify." A part of me was not going to allow the passive woman any respect.

At home, I decided to let the child draw whatever she wanted. At first I drew only childlike stick figures of my family, my brother and sister, small and distant, standing behind my parents. Then I drew my mother at the kitchen stove "I love you, Mommy," I wrote in big childlike letters. Then finally came a rough drawing of a house with basement windows, the whole thing scribbled over with heavy black crayon.

I showed them to Glenda. "The child has eyes but no mouth," she commented "The whole family has no hands except the father, whose hands are clawlike. The mother is a mere stick."

I had noticed none of those things. I said, "Isn't that just the way children draw?" But I knew the scribbled over house with the black basement windows held a child's rage.

At home, I again went back into the left side of the house. I saw the passive woman, the caretaking man, the bandaged girl, knew Sneaky Snake was in the wall. *When I look at the creepy man, the one who tries to touch and caress the passive woman, I can not see him clearly, I can't see his body, from the shoulders down . Then I realize he comes from the other side of the house; he comes through the wall. That's why I can't see the rest of him. His shoulders are clothed, a white shirt, an old fashioned vest. I can't see his face. He seems to be older, like 40, yet he reminds me of my grandfather. He also reminds me of Mr. Gardella and Job, old creeps I've known. He is slimy, ingratiating, disgusting. He seems retarded in some ways, groveling to get what he wants, sex, which mindlessly drives him. He doesn't loath himself, but he is loathsome and puts up with loathing for what he wants.*

Creepy Crawly puts his hand on the child's thigh. She feels it but keeps trying to be asleep. She sees her mother at the front door sending someone away. The child knows she has to be quiet. Maybe he will quit, the creepy one.

I was beginning to think that my grandfather, who always wore a vest, was the man in some of the memories. I remembered walking in on my mother and grandmother when they were talking about my grandfather. I knew they were saying something bad. They got very quiet, and something about the way they looked at me made me think I was involved. I remembered my father's eyes when he said of my mother's father, "I hated that old bastard." Were they two of a kind?

Another day: *My mouth opens in a silent wail, my head turns side to side, but there is no feeling in the center of me. I can feel my hands, like claws. I am rocking and saying I - I - I—My clawed hands are ready to attack anything that threatens anyone under my wings. I'm shrieking warning, like a hawk, my mouth wide. Then a big penis is thrust into my mouth. Choking, blacking out, I fall back, collapse, hands, claws, out to the side, useless, helpless.*

So there was an encompassing part of me, I thought, that had tried to protect me, like a mother hen; it had shrieked and fought, but it was helpless against that larger body, unable to defend the child.

I recognized that part of myself; sometimes I called her the Bitch Queen. When she was threatened or frightened, she shrieked ineffectively, covering her inadequacy even from herself. She had no confidence that she could prevent any disaster, because so early in her life, she couldn't.

That was the part of me that, frightened by Ken's emotional and financial morass, had become a Bitch Queen, squawking ineffectively at him. That was the part that squawked at Carl for not leaving me alone when I was so preoccupied and frightened.

In meditation, I went back into the house. I could see all the people on the left side but could see no one at all on the right, the larger side:

I shift into my own body; it is reacting. My thighs are twitching, my breath is in my head and chest, I consciously bring it back to my belly. I realize the reason my father has no chest in the drawing is my eyes are closed, and I'm under his chest. My hands are helpless and I have no feeling at all in the genital area of my body. It just isn't there.

I experience a flash of rage. "Do that all you want, you bastard, I just won't feel." Then I feel my hands, clawed like the ones I drew on my father.

When I come out of meditation I can feel my hands! They have energy. They could kill somebody. As I write this I get dizzy.

I came back to myself lying on the floor, breathing into my belly. I had already remembered more than I wanted to. I was sure now the incest didn't stop with one incident. There was more. I didn't know how to get through the pain. I was ill all the rest of the day. I slept, I cried.

I put a blanket and pillow on the floor in front of the stereo and, doubled up, wrenched with grief, listened to Pachebel's *Canon*. I played it over and over, the high joyous violin weaving itself into the slow sorrowful cello, until I was calm and empty.

Inside my own chest, I felt the chest of a tiny little child, sleeping. I told her when she wakes up, she will not have to endure any of that any more. "I will not let anyone do anything to you. You will not have to do anything you don't want to do. Maybe you had no one to protect you then, but you do now. I have hands and I'll protect you." I wrote in my journal, "She slept on, but I thought she heard me."

The day I was supposed to pick up Carl at the airport, I had a panic attack. It began with compulsive pacing, then screaming and crying. I went into the closet and screamed into a down pillow. Images flashed of glass shards. Terrified of getting cut up, I crawled out of the closet like an animal driven from its hole.

I took my canoe out on the river, let the serenity of the upper Mississippi reassure me. Drifting past reeds and water lilies, listening to the aggressive brash calls of the red-winged blackbird, I calmed myself.

I asked the mature woman, the absent owner of the house, to take charge. I told Passive Woman she didn't have to be a wreck with Carl. I planned how I could best tell him I wanted a three month moratorium in our marriage. Then I got dressed and drove to the airport.

Carl, calm and self assured as always, listened to my explanations as I drove him to his house. He said he wasn't surprised. "I suggested it myself earlier, but you said that would be letting her win. Remember?"

I didn't answer.

"Remember?" he asked me again.

"I said *her* , even back then," I said, feeling spooked.

Carl gave me a kiss as he unloaded his suitcases from my car. I realized he was probably relieved to be back in his own routine. After all, he was nearly eighty. That made me feel a little less guilty.

A journal entry a few days later showed I was furious with Carl.

That tiny kiss when I told Carl of the incest, when I was vulnerable and fragile, was his first betrayal of my vulnerable child. I passively go along the caretaker saying, "Its ok, he will take care of you, he gives you expensive gifts, he is a good person, good for you, I even go along with marriage, but the betrayed child has a champion, and she lives in the wall and she is Sneaky Snake and she comes out. She can't stop what's happening, she has no arms or legs, but she can cause trouble, she can loath and hiss and bite and keep her sex for herself, even if she has to be sneaky about it.

I cried when I read that journal page to Glenda. "I don't know if I will ever get Carl separated from Creepy Crawly or the Caretaker."

Meantime, I continued to manage a sane public life. I would shop for groceries, do my chores and errands. I would dutifully stop by to see Carl. We would talk safe topics, family and friends, for an hour or so. I felt nothing for him, just my own separation and grief. I wrote in my journal:

I have been feeling like we aren't married, were never married, he's just an old acquaintance across the lake, with no more privileges than that. I'm almost surprised when anyone assumes we are married, or asks about him.

When I got home late one night from a trip to the cities, the rocking chair, which had a broken arm, was in a vice, being repaired. I realized Carl had been there in my absence. I felt deeply violated. I told myself, he's my husband. He has the right to come in, he has his own key. The next morning, when I got up, there was a note pinned to the cupboard about the repaired chair. He'd come in again while I was still sleeping. I felt even more violated.

When Carl and I went to dinner with friends that night, it was even harder for me to make polite small talk than it was earlier. Afterward, when we were alone, I explained to him the two levels of my experience. "On one level, you did a very thoughtful thing, coming in and fixing the chair. But on another level, you were dealing with a child who had been violated; whose boundaries had been trespassed."

"My child is already furious. I've done to her what my mother did to me, forced her to deny her own experience then allowed her to be used by a man. That child felt violated when you entered my house." Carl said he understood, but he did not seem particularly disturbed. I was beginning to wonder if he had any greater sense of reality in his life than I had in mine.

This morning I wake up from a deep deep sleep. Dead with exhaustion from all this. I ask the sleeping child if she could tell me anything else that happened back there. She sleeps on. I tell her it's safe now. She says, no it's not. He's still coming over.

Carl called. I couldn't talk to him, except to say yes or no. Later, he dropped by. As we sat on my deck, having tea, I became so nervous I couldn't bear it, and finally said he had to go. He resisted. "Surely we can spend a few minutes together."

I had to almost push him out. I leaned against the door, nearly in tears and shaking all over. I felt as if I had a rapist in the house with me. He was no longer Carl to me; he was so entangled with the figures of the past that I could no longer sort out my responses. A heavy headache clamped down. I screamed into a pillow. The headache released its hold.

Sessions with Glenda were like an emotional washing machine. I would sit down in the chair feeling in control, then immediately fly off in every direction; past and present were one. Terror, anger, sorrow, shame, bitter laughter, all mixed together.

In one breath I would say my teddy bear had started to remind me of Carl. "He's in the closet, he can stay there, he's loathsome." Then in the next breath, I was saying how bad I felt, how guilty I felt about Carl.

More rage was emerging, and though it frightened me, I knew my sanity depended on allowing it.

Woke up this morning thinking about that teddy bear I threw in the back closet, about killing it. Then I decided to put my father's picture with it, and kill him. I went to the kitchen and took out a sharp pointed knife. I had to tell myself it was only cloth and paper. I tried to do it, couldn't, went back to bed. Then I got up again and drove the knife clear through the picture and the bear, over and over again. The eyes made me feel guilty so I cut them out too, then I took the whole thing out to the burn barrel and watched it flame and flame and finally burn down to nothing. I came in and got my mother's picture and tore it up and burned it too. I felt slightly paranoid for awhile, fearful of the smoke sticking to me, haunting me. As I took a

shower, I sent a mental message to my father, You come back I'll
strangle you with my bare hands!

I wrote a letter to my father, though he was long dead:

Today I took your smirky picture down off the wall, stabbed it a hundred times
and burned it, a big blaze, along with newspapers and a teddy bear I can't even let
myself love because it's male. You did that to me. I don't know clearly everything
you did, but you do, and the results are clear, I am full of pain and anger that has
interfered with my whole life.

I hate remembering your creepy remarks about me in shorts, or with boyfriends,
you made me feel like a worm. Your threats, your dire forebodings about being
pushed out of cars by boys who raped me. Your embarrassment at women's breasts
or pregnancy, your contempt for raped women. All that I remember clearly. The
early stuff I have too much terror to even see clearly, but it must have taken from
me all my child's trust in the world and my place in it. I've been alone since I was
two or three, essentially, though you and Mom both played the good parents.

I know that you sexually abused me, and even blamed me for it, allowed me to
carry your shame and blame. You are not deserving to be my father and I now
disown you. Forever. I don't even want your name.

I called Carl and said I was coming over, and I was angry. "If you don't
think you can take it, tell me not to come, no heart attacks or anything."

He said, "Come ahead, I've been expecting it."

Shaking and sometimes crying, I sat across the dining room table and
told him. "From my perspective you have abused the trust I gave you
when I told you about my incest therapy. First, your response to that
broken vulnerable person was a kiss. Within days after that you told me
your sex dream about me, your "tumescence," the equivalent of exposing
yourself to a vulnerable child while her adult was away. Soon, you took my
hand and put it on your crotch. Next, you dangled marriage in front of
me, though you said yourself I turned into a frightened child when you
suggested it. Later, when I demonstrated panic, you dangled $60,000 in
front of me, more money than I've saved all my life. That was like candy
to a child."

He started to make excuses but I interrupted. "I just need you to listen,
I'm not interested in what's right or fair, I just need to say this to you. You
did all that knowing I was in and out of therapy for very serious and
complex abuse involving my father, and often said yourself you were
surprised I'd be interested in a man old enough to be my father."

He sat across from me, looking helpless and bewildered. "But I care for you ... I had only your best interest...."

"If you only my best interest in mind you'd have kept your hands off me until it was clear that I was really strong and healed, a process you knew takes years. You are supposed to be a healed and capable adult. Now I hate sex and can't imagine that I will ever be interested in it with you again."

"What can I say?" He looked at me helplessly, palms up.

I said, "Can you tell me you're sorry?"

He said, "I'm sorry for all you're going through."

I said, "No, sorry for what you did." He said he was sorry he hadn't been more sensitive, hadn't understood how serious it was. Then he went on to describe the operation of a new garage door opener he'd just installed. I felt that my pain was unimportant, trivialized, that he couldn't see it or acknowledge it, couldn't see or acknowledge me. I felt he treated me just as my father had.

I said, "I've got to go," and left, drained and exhausted.

I had a dream: *Funeral or something. Plants hanging on a balcony. Some important decision has to be made. The young man makes it because all the others are too emotional to make good decisions. He's not an arrogant dictator, just accepts the responsibility. Whose funeral? I don't know.*

Things were growing on the balcony of my dream, the place from which I overlook the rooms of my house. Some growth was taking root in the place that used to be full of old bedpans and trash. The important decision the younger man (my rational male self?) was making, was not to see Carl any more, not to go back to the old house of horrors. Though I didn't know it yet, it was the funeral of our marriage.

"I'm getting worse," I told Glenda. "It's not normal, the way I am about Carl, about my father and mother."

"What's so good about normal? Half the people around here are normal, shut down, half alive. It's not normal to have pictures on the wall of people who have abused you."

"But it's my family, " I cried. "Is it wise, letting all this anger out?"

"Absolutely," Glenda said. "You have to get your hands and legs back again so you can do everything you want to do." She told me not to get discouraged, "I'm confident in my skills, and confident of your ability to get through all this."

After that session, Carl called and asked me to go dancing.

"Carl, didn't you hear what I said to you? Don't you understand how angry I am with you?"

He said, "Well, I thought that was just one of your other personalities."
I was furious. "This is *me* talking. Me!" I was loud. I hung up.
I felt cruel, uncaring whether I hurt him or not.
Glenda said, "I think you're learning to trust the Hellion."
"Yes, I like her now. She's my favorite. But another part of me does care about Carl. How can I do this to him? How can I treat him this way? I *married* him. I did have some feelings for him. He got caught in something he knew nothing about." Then I could feel my attitude, my voice, and my expression change. "Bull shit, he saw an easy mark and went for it. Now he's in fantasy land about how much he loves me."

Glenda said, "Helen, when you're at odds with yourself you can't have much empathy for others. When you learn to be more empathetic to yourself, you will find it easier to be so with others."

One night I woke up frightened, sure there was someone else in the room. I saw the glow of my father's cigarette. He was sitting at the end of the bed, smoking. I remembered him doing that, remembered my fear of what was coming. Even when I saw that the red cigarette tip was only the red dots of my digital clock, reflected in a mirror, the fear did not leave. My body continued to reproduce, to reexperience, the triggered memories: *My legs are apart. I feel like there is a big long hole below my belly. I hurt like when I had an enema once, but the hole doesn't hurt, it's empty. Someone—my mother?—is looking at it to see if I am all right. I am all right, she tells me. My belly hurts bad.*

I lay in the darkness, curled on my side, a pillow clutched to my stomach. I told myself, *It's all right. It will heal. You can remember and it will be over. You can have your own little place back, you can close it. You can feel it. It will have feelings again and nobody can touch it but you unless you want them to.* In a few hours, it was over. I just wanted to sleep.

When I woke again, I felt weak. I felt a need to cleanse myself. I drank cup after cup of herbal tea, found myself eating nothing but fruits, oranges, figs. I bathed, washed my hair, polished my nails, shaved my legs. Then I took the sheets off the bed and washed them.

In therapy the next morning, talking about all the bathroom or toilet dreams, another memory fragment was triggered. *I am in the bathroom. Something is coming from behind, catching me from behind. I kick through some glass...* I shrieked and cried and struggled in terror. Glenda watched silently, without interfering.

After the flashback, I sat staring at the floor, tears streaming. Slowly, I returned from somewhere very far away. For the first time, I looked at

Glenda. "I still have trouble believing, even though she becomes seven, has all the terror of a seven-year-old when it's happening."

Glenda said, "If you could see yourself, you would believe it. If you had a video of yourself, you would believe you."

"I know I need to believe in myself, my child, my memories, if I'm ever going to be able to trust in myself." My voice got stronger, as if with a new recognition. "No wonder she won't tell me, if she thinks I won't believe her either!"

"Can you draw that bathroom scene?" Glenda asked me, just as I was leaving.

At home I got out paper and crayons. I felt some resistance. What is there to draw, the broken glass? But as I pulled the red crayon across the rough paper, the memory returned. *I have just finished my bath and am naked. My father comes in the bathroom with no pants on, sits on the toilet lid, grabs me from the back. I kick through glass. I am badly cut.* The picture was childlike, like one drawn by a child no more than six. A man with a very large red penis is pulling a kicking child down on his lap. After I finished the picture, I wanted to scribble black over the top of it.

I wrote in my journal:

> *I look at it now and say, this is sick. I have to remember, it is not me who is sick for drawing it, it is he who was sick for doing it. But that I'm connected to something so sick sickens me. I am full of loathing and my belly hurts with tears and pain and sucked in air.*

As I sat there with the journal, I started to cry. I was remembering my mother, hard faced and angry, bandaging my leg, and putting me to bed. I remembered going to sleep, a drugged sleep, before the pain could set in.

Sitting in my living room alone, I wailed, "My daddy. My daddy," knowing the one I loved most was the one who hurt me. I sat in the rocker then and talked to my little girl. "Your daddy was bad to you. I'm sorry to have to say it, but he was. I'll take care of you."

Then I heard the child say, "You make me do it, too."

"I know I did and I'm sorry and I'll never do that to you again."

We cried together.

One morning I lay in bed, realizing how little joy I had on waking. I was thinking about how puffy my belly had always been, how I protected it, how it had always felt tender and vulnerable. I turned over on my belly and thrust my stuffed animal under me, and for a long time lay there, experiencing the chronic pain. "Have the organs all pulled up into a ball?" I wondered. "Were they thrust there? Or do I pull them up?"

After awhile I felt some life stirring in the hard walls of my belly, not just pain. I thought, that's Sneaky Snake. That's the wall sneaky snake lives in. I remembered how in the past, just before breaking off with a man, there was usually an incident of seeing his penis as grotesquely large and threatening; perhaps it was close to my face. I wondered if those moments, lightly dismissed, barely noticed, had actually triggered the signal for the gate to drop, the end of feelings, the end of the love affair.

Determined to flush out, to face, all that I might have buried, I took the few snapshots I had of my early childhood, and examined them again and again. In one, a '20s model car was parked in the background. I kept returning to it; something about the curve of the sunshade across the windshield held my attention. I could remember what it looked like from an angle low on the seat, its rounded cup shape.

That led to another memory. *I am going to the store with Daddy. I am happy. Daddy stops somewhere where there are trees and we get in the back seat. I can see the tops of the trees. He is playing with me, I try to crawl away, but he drags me back by my panties. It is going to happen again. The big penis, I can't breathe as it is shoved down my throat, I blank out. Afterward, he cleans me up, puts me in the front seat.*

We drive to the store, and he goes in for cigarettes. When he comes back out, he gives me a candy sucker. "Didn't we have a good time at the store?" he says, patting my leg. As we drive home, me beside my handsome daddy, in his white shoes and his white hat, I am very happy. Daddy loves me.

Glenda said there is often pleasure involved with incest. The closeness, the feeling of specialness, being the chosen one. I resisted that; I didn't remember ever feeling like the chosen one, ever enjoying any of the sexual act.

I hated the ugliness of it; it made me feel shameful, slimy. I didn't even want to deal with it in therapy. "Should I be doing this?" I asked. "Spending all this time wading though all the muck, the garbage?"

Glenda encouraged me. "Give the turmoil all the time it needs. Go through the muck."

The worst of it was out now, I knew that. Some fragments followed, until gradually I put it together: my mother whipped me either because my father said I was seductive, or because my mother knew what he was doing, or because the incest created excessive masturbation. That's why she called me Hellion. My father said I lied when I tried to tell him about the whippings. I did not dare tell my mother what my father was doing, or I would be whipped for that.

I had been chosen to carry the neurosis of the family, their lies, denials and secrets. No wonder I found it so hard to believe in my own memories. I was taught even when it was happening, that it was not. Sometimes they said I lied, sometimes they said it was just a dream. If I told the truth, I was a "bad girl." When I kept quiet, things were more bearable in my family. I was a "good girl", when most of the time, I felt very very bad.

Why did it stop, as I knew with certainly that it did, when I was around seven? The books I was reading on incest perpetrators said some types are only attracted to soft babyish bodies. It was also possible it stopped because my mother and father could no longer convince a seven-year-old that it was my own fault, or that it hadn't happened. It is also possible someone found out, or they were afraid someone would. They moved often, I remembered.

There was some relief in facing the horrors of my early years, admitting it, giving up the denial. But all the feelings the small miserable child had kept in denial surfaced in the present.

The adult me, who had built up great strength over the years, who had overcome so much, reverted to the unacknowledged feelings of the five-year-old. I felt shamed and shameful, "bad," "dirty." I avoided people. I made disparaging or derogatory remarks about myself, even about my therapy. I felt unloved, unlovable, and victimized.

My child became my only companion. I drove all the way to the city to find just the right stuffed animal for her. I talked to her on the trip, asking her what she wanted to eat, where she wanted to stop. I'd ask her with each place, shall we try here? I'd show her all the animals. How about this one?

I finally found a huge lioness and lion. *They are magnificent animals, so beautiful and comforting. My child is still afraid at night. I tell her the lions and I will protect her, but neither of us is sure I can.*

I was constantly having to push back other voices, voices that said I was wasting my time, that I should be working, that I was too self-absorbed. I would remind myself that I was working for my very life, and I would continue to do it for as long as it took.

I no longer had any relationship at all with Carl. I knew the woman he had married did not exist; his was an arranged marriage. The Caretaker and the Passive Woman had arranged it. Creepy Crawly cooperated. Sneaky Snake and the wounded child were violently opposed, but the child was powerless, and Sneaky Snake covert.

I had not felt such strong aversion to my previous lovers; in fact, I usually hung on long after the affair was over. I decided it was probably because Carl was my first lover after the lid was off the memories. Before that, I had been living in denial, as if it hadn't happened. Now I just wanted the marriage to be over. All the books said not to make any major decisions for at least a year after going into therapy.

I was afraid it would be hard for my friends and family to understand how a marriage that seemed so promising was already dying. I called my friend Nanci in California, who had stood up with us at the wedding. Nanci said, "I thought I saw this coming in your letters." Never one to be divided against herself, she said firmly, "If the day comes when you're all over this and you don't want to stay married, you're not going to be able to stay married. It's embarrassing to call it off, but that's it."

My son Mike, distancing himself, said I had to do whatever I had to do. I could hear the sadness in Scott's voice when he asked me if I was sure, but I knew the sadness was for me, not for Carl. Still living in the world of the victimized child, I was amazed that my friends and family still loved me, no matter how "crazy" I was.

I wrote Carl a letter and read it to Susan on the phone: "... Chances of our marriage recovering are very low. I didn't mean to hurt you, I thought I could do it, make myself into the kind of wife I wanted to be for you. I don't see you clearly, I know that. You are all tied up with my perpetrators. I don't think you see me either. I know you want to help me, but I don't need a caretaker; I'm going to make it through this. I've found out we can get an annulment. Of course, I won't take your money. I'm sorry about all of it."

Susan encouraged me to send it. "It's the truth. He needs to hear the truth."

Glenda said, "This could change, but if you tried to live with Carl now it would be like prostitution."

Carl wanted to wait until I was sure. I told him quietly, but firmly. "I'm quite sure. This isn't one of my personalities."

He was kind, understanding, said he would cooperate, even pay the lawyer.

I was grateful that he was not tragic. He even made a joke. "Maybe my better half and your better half can get together at the Union."

He laughed and so did I.

When I hung up the phone, I was shaking all over. I felt some pressure at the top of my spine. Perhaps, I thought, the passive woman is coming through, taking her place in her backbone.

Dream: *I am at a conference with other men and women, all nicely dressed. There is the usual looking one another over, dropping hints about whether we're sexually available, etc., I'm married but drop a hint I've been known to stray. At a banquet it is discovered that one of our members has been caught stealing. She has stolen a wallet and is turned over to me, as the gentle but responsible one, to keep an eye on her. I have her on a string until the police come for her. She is a genteel person and is slightly embarrassed. A part of me had glimpsed the wallet on the floor of the hall. It was on a string. The next morning she is back among us. We want to know how it went at court, how she got let off so soon. She said if it had been an impulsive thing, they would have seen her as out of control and therefore likely to repeat at any time. But she was not a menace to society, so was only fined and then released. We accept her back, but it's not the same. We know now she is not to be trusted. She doesn't seem to feel guilty, just matter of fact. It didn't work. She is an attractive person otherwise, and goes about having breakfast with the rest of us.*

There is a change in the conference. Because of budget cutbacks, programs will have to be limited, no transportation, meeting rooms, etc. Not even name tags. We'll have to put notes up for one another.

I realized the dream was all about going after Carl's billfold, his money, though I didn't admit it to the rest of the conference (to other parts of myself). The wallet was on a string, had strings attached, a setup. The inner personalities caught me and held me until the police came, my inner law courts. Because it was not a habitual thing, or impulsive, the law decided I was not dangerous. "She won't be trusted by the rest of us again." How could I trust the decisions I made after what happened with Carl? "She is back with us, presentable as ever," but there will be a change in conference budgets. I'm giving up Carl's money and the program that went with it. And now the conference participants will have to communicate with notes to each other.

I thought perhaps I could go into meditation, see where the people in the big house stand: *The caretaker insists he was setting up something really good for the passive woman. I send him away for awhile with the creepy guy, leaving the passive woman alone with the bandaged child. I think maybe they will talk if they are alone. For awhile, the passive woman just lies there on the table, the child stays in the corner. Finally the passive woman says, "Why don't you come over here so I can see you?" The child does come closer, but she just stands there, the way I did as a teenager, when my mother was dying. Sneaky Snake comes out of the wall and starts talking to both of them. "You've got this sex thing," she tells the passive woman. "You've got to come out of the corner sooner or later," she tells the child. The two of them gradually enter the conversation. The child finally says to the* passive woman, "I don't remember what went on, but if I'm going to come out of the corner, you've got to get into the backbone."

I wrote in my journal:

The minute she said that, the passive woman was just sucked up off that table and into the backbone. Then there was a head at the top of the backbone, and a body with the hands of a fierce bird. Now the Bitch Queen has a backbone: she won't have to be so bitchy. The child and the passive woman have communicated. So now they know it's like this: The child will live in the heart, Sneaky Snake will live in the genitals, and the passive woman will live in the back bone. The caretaker, when he comes back, will only be allowed to pay bills, maintain the house and keep the calendar. The creepy retarded man has to go. Period.

I emerged feeling shaken, a little tentative, but stronger.

"Sneaky Snake would like to get something sexual started, maybe get ahold of Ken, but I don't think I'm strong enough in the backbone yet, or the child strong enough yet to get into that. Besides, the child tells me, 'He didn't treat you so good either, Gramma. He proposed to you and then started talking about catching the next bus out of town. Get real.' Well, she does see a lot from her little corner of the room."

Glenda said she thought I was listening to the right voices now. "You were all over the place when you first came in. 'Save my marriage, my wonderful marriage to this wonderful man.' I think you're much more in touch with yourself now."

She summarized our progress: "Your outer personality is well integrated, you take care of the essentials in your life, your job, your health, your home. Your personal self is not. You will have to learn slowly to build and rely on your own perceptions." She encouraged me to keep journaling and drawing and talking to my little girl. "I'm impressed with all the work you've done, the art work, the dreams, the journal entries."

When I left that session, I felt my child skipping with glee.

A dream: *I go to find everybody and somebody says they have gone to help a friend get her book published. I said, "Well, I've got to deal with all my envy and jealousy then," and we started off, me leading, down a side alley. In a shop we saw this wonderful crystalline cube. We knew we could change it just by thinking about it or touching it, but what was in mine (there were others) was part of a face, very sensual lips and part of a cheek, and behind it, the rest of a compressed body. The colors were mauve and purple and pink and red, very sexual colors, and it was alive,* moving, seductive. It was like those cubes they make out of entire cars, crushing them for recycling.

I took out my water colors and painted the cube, just as I had seen it in the dream, with all the subtle shades of mauve, blue, and red. I loved the painting; it fairly glowed.

I showed it to Glenda. She said, "The cube is you." I already knew it. Like the crushed car, all of my sexual self was still there, but it had been so tightly repressed, that it couldn't move. Only the young sensual me still occasionally showed through, alive and wanting out.

The first part of the dream, I told Glenda, the part about the friend going off to get something published, was easily recognized. "I've been jealous and envious of friends who are doing their writing and getting published while I'm not doing much with mine. Instead, I'm doing therapy, down the side alley."

Glenda said, "Why don't you write about this?"

I lit up, remembering Larry's suggestion over a year ago— How'd you like to bring the two sides of yourself closer together?

"That would be putting the two sides together!" I said, and this time there was no ironic commentary in my mind, *"That'll be the day that I die."*

While I was sitting in the car after that session, the windshield, the rain, a chain link fence melted together with my tears, turning the chain link fence into a web of crystal, a thing of beauty, like the view from inside the cube.

After I got home from that session, I wrote:

And now, here I am, the writer woman looking at herself. Around me are my journals, books of them, full of secrets and dreams and love and hope and pain and rage; and my writings, my half finished books and stories. What I'm remembering from my session is: You can write. You can write about this. You want to write and you want to do therapy. You can do them both"

Not exactly a happy story I would be writing, and yet I had never seen it as an unhappy story. A love story of sorts. I thought it would begin:

The child roamed the dark house, a heavy hammer tugging at her wrist. Its head dragged on the floor, the sound muffled by the heavy carpet....

13

American Auschwitz

After months of near isolation, I was ready to start reaching out to the larger world. I wrote my brother John in California, warning him that I would be calling, and why, so he would be prepared. Because he was four years older, I thought he would remember more of the Richmond years. We had never been close, but I always trusted that he cared about me. I stuck up for him too. Our father never spoke a kind word to John, constantly criticized him, despite the fact that John was always a good kid. A few years before Dad died, I asked him why he had treated his own son so badly. At first Dad denied it, then he said it was because John reminded him of Mother's father, "that old bastard." I hurt, thinking of the beautiful curly headed child, carrying all that hate that was not his.

I kept John on the phone over an hour: Where was the basement? Why did Mom and Dad quarrel? What did he remember? Was I the bad one?

"Dear, I remember everything, clear back to when I was a baby," he said. "But I don't know how much help I can be to you, because I only remember my own little world. I don't know if they thought you were bad or not, but I know they thought I was.

"One of my first memories is crawling out of my crib and dragging pans out of the kitchen cupboards, banging the lids. Dad jerked me up, threw me back in my crib and fastened me there with a clamp on my penis." Anger thickened his voice. "I even remember where the clamps came from," he said through clenched teeth, "the laboratory where Dad worked at Standard Oil."

He went on to describe in vivid detail how by age 5, he was already considered a bully and troublemaker. "So they tied me up in the back yard in a harness, like a dog," he said bitterly.

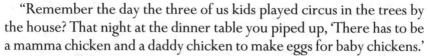

"Remember the day the three of us kids played circus in the trees by the house? That night at the dinner table you piped up, 'There has to be a mamma chicken and a daddy chicken to make eggs for baby chickens.'

"Dad just blew up. 'Where in Hell did she learn a thing like that!' You left the table in tears."

I didn't remember, but the shame felt familiar.

"The worst part," John said, "was their quarrels, Dad jealous, Mother provoking it. They would go at each other for hours. We would lie there and listen, scared to death."

John said Mother's father was so verbally abusive of all his kids that one, Ruth, ran off with a sailor, then committed suicide. Another of the girls drank. One son disappeared forever. "Remember, Mother would have been pregnant with me when she was only fifteen, and Dad was over thirty. She just wanted to get away from the old bastard."

Then he shifted to years later, when Mother died. "She always took my side against Dad, even if she had to wait until he wasn't around. He'd say that I couldn't go skating or couldn't go to the movies. Mom would give me the money and tell me to go. Then he'd raise hell with me. But he was going to raise hell with me either way." A bitter pause. "Mom ignored the lump on her breast a whole year because she had a death wish—she was so miserable."

Then, with all the pain of the past in his voice, he told me how he tried to keep the 8-Mile House going, with all the creditors hounding him, an impossible task, when he was hardly more than a kid himself. "We had to watch it all go down the tubes, the house, all of it. No wonder you married Jimmy. You had no family.

"I confronted Dad with the truth in later years. I told him he never loved any of us."

There was silence on the phone while he recovered. His anger turned to hurt. "I can't let anybody close, even my wife. The kids are still sometimes afraid of me." My brother, who always took such good care of his family.

I felt a deep sorrow, remembering how he had always said, "I'm fine," with a broad good-kid smile, no matter how difficult things were for him.

He said, "I'm sorry, Dear, that I couldn't be more help. It seems like all of us just lived in our own little worlds."

"You have been a help, a big help," I assured him as we said goodbye. Now I knew that my brother had no trouble believing our father had done exactly what I remembered. John at least saw clearly, remembered clearly, the truth of his life, rather than whitewash it, as I had.

He had said: "You married Jimmy. You had no family." It was the first time I ever had it acknowledged that my life was less than okay back then.

I called my sister Beverly. I told her the whole truth, what happened with Carl, the flashbacks involving our father. She was not surprised. "You were kind of circling around that the last time you were down here," she said, quite matter of fact. I told her I was coming to see her, and I wanted her to try to remember as much as she could.

Driving through the woods of the Michigan peninsula, I found myself daydreaming about men, imagining calling old boyfriends, spending the night with Ken, meeting a new man on the way. I hadn't had any interest in men in months.

That night, I stayed in a little motel and woke up the next morning berating myself for the failure of one more relationship. I felt so bad, I thought I might be ill. I realized then I was doing what I always did when an affair was over; beat myself up, just like in the dreams. While I showered and dressed, I thought about who does the beating, who takes the beating, and wondered how I could interfere with that process.

Back on the road, I still felt so bad I had to pull over. I started talking to my bandaged child. *She tells me how bad she feels. I ask her who has been making her feel so awful. Her mother, the Bitch Queen, has been telling her what happened to her wouldn't have happened if she hadn't been bad to begin with, if she hadn't been sexual and showing her genitals and slithering around on Daddy, being a Hellion. The child feels bad and wrong and slimy. She feels so bad, so terrible, she can't bear it. "The only person I can go to that makes me feel better is my daddy," she says, "and he's the one who does it to me."*

Then I understood why I was having fantasies of calling Ken; I couldn't stand to feel so bad about myself. The child desperately needed someone to make her feel better. Desperately needed her "hit." *She wants her daddy.* Daddy comes to comfort her and to be comforted. There is some pain, but she blanks it out. The high is worth it. Later, she will take her punishment. She goes to sleep in his arms. I understand. That's what I have done with men, in different ways, over and over.

Over the years, people had told me I was flirtatious, seductive, and manipulative. I didn't understand what was wrong with that then. Wasn't everybody? When I got involved with men, they *had* to love me, I'd make them. Even if I didn't love them. I couldn't stand the pain if they didn't love me. I had used sex the way some use alcohol or drugs.

I promised myself now I would learn to break those habits: I would find other ways to comfort myself, I would recognize when I had taken over my mother's role and stop beating on myself.

I arrived at my sister's house determined to talk about the past, to find missing pieces for my puzzles, to gather evidence to support my memories. Beverly immediately took me upstairs. "Don't talk in front of Martin. He already has enough reasons to tell me there's something wrong with me."

I turned and closed the door. Beverly opened it. "He'll think we're talking about him." We sat on the bed and in a low voice I told her, "It looks like Dad was doing this sex stuff with me for probably four years, the whole time we were in Richmond."

Beverly's face kept the same resigned calm. "I'm not surprised. I don't remember anything from back there. Just being terrified all the time." She didn't remember anything before she was five or six. "It's just a blank back there. All I remember is that I was scared all the time, but I don't know why."

She couldn't remember any physical or sexual abuse. She remembered almost nothing about me, even though she was older.

"We all lived in our own separate misery," she said. "I've always felt guilty. Even today, walking downtown, I think there is some reason people will think I'm doing something wrong. I can't remember ever feeling any different."

I said, "But I always thought you were Dad's favorite. He always talked about how pretty you were."

Beverly looked scornful. "All I remember from him is criticism. I couldn't ever do anything right. He was always yelling at us, so I just learned to keep quiet and stay away from him. I never trusted him."

I wanted to keep talking, wanted to trace it all back, but we had to go downstairs then because "Martin will be thinking we are talking about him." Downstairs Martin was watching TV, "sulking" Beverly said, out of his earshot.

The next day, we found time to talk when Martin was in the shop. There were no major breakthroughs, but the small things added up. "Remember Dad's friend Glenn?" Beverly asked.

"How can I forget? Glenn made a heavy pass at me when I was about thirteen. Even before that he was always trying to put his hands down our swimsuits." I laughed. She didn't.

Beverly said. "I never liked Giardello either, always trying to get us on his lap. And Umberto got picked up by the cops for molesting a high school girl, remember?"

I had only remembered them as affectionate old men. But now I remembered reading that abusers usually have friends who are abusers too. "I must have been whitewashing everything by then. 'If you don't see it, it isn't happening.'"

Beverly stopped talking; Martin was coming in the back door.

Soon I saw that everything was geared to what Martin might think. In town, Beverly couldn't let me buy her a pretty sweater because Martin might think she was dressing up for someone else. She can't run to the store to get eggs because Martin might think she was going to meet someone. She couldn't show him the bookkeeping, how bad finances were, because he thought she was deceiving him. "He gets mad and yells at me."

I knew those were the symptoms of an abuser. I asked if Martin had ever hit her.

"No. He probably would if he got mad enough. He grabbed me by the throat one night and slammed me against the kitchen cupboards."

Beverly's expression was flat and emotionless; she could have been reciting a grocery list. "Beverly, have you talked to a counselor at the battered women's shelter?"

"No. Martin would be furious. And besides, it's fifty miles away. I can't call 'em either, he'll see the long distance bill."

I cried when I left my sister's house. She had become our mother, married to our father.

"What old stereotypes we have become," I told Glenda, "Caricatures of earlier selves. Such wasted lives."

"People live like that because they get something out of it," Glenda said. "Beverly's bungling the books and making Martin angry may be the only ways she can feel some power." In some ways my mother had sabotaged my father. " Cycles do repeat themselves, unless we interfere, unless we take charge of our lives."

Beverly's guilt reminded me of how much guilt I carried around all my life, how much effort I'd made to build a whole personal life, successful, self assured, on top of a base that felt like garbage.

"There is no reason for the guilt. There was hardly any way you could have been more powerless," Glenda reminded me; "Size, age, family power, all of it. You had none."

"I know that, but how can I ever have a clean healthy relationship when I still have all this garbage I'm carrying around with me from the past?"

"Name the garbage." Glenda said. "Sort it out and name it."
So I did.

🌴 *Guilt*—Feeling guilty for participating in that early incest, even though it wasn't my fault and I had no choice. Feeling that I am guilty for terrible sexual things, my own sexuality which I thought caused the incest, and guilty of the isolation between my mother and me. Guilty of being competitive with my sister and my mother for my father's attention. Guilty of not being good enough to make things okay, to fix it.

🌴 *Disgust*—My father found me to be disgusting, contemptible, because in his eyes I was a sexual object, and probably because I was helpless and vulnerable, submissive, and needy for attention and love. I felt contemptible and disgusting.

🌴 *Rage*—Rage at being emotionally neglected by both of them, rage that my mother whipped me for my sexuality, rage that my genuine, natural, sexuality was taken from me, rage that my father used me then threw me aside like a piece of garbage, covered with his own disgust and contempt.

🌴 *Despair—Hopelessness*—The feeling that this is the world, this is the way it is, anything that seems to be good will always end this way. Sexual or emotional pleasure will be followed by guilt, rage, and disgust.

🌴 *Shame*—The feeling that I am just inherently bad, that badness is part of who I am, no matter what I do, that at the bottom of it—I am bad.

🌴 *Distrust*—I am not to be trusted, no matter what I do or say, or even think to be the truth, I am not to be trusted. Nor is the love of others to be trusted.

🌴 *Fear*—The world is not a safe place. Bad things happen to me. No one is going to care or do anything about it.

🌴 *Misery*—Chronic sense of darkness, no joy. Don't expect or deserve joy.

☥ *Loneliness*—No one is going to want to be with me, to care about me, to think I am worth the trouble I cause. I will have to take care of myself the best I can, make myself happy the best I can.

☥ *Desperation*—If I can get Daddy to see I'm ok, if I can make him love me, then everything will be all right. If I am just in some way good enough, or do enough, or act happy enough, I can get through this pain.

"Quite a lot of garbage to build over the top of," I told Glenda as she read the list. "A regular landfill."

"That's not your list or you wouldn't still be here today," Glenda said, handing it back to me. "That's the child's list. And you're going to have to help her get rid of all that stuff. It's going to take time."

Then we discussed whether I was strong enough to attend a national survivors conference that was coming up in Illinois. The work there would be intense.

"I know you're quite competent, professionally," Glenda said. "You've travelled all over the world. But this is different; this is going to be all about your personal world."

Was I ready to handle it emotionally? I thought I could. "Maybe there would even be some comfort in knowing I'm not the only one."

Glenda nodded. "Good. Just keep listening to the child, paying attention to the belly and the head."

When I arrived at the VOICES conference, I registered, picked up the program schedule, and headed for the elevators. It was a first class hotel, quite elegant, but I noticed the clientele did not have the slick appearance one usually finds in such hotels. Waiting for the elevator were two overweight young women in bulky sweat suits. One was carrying a large teddy bear, its synthetic hair an unnatural, poisonous-looking blue. The other carried a rag doll, its eyes gone, its wool hair matted. On the way to my room, I passed two more: one was a small hunched figure who did not raise her head as she scuttled past, another a large woman talking loudly to her teddy bear. "It's Okay, Sarabecky, I know you're afraid, but I'll take care of you." They disappeared into a room marked *Safe Room*, where several others sprawled on couches or on the floor, while a rather professional looking woman knitted. I felt a chill as the hotel segued into something uncomfortably like a hospital or asylum. Twenty years earlier, that's where they put women going through these things. I did not want to see myself as one of those people.

After unpacking, I went downstairs to the restaurant. There were more people in the lobby, the lounges and the dining room carrying stuffed animals, dolls or blankets. Mostly women, some men, they gave themselves away in minor ways too, an exaggerated defensive lift of the chin, a refusal to make eye contact, a slumped position, eyes that searched for danger, or for safe corners. There were more than four hundred survivors at the conference, I learned. These were only the ones who were well enough to come, I thought, the ones who could afford the expensive fees and the long trip. How many more must there be out there?

After dinner, I sat in the lounge, trying to read. A woman in her thirties, carrying a doll that looked about that same age, sat down next to me. "This is Suzy Q," she said, loudly, as if I might not hear well. "I got her back from my grandmother. Didn't I, Suzy?" She held the doll upright so its plastic lids flew open with a startled click.

She tugged its neatly ironed dress down over its stuffed cotton torso. "She took Suzy Q away from me but I got her back." Her expression was aggressive and her voice carried defiant pride.

"Why did your grandmother take Suzy Q?" I asked.

"To punish me. Because I told." She looked around the room, as if her grandmother might still come and snatch Suzy Q from her hands.

"How long did she keep Suzy Q?"

"Twenty-five years!" The woman's heavy lidded eyes brightened with triumph. "But I got her back, didn't I, Suzy Q? I got her back."

In my room that night, I could not allay my anxiety. I didn't want to be around all those other victims, I didn't like to see what had happened to them. I didn't want to be called a survivor either. I went to bed, but could not sleep, my legs twitched, my arms itched, my head ached. I kept hearing a rhythmic chime, like a soft alarm, but there was no clock radio in the room. I talked to my child, who was mad because she didn't have her stuffed animal, and everybody else did.

The next day, I attended a lecture by Linda Sanford, a therapist who had worked with survivors for ten years, and then worked with perpetrators who had been mandated into therapy by the courts.

Her statistics put to rest my lingering denial: *People don't do things like I remember.* People do. Great numbers of them. A 1985 survey estimated that 38 million adults were sexually abused as children. Some 250,000 cases were referred to the Child Sexual Assault Treatment Program. One in every four women and one in every seven men are sexually abused by the time they reach the age of eighteen. Another survey showed 27 percent of the women questioned and 16 percent of the men said they had been sexually abused as children.

Sanford said the perpetrators she worked with openly admitted sexually abusing their daughters, stepdaughters, sons, nieces. "She liked it," they would say of a one-year-old. "I always saw her as my sweetheart," one said of a six-year-old.

When I woke in the night, I read for distraction. Wenday Maltz, a speaker on the program, had written a powerful book: The *Sexual Healing Journey*. I cried, reading about how memory loss protects the child, and the adult, from feelings of the past. I felt my own feelings recognized and acknowledged. "Sexual abuse is often confusing, painful, upsetting, shame inducing, and humiliating." I checked off the list in the book practically every unwholesome response I had to sex, the whole range, from total rejection to exaggerated aggressiveness.

The next day I went to a session on *Helping Yourself to Heal*. At first, I wanted to leave. The speaker, Karen Spolyar, looked so straight, so middle class, so ordinary. How could I identify with anyone so wholesome? "It is very difficult for most of us survivors to combine feeling and thinking," Karen began. "We usually separate feelings off." I recognized that in myself, and noted the suggestions: combining work and music, decorating a work area with passionate art, wearing soft colorful clothes while doing household chores. I ended up admiring the "ordinariness" of the speaker.

I attended a workshop called *Family Reconstruction*. Chosen as the "explorer" to model the reconstruction process, I was asked to choose people from the group to sculpt as my alter ego, as my mother, father, grandfather and grandmother, aunts and uncles.

I picked Karen, the woman from the last workshop, to be my alter ego. What I wanted and needed was the very wholesomeness I had been suspicious of. I said, "Tell me when you think I'm not telling the truth, or lying to myself."

Karen said, "I trust everything you say." That brought tears of gratitude, as well as grief that I was unable to trust myself as totally. After that, I wanted Karen right behind me every moment, wanted to be able to reach back and touch her. I wanted what I never had as a child.

My mother had been from a huge family, eight or ten brothers and sisters. I felt overwhelmed when all the people I chose to play them stood around me ... the one who committed suicide, the one who ran away, the

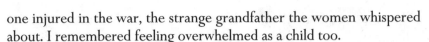

one injured in the war, the strange grandfather the women whispered about. I remembered feeling overwhelmed as a child too.

The circle of women closed against Grandfather, who liked it that way because there were "too many of them." Grandmother, who seemed to have nothing to say about her life, really had the central role in the family, adversary to her husband. I myself had done that. The man playing my grandfather said he kept himself alone because he liked it. A minister, he liked the control of the ministry. I had almost gone into the ministry myself, years ago. I kept myself alone. I had never realized how similar I was to my grandfather.

Responding intuitively, people came uncannily close to the facts of my mother's family. The daughters said they had only two choices, to be nurturing good women or suicides and drinkers. I kept asking my Grandmother why she had all those kids, why she had sex with Grandfather if he was such an old bastard? Grandmother said, "That's just the way it was then."

After recovering from all the old feelings of that visit to my past, I went to hear a multiple personality, *Jane and Company*, talk about waking up in the morning to find she's done three paintings in the night, none of them good; looking around at lunch to find she's at a restaurant she's never been to, ordering something she hates; looking in the closet and seeing clothes she would never wear. Jane had a humorous contempt for "singletons," who seemed cloddy in comparison to her own houseful of personalities.

I don't have experiences like that, I reassured myself. Sometimes the host personality got pushed aside when another personality took over. Like getting married, running from Carl's house, having the accident. "That doesn't make me a multiple." I felt a flash of rage.

In my room getting ready to go to a mask-making workshop, I glanced in the mirror, and a felt another flash of anger. I controlled it, telling myself not to act crazy.

Another part of me objected. "I feel what I feel, goddamn it."

I cried with relief after all those years of shutting feelings down, "I can feel what I feel," I would think, and just the thought would make me cry again, with tears of freedom.

I spent a morning making a mask with paint, glue, colored paper, yarn, and whatever else I found in a pile of art supplies. Then I told other participants what it represented to me.

"It's blue—she's an intellectual, thinking rather than feeling. Blue also represents not breathing deeply. Or not at all. She has mirrors for eyes—

helps others see themselves but doesn't show herself. Black in the mouth—what her father's stuff makes her feel like. No eyebrows. Vague definition of herself. There are heavy frown lines on the forehead—her father's rage, his criticism. In one eye there is a heart—looking for love and vision blocked by that—and there is razzle dazzle stuff in her hair—her sexy personality, at times."

I had pasted wide black and purple rays behind the mask, to make it look bigger, like animals that fluff their fur to look more fierce. "It's survival technique," I said.

"I think it's spirituality mixed with fear," a woman said.

I did not mind showing others my mask. They were all survivors. They understood its ugliness. But back in my room, the ghastly glittery mask made me uneasy. I threw it in the waste basket, with pangs of guilt that I could not accept myself exactly the way I was.

That evening I went to a poetry writing session. Thirty others expressed their pain, anger, loneliness, despair, their intense loyalty to others who had been hurt. I felt an increasing admiration for these wounded people, for their courage, for their determination to work through art, therapy, any way they could, to get back their splintered selves. In that poetry session, I wrote an admission that I was one of them:

Arrival
Who are all these strange people
carrying teddy bears and dolls? Looking at their shoes?
I'm in my room, alone.
That's not strange?
I am so frightened in the night
I can't tell
if the soft digital bell—ding ding ding
is in my head or in the clock.
I sit in different chairs, first one, then another.
The bell starts and stops.
In bed I twitch.
All day I take notes, a lecture, while in another room,
people are dancing, crying, moving. I want—I want —
I want to be there.

As I listened to the poems of others, their grief and anger, I felt my own sadness. Then I went to the art gallery and saw their tortured drawings, black and red, mostly, children's crayon scrawls. Huge black figures leered at cowering small ones. An outsider might say these were the drawings of sick children. I knew that they were the portraits of sick families. The drawings triggered more sorrow for others than I had ever felt for myself.

Again, I couldn't sleep. I tried to read a book, Fredrickson's *Repressed Memories,* which talked about the power of smells to bring memories flooding back. My room smelled of liquor, familiar in our household. As memories edged to the surface, I tried to twist away from them. I was crying. "It wasn't me, it was her." My vision went askew when I tried to correct that in my mind. "It was me. She was me. She is me."

I got up and went to the 24-hour help room. Several people were there, sprawled out alone with their teddy bears, or talking quietly with each other. I didn't like the look of the stern looking helpers. Two women lay on the floor, one trying to quiet the other, who was whimpering and shaking. Then two men came in, lifted the frightened woman up by the arms and took her out in the hall. I saw them strapping her on a stretcher.

Another woman came in and sat down. "They hauled somebody off!" she told me, eyes wide. "Freaked everybody out." I felt like I was in a psych ward. My own fear was rampant. Still, I felt intuitively that I must face my fear, accept that I was one of these flawed hurt people. I couldn't keep running from it.

The culmination of the conference was an anger workshop. For many of us, it was the most frightening. Would we lose control? The leader was a survivor, Ariel Jordan, a New York filmmaker from Israel. Handsome and tall, with a charming accent, he talked about his abuse, not without compassion for himself. He even showed us, lying down on the floor, what it was like for him when his father taught him at age five how to be his sexual partner. All he had wanted to do was please his father. "Is this right, Daddy? Is this how I do it?"

Ariel asked a few people to talk about their experience. Hearing those stories was like a visit to Auschwitz. There seemed to be no limit to the number of ways people can inflict their sexual sickness on their children, grandchildren, stepchildren, any child they can get control over.

One woman was shut out on the fire escape in freezing weather until she was so grateful for her grandfather's "rescue" that she did whatever he wanted. Another was tortured by her mother, who burned her labia with cigarettes. A young man was taken as a lover by his mother when he was six; he learned how to masturbate her to sleep every night; if he didn't do it right, she lay on top of him, trying to satisfy herself, nearly smothering him in her huge breasts. A sixteen-year-old girl had been kept sexual hostage by her father for years.

As we listened to the horror stories, numb with shock, Ariel would say, "Respond from your heart. Get in and feel for this person from your heart. Tell them what you feel deep inside." His face was alive with compassion.

My own tears streaming, I told the sixteen-year-old, "It breaks my heart to hear what happened to you." The girl looked at me blankly. I understood the look. The girl had not heard that from anybody then, and now she could hardly believe she mattered.

The stories triggered our own grief and anger. Almost everyone was weeping, some wailing, some beating on the floor, sobbing. From across the room, I heard the woman with the doll repeating loudly, like a stuck mechanism, "and then my grandmother took her, but I got her back, I got her back! Didn't I, Susy Q?"

The room became Bedlam, as the pain that could not be expressed years ago filled the air with cries. Aerial reminded people to respect themselves. "If you can't handle it, put your hands over your ears or leave," he said, calmly but firmly. "Be responsible for deciding just how much you can take." One person left the room with a trained attendant.

In dyads, twos, we each told our partners what happened to us as if it were happening now. Then the partner was to say what that child most needed to hear, and didn't. My sobbing partner was a thin young woman who for years had been used by her father for what he called, comforting. "It wasn't your fault," I told her. "You could not take care of your 'poor father.' He was a bad person. You were a child. It was *his* job to take care of *you*." I felt fiercely protective of my dyad partner. I would have torn the father's miserable eyes out.

When it was my turn to tell my story, I stayed in control of my feelings, fearing that my already fragile partner would not be able to handle anything more. I calmly told of the first abuse, in the basement when I was two. It was very painful for my partner to hear and she looked away. I insisted on making eye contact. Then I told her what I needed to hear from her; "Tell me my genitals were not bad, this didn't happen to me because I had a girl's genitals." Once she knew what I needed, my partner was able to say that, and mean it. She was able to hold me and cry with me.

There was much tenderness now as partners held each other and shared their grief and pain.

"All those tears, all those abused children, so many years later," Ariel said, surveying the room full of people spread out across the floor weeping in one another's arms, or curled up alone, like survivors of a hurricane or a plane crash.

Ariel showed us what just hearing someone's rage triggers in a child who has grown up feeling helpless. He lay down on the floor, banging his hands and feet against the floor, yelling himself hoarse.

I felt my own body go stiff, my own breathing go shallow, as it did when I was a child and my father was slamming around the house, banging doors, turning over the coffee table. I would get very quiet, fearing his rage might be directed at me. As for my own rage, it was stifled. There was no place for that in my family. Now I looked around at the other participants. Most, like me, were wide-eyed, white faced, silent. Some put their hands over their ears. Some trembled, cowering.

Ariel invited us to do what he had done, to express all the rage the child had felt, as the child wanted to, needed to, but couldn't. As I pounded and screamed, I felt the familiar pain, the hair ball, gradually leave my belly. I felt emptied of old stale breath held for more than fifty years.

Then we stood in a circle, color and excitement in our faces. We held hands for safety, and yelled at our perpetrators.— "Fuck You!" "Get Away From Me!" "You bastard," I yelled, bending my knees and jumping like an ape. I felt powerful. The energy in the room was high now, tangible in the air.

Ariel joined the circle, asking each of us to take a big step forward and make a claim, speaking as if we already had it. I jumped into the center right away. "I have my genitals back!" I felt great. Everyone applauded. Others followed: I have rights! I can say no! I own my own body! I can say no! I can protect myself!

"That's it," Ariel said, laughing. "Before we go, give somebody a big genuine hug." I leapt up, threw my arms and legs around him, and hugged him. Then I was horrified. I apologized for wrapping my legs around him, a survivor. He said, "I know you meant it in the best way. You are a wonderful spirit. How about another hug?" I made that one more restrained. I left that workshop feeling more confident of my ability to handle my often overwhelming feelings. But I would have to learn how to relate to men in less extreme ways.

For the ceremonial closing of the conference, two survivors created a beautiful dance. One represented the inner child, ignored by the busy woman, feeling despair, reaching out to others to fill the empty place. Gradually, the woman connects to the child, who slowly learns to trust, and they dance off, talking happily together. It was a touching farewell.

Sitting in the foyer of the hotel, waiting for the airport limo, I found myself looking at two ficus trees. One grew straight and strong over a thick trunk. The other had three pencil-thin trunks, woven together like a braid. I wondered about multiples. They tell us we are strong, creative, I thought. Artistic, yes, more stylized than the straight trunk—but the braided tree looked more delicate. It had come to be the way it was through torture; its trunks had been bound until it took that shape. Now it had its own special kind of strength and grace. Not better than the other, not worse, I decided, just different. I felt some peace in that.

When I got home, Ann told me Carl had called, even though I had asked him not to contact me anymore. Then she gave me a cartoon strip she had cut out of *Frank & Ernest*. A woman, unlocking her door, says to her date, "I'll see you in my dreams—unless my therapist can do something about it." It was good to laugh.

When he called again, I answered, and found I could barely speak to him. When I hung up, I was dizzy, my legs weak, like a person who had just had a brush with a rapist.

A visiting friend, a Jungian therapist, explained what she thought was going on with me: "When we are caught in an archetype, the projections are going to fly out everywhere unless we get a hold on the archetype, see our various roles in it. Then we can rise above the puppet parts and make choices as an observer, rather than responding to the repeating pull of the archetype. I think it's important that you begin to react in this scenario in a different way. Break free of treating him like your father. Write a new script for yourself where it's two adults." I heard her as from a distance. It just didn't seem possible at the time.

Dream:

I'm on a trip with a lot of younger people. I know they think I'm different, because I'm so much older, but I act like myself anyway. One of the men is the group leader. He is very attractive to me, though I hang back, away from him. He is gone with some of the others, gone somewhere to eat, I think. I am with a lot of other people (strangers) at some kind of street fair or something. A great big man, I know he is not a good man, he's dangerous and ugly, picks me up and puts me on his shoulder and starts running with me through the crowd. I am exhilarated and decide I might as well enjoy it, rather than scream and hang on. I stretch out like a dancer, and pose for the crowd, loving it. Then the leader comes back. He is very disapproving. I leave the big man and go and hang adoringly on the leader's chair, a director's chair, like we both know I am his. Then

I see something behind me, where the other man was, in a kind of dark cave or hole in a hillside. It looks at first like blueberries, as I go to see. Then it looks like a cluster of grapes, but up close it turns into something sticky and stuck together in some kind of sick way, like grapes that have been boxed and turn rancid. Only they're not grapes. I don't know what they are. Even though they look repulsive and unhealthy, I am divided about them, I think I am going to eat them anyway.

Awake, my mouth turned down. I felt sick that I was about to eat the grapes, even though they might be poisonous. My mouth and throat felt full of something loathsome.

I told Glenda I understood the dream: "I can have the grapes—sex with daddy—or other men— if I don't see the grapes are rotten. I can have the thrill-ride if I ignore the man is ugly and dangerous."

Glenda said, "I think the man carrying you around was Carl."

"But Carl is not all that big."

"He's big with power, money, prestige," Glenda said. "Remember the wedding, receptions and all that? You were like that dancer on his shoulder. And the ugliness, the poisonous grapes—that's how you felt about sex with him." Grapes I associated with Carl; he grew them, took a picture of a cluster in his hands, and even wrote a poem about their "breastlike succulence." I registered that sense of fit I always had when both interpretations, that of the inner and the outer world, fit nicely together, like those little nested boxes in Chinatown.

I told her Carl called. "I hung up on him. I can't even act like a rational adult around him."

Glenda said, "Perhaps you're just allowing yourself to feel the fear and loathing your child could never allow herself. You need to be free of all that with Carl while you do your own work."

Going back to the old journals, pulling out patterns and dreams, I came on an entry I didn't remember ever seeing before. It was simply written there, with no comment.

A man takes me, a child, into the Ladies Room, goes into the booth with me. I call for help. Then we are outside somewhere, and he is getting beaten up badly. I can't stand to watch it, it's my fault, and I am screaming for them to stop.

Had someone been beaten for molesting me, and I forced to watch? I didn't remember.

In August, even though Glenda had asked me not to do it yet, I began reading a popular book called *When Rabbit Howls,* by Trudy Chase and the Troops. The title reminded me of the time when my father caught a wild rabbit in the basement. It fought so hard to get away, one leg was torn off.

Trudy Chase's story was a horrifying account of incest, violence, and sadism that resulted in her personality splitting into dozens of multiples. Certain pages touched me so deeply, I would have to stop reading until I could see again through my tears. Sometimes I would scream into my pillow until a headache came.

I identified with the woman who had experienced nothing but fear and a compulsion to do right all her life. I identified with the woman who saw herself as a conduit for everyone else's emotions. I recognized myself in Trudy's description of her entangled affairs with men.

As I read, I often felt dizzy with vertigo, as if I were being spun around and around.

When I told Glenda I'd read the book, I started listing all the reasons why I could not be considered a multiple. "I don't have blackouts, I don't find other people's clothes on my bed. I'm not unaware of the different personas I use for different situations."

"You're pretty upset," Glenda said. "I hadn't expected you to diagnose yourself. I just wanted you to see the severity of the damage incest can do."

"This woman was dangled into a well, she had snakes dropped on her. My childhood wasn't nearly that severe."

"Yours was horrifying. Just because somebody else's pain is more grotesque doesn't diminish our own."

I continued with the reasons I was not a multiple personality. "The things I do are just the things everybody does, everybody forgets sometimes where they are, everybody has different parts of themselves that deal with different situations."

Glenda said, "You are really defensive about this."

I quieted down. "Okay, so I'm a multiple—a modified, moderate multiple."

Then I started in on Glenda. "But what about you? I don't know anything about you. You sit there like some voyeur, the therapist observing objectively while the client pours out her guts."

"Now I'm going to get defensive," Glenda said. "I'm very protective of my clients, very concerned about them." She went on to give examples, but I already knew from my own experience how protective Glenda was, and was grateful for it.

"I think I'm just responding to my discomfort at being seen, after all the years of cover up. Trudy's therapist tells her to let the chips fall where they may," I made a wry face. "Easy for him to say."

"To be totally out of cover is risky," Glenda conceded. "You have to make choices."

After months of essentially living my therapy, I was planning a trip to California to see family and friends. I was quite apprehensive about it. My son Mike had already told me that my letter had said more than he'd wanted to hear. I'd apologized. We agreed that I would not do it again, and he would tell me when I went over his boundaries. My other son, Scott, was very supportive, as was his wife, Joyce. Still, I was nervous. I felt a compulsive need to talk about my therapy, my past, perhaps because of an anxious desire to prove that people would not reject me as dirtied or fatally flawed.

Glenda encouraged me to talk all I could about what I was going through. "Don't keep it a dark secret."

In California, I found it was difficult and exhausting to be around normal people, even those who loved me. I was essentially very isolated and still confused about who I was, "now that the roof is off the house." With friends, it was sometimes tiring to pretend everything was just the way it had always been.

Joyce said she had seen glimpses of my multiples. "Once was when you said you weren't ready to get married, then you went out and bought a wedding suit. And I saw the frightened bandaged child once when you accidentally broke an ornament in a store, remember? You looked like you had done something terrible. Then when you smoked up the house that time, burning papers in the fireplace. You looked so guilty." I remembered with embarrassment those first primitive drawings of disgusting memories.

Everywhere I went, telling my own truths brought up old emotional wounds of others. One very centered and competent friend told me about his alcoholic parents, quarreling in the car, himself, six, between them. "My mother opened the car door, and, dragging me with her, threw herself out. I remember sitting by her in the middle of the highway, waiting for the ambulance to come."

Nearly everyone had some terrible agony in their past, alcoholic parents, battering brothers or spouses, date rape. I remembered a quote from Hemingway: "The world breaks everyone. Some are just strong at the broken places."

My sons were taken back to the physical abuse in their own childhoods. They watched *Radio Flyer,* a disturbing video about two boys and their mother, and a stepfather who abused them. Watching the video, I relived those years through their eyes. How afraid they must have been most of the time. I reexperienced the pain of watching my sons get treated violently, watching their sweet trusting faces change to fear and guardedness. I saw them again and again reach for love, again and again rejected and even terrorized. After I came home, I wrote a letter to their father, demanding that he tell his sons how sorry he was, but I didn't send it. It was their fight now. I felt dizzy writing it. Dizzy and overwhelmingly sad.

In August, I had one of my last anxiety attacks. I heard myself crying, rabbit keening, while my whole body moved and remembered: he put it in my little ass hole first and then my little vagina. My body undulated, feeling both sexual and ripped open, wanting resolution of some kind, crying, hurt, until the headache came and made it all stop. Afterward I felt empty, like a discarded gum wrapper. The rest of the day I was tense with anger. I imagined putting my spike heel through a man's balls.

I wrote: "I can speak to my child lovingly, soothingly, but we are both afraid that we are messed up forever, sexually."

My struggle to escape the past was reflected in a dream I had in August: *I have been kidnapped by a family, a rather strange stupid family, a little foreign. They live in a three story house. They are going to murder some man, and I either see it or will see it, so the men turn me over to the women of the family, whose job it is to drug me; the hypodermic needle is so big and will be so painful that I can neither look at it nor feel it. Then I am face down under a sink for some time. Next day, I am left in an upstairs room where the other children of the family sleep. I'm given a lot of freedom, the other kids ignore me. There's a street sign in the middle of the ceiling but I can't read it, or only can read one side, or I can't remember what it says or I'm not sure it's really the address, so when I manage somehow to slip away unnoticed to a women's luncheon, I can't tell the woman I talk to where I am ... too embarrassed and inadequate to explain, I tell her not to show any response because I may be watched to see if I'll tell. I leave without being sure she even understands or believes me.*

Back at the house they don't seem to know I've been gone. I make a batik sign and put it in the kitchen window. They may think it's clever or they may punish me. I go in the closet to hide so they'll think I've escaped. It's becoming less and less important now, they're getting used to me, I'm becoming used to them, but I am still looking for a way to escape. The street signs are gone now. I look up the address and try to memorize it, with difficulty. I know the man will send the woman to make sure I have not given them away when they see the sign in the kitchen or find out I was gone for awhile. They check on me, but I am just playing in the dirt in the back yard.

Awake, I feel flashes of anger; I want to cry and rage. It's my life. Geno is the godfather-like figure who runs the house, he is the head of the mafia. It was Carl who was murdered by the Godfather because I was using him to try to get out. I have been trying to slip out, telling women mostly, Glenda, Susan, but not sure if I can be rescued. I don't remember where I'm at, I'm drifting into acceptance of my situation. Still, I was kidnapped, it is not my house, though it is all I can remember.

I still felt controlled by my past, had not built a "house" of my own. I was still shaky about my identity, unsure who I was. That fall I wrote a very strange letter to my friends and family, like something I would have written as a teenager:

Things are calm around Lake Woebegone after a traumatic summer when that far out Californian went and got herself hypnotized, recovered memories which if you ask me, were better off where they were. 'Cause if she'd just left 'em there, the chances are that she would never have drifted into some numbed out marriage with a bemused ol' widower.

Her friend Susan is probably the only reputable person in Minnesota who would get close to her, after she practically announced on the radio that she was an incest survivor. Folks don't talk about things like that in Minnesota. It is considered an embarrassment best left under the bed, perhaps the bed it all started on would be a good choice.

Thanks Garrison Keillor, for your perspective. If you don't mind, I'll borrow it occasionally, since I don't have one of my own.

Scott called. "It's not funny, Mom." He saw how victimized I felt, how I minimized my own pain, belittled myself. He encouraged me to do my "soul work," reminded me I had never been afraid of rocking the boat in a community before.

Joyce said, "I'm afraid you've thrown out too much, good with bad."

I asked Glenda what she thought of the letter. Glenda noted that I used *she* instead of *me* and made fun of having hypnosis. "You seem to belittle yourself and the whole therapeutic process."

I hadn't realized I was doing that when I wrote the letter. As a teenager, I often made fun of my own pain. My teenaged version of join the enemy, it was a survival technique. My father taught me that by making fun of my pain himself. "Funny it should come back now," I told Glenda. "I'd like not to do that any more." Now I realize I had progressed from the traumatized child to the clowning teenager covering her wounds. A maturing process was taking place, one I could evaluate and trust.

I was now reading every incest healing book I could get my hands on, recognizing how common my symptoms were. The books, like Glenda, stressed how important it was to get in touch with feelings. I had always struggled to do just the opposite, to find ways to go over the top of how I felt, find something to read, focus on something good. I had to learn to feel, not avoid feelings.

The feelings coming up as I continued to face my past were often shame and embarrassment as I realized how much sugarcoating of the truth, how much intellectualizing or rationalizing I'd done over the years to protect myself from the pain of the truth.

I wanted to write a personal account of the results of incest, the repeating cycle, the indicative dreams, the repressed memories, so that others would know they could trust their dreams, trust their memories, trust themselves. But now, reading the journals, I was no longer sure I had the courage to write about all that messiness, to tell the truth about my often sordid life. Yet, if my story was to mean anything, if it was to be useful, I had to tell the truth, all of it, even the parts I was ashamed of.

I told Glenda how sick I felt about my year with an abusive man, about all the other men, how I'd used sex. "How could I have done that to myself? How could I let myself get hit, get used, get hurt like that?"

"Don't blame the victim," Glenda said. "There's enough of that out there. You had been taught all the wrong things. You didn't even know what was wrong. You were fighting, even then, fighting your way through to get to where you are now."

"But my God, over and over and over..."

"Helen, you didn't become a suicide, or a drunk. You didn't get hung up on drugs. You didn't cave in to a second-rate marriage. You refused to quit trying!" She calmed her impatience. "Survivors always have trouble with relationships. They often settle for crumbs."

I laughed cynically. "Relationships, that razzle dazzle prize. I don't think I will ever be ready for that again." But some part of me, perhaps the child, heard, and remembered, the pride in Glenda's voice. "Helen, you didn't quit! You were fighting, even then, to get where you are now."

In time, I began to think differently about my past. I had fought my father; when he called me a bitch and a whore, I had left rather than put up with it, despite his threats to put me in a detention home. I had fought Jimmy off the children and left him, even though I had no way to make a decent living for the three of us. I had recognized the deadness of my second marriage, fought to create something more alive. I had fought, and left, the men who abused me, and the men who exploited me. It was not easy being a single woman in those years, still wasn't, but I had raised and unconditionally loved two fine sons and built a career for myself. Standing up for myself against my own internal criticism was a new and freeing experience.

Another dream: *Someone is looking at the way I make decisions. Primitive, they say. They'll teach me how to make better ones.*

I still had no trust in my own decisions; my marriage had thoroughly undermined that. My personal world was still riddled with confusion. The persons who roamed my dreams and ran my inner communication system—the Caretaker, Sneaky Snake, the Bitch Queen, Creepy Crawly— still had to be accepted and integrated, especially the hurt child. My therapist, my family and friends had shown me they believed in me. I was only starting to believe in myself. I still avoided anyone who might not believe me, or who might criticize me.

14

Coming Home

When I had lunch with Susan that fall, I felt almost normal again. I could listen to her, respond to her, not just talk about my own obsessions. I apologized for my past self absorption. Susan said, "I'm honored to be part of it. The whole process is like giving birth."

"Remember that night two years ago, we had similar dreams on the same night?"

"Oh, yes!" Susan recalled. "You were giving birth to a fine healthy baby, and I was the midwife. So this is what it meant." We looked at each other, awed by the mystery of dreams.

"What are you doing Saturday night? I've got some friends coming over to play Pictionary."

I looked down at my hands. "I'm going dancing with Les."

Susan gave me a look. "Why? Its been four years since you broke up with him. You want to get into all that pain all over again?"

"I'm not sure why. I like to dance, that's why."

Susan raised a skeptical brow.

"I know," I said. "I'm going to talk to Glenda about it tomorrow."

When I got home, I fed the dog and cat, changed into my jeans for a walk along the lake. Ann had left for a job in Texas, and though I was happy for her, I was faced with my own loneliness. Be careful, I reminded myself. Stay steady. Right after the annulment, I had fantasized getting something sexual started. "Getting your quick fix," Ann had called it. Glenda had said, "With all you're dealing with now, you don't need that." But I would yearn and yearn.

In time, that reversed: now I was nervous about going out at all. Like a recovering alcoholic, I knew a surge of loneliness could throw me back into old patterns.

The next day during our session, Glenda supported my decision to go dancing. "You need friends and a social life, too. And besides, it might be a good opportunity for you to practice some new skills—boundary setting. What do you think? You look a little apprehensive."

"I am apprehensive. The caretaker says okay; he's ready to move fire escapes, communications systems and luggage at a moment's notice."

Now it was Glenda's turn to look apprehensive. I laughed and made a droll face. "I told him not to jump to conclusions, to do nothing without explicit instructions from me. The passive woman wants to get ready to charm and go totally co-dependent. I told her she might like to try a friendship with a man, she's never had one."

Glenda nodded with relief.

"Sneaky Snake wants the body heat, wants sex, she wants to razzle dazzle, but she's going to put that energy into helping Passive Woman stay in our backbone for awhile."

"Sounds promising," Glenda nodded again. "How about the child?"

"The child is shivering and feeling bad. She says Les is like our father, thinking he's entitled because he's male, making us feel like we're never quite good enough, embarrassed about being female." I sat in silence for a moment, reconnecting with the child. "I promised her I would be on the lookout, and if I saw any of that, there would be no friendship. Certainly no sex."

Glenda smiled. "Sounds like you're in touch with what you want. What are your fears?"

"My biggest fear is that I'll just slide right back into a sexual relationship with him, right back into the old stuff."

"Maybe this is an opportunity to show yourself that you're the one who chooses to do that, or not to do that," Glenda said. "Then you'll feel a little more sure of your ability to set your own boundaries and hold to them."

When I met Les at the restaurant, I didn't do my "razzle dazzle thing." I sat back and observed, paid attention to what was going on in myself, my own feelings.

"You're wearing my favorite sweater," he said, smiling suggestively.

"I didn't know it was a favorite of yours," I said, genuinely surprised. "I like it myself." Before, I would have let him think I had worn that sweater to please him. "You look nice too," I said, noticing how healthy and fit he looked in his blue shirt and tan corduroy jacket. I had seen him on the trails around the lake, his strong legs in graceful, effortless motion. "Still the athlete?" I asked.

"I still jog about five miles a day." He had brought pictures of his grandchildren. Seeing them brought a pang of regret; I had enjoyed them too. As I told him about my own family— "Scott's buying his own airplane." "Mike and Jean are going to home-school Lea"—I began to feel the warmth of the old connections we used to share.

He asked if I was still in therapy. I nodded. "This is one of my first forays out in the single world." I felt a rush of vulnerability as I said it. When we left the restaurant, he took my hand. His touch was comforting.

Sitting on the passenger side of his car, I recognized the pleasure of being no longer in the driver's seat. It was nice to just sit back sometimes, let someone else take over the wheel. But with it came fear. "How are you feeling about our agreement to be friends?" I asked.

"I thought we were always friends," he said.

"I mean, just friends," I said, feeling awkward as a teenager.

"Well, I think that is harder for men than it is for women, but I'm working on it."

At the club, it felt good to fit myself into Les's arms and move across the dance floor. "You're a better dancer than you used to be," I told him. "A stronger lead, more responsive to the music." He moved me away into a twirl, pulled me back into his arms, then led me into a reverse twirl. I matched him step for step, enjoying the graceful swirl of my skirt around my legs. He grinned then, and I realized he had been trying to see if I could follow the tricky maneuvers. "I don't know how you do it," he said.

"I've been paying more attention to your body language," I laughed. He couldn't know how much I'd been paying attention to my own body language.

We drank Cokes, ate popcorn, and talked between sets, with the comfort of people who had known one another for a very long time.

When it was getting late and the band played a slow number, we danced closely, moving in unison to an old song, "Deep Purple." I felt myself sliding into the old feelings, sexual, romantic. They carried a kind of sickly nostalgia, like wine that is too sweet.

I moved back from Les's close embrace. "I've got to slow down. I don't want anything more than friendship right now." He stiffened, and I noticed the muscle of his jaw tightened.

Later, when I slipped out of his car and into my own, turning away from a kiss, Les told me, "I don't think anybody but me would put up with this."

He had asked me out again anyway. I told Glenda. "I really enjoyed the warmth, the closeness, the dancing, but I felt like I was back in high school. That's how it was then. 'Put out or I don't take you out anymore.' Too bad, because I really do enjoy him. He tells me I've changed. He treats me with more respect. But I don't want to get back into it with him."

"There are good relationships," Glenda assured me, "where people enhance each other, rather than giving up their own identities and going co-dependent."

Glenda talked to me about what a healthy relationship with a man could be, and how to recognize the patterns of unhealthy ones. "What you had with Les in the past was addictive intimacy. Addictive intimacy is more work than healthy intimacy. If you could do that, you can learn to do healthy relationships, and it will be easier and more satisfying than you can ever believe. One could decide living alone was good and nothing less than a good relationship would be preferable to that."

"That's hard for me to imagine ... a healthy relationship," I said. "And I don't mean that in bitter way." I reflected a moment. "For the most part, I've chosen insightful men who told me the truth about myself. Even Les, by taking such good care of himself, knowing what his boundaries are, taught me to take better care of my boundaries."

"Which is why you chose them," Glenda reminded me. "Don't give them so much credit. They learned a lot from you too. Well, I don't hear you worrying about Les now, trying to make him different than he is. Or trying to make yourself over to suit him. I see you paying attention to your own wants and needs, and staying honest with him about it."

"Progress," I said, pleased.

"I'll say. The average time it takes for people to go through incest therapy is nine years. Probably because you could devote so much time to it, you've done it in less than three."

I was starting to come out of hiding. I mentioned the fact that I was an incest survivor in my Women's Issues class. I published two autobiographical poems. I did a radio commentary on early incest survival. I was invited to speak at Take Back the Night, an annual gathering for women who claim their right to live in safety.

I was pleased to see a few familiar faces in the several dozen turned expectantly toward me. This would be the first time I told the truth of my past to an audience; I was fearful of disbelief or rejection. But many of this group were survivors themselves; I could be sure of their acceptance.

I waited for the rustling to die down and began. As I briefly summarized my story, I looked closely at the faces. They were attentive, expectant. Hopeful still. I took courage and went on.

"It has now been three years since I went to that first hypnosis session where I experienced and spoke the word—incest—it was my father—I was two. I wanted to avoid the messy work of cleaning up that festering abscess by turning myself over to a caretaker, a husband, and pretending nothing was wrong. But the past had to be faced, the trip through darkness had to be made. With the help of a fine therapist, I am working my way out of the muck of the past.

"Thank you for listening so closely," I finished. "Telling my story has helped to free me from the shame and guilt I carried for so long. My respect is still growing for that woman, my Self, who picked herself up time and time again and fought, struggled, wrestled with what kept going wrong. Like Jacob wrestling with the angel, she said, 'I will not quit until you bless me.' At times, I still wrestle with the dark angel."

I paused, looking out over the faces, many of them like flowers in a garden after a rainstorm, bent, smeared, muddy. I could see some heads nodding, a few tears as some recognized their own experience, as others empathized with me.

"My wish for those of you who have suffered the violation of your will by someone else's trespass is that you do not give up. Ever. Healing is not only possible, it is nature's way. But we must have the courage to go through the pain."

Perhaps it was just the way the light came in from the high windows, but I saw over them a kind of radiance. "I see your angels hovering over you. They will bless your journey."

Having lunch in the Student Union, I told Susan I felt triumphant. I'd taken another step further from shame, and I had freed several women to tell me afterward of their own rape or incest.

"The real test will come if I ever have to talk to people who don't really know what I'm talking about. Worse yet, an audience with an oppressor or two in it. I just collapse in the face of verbal bullies. Takes me right back to when my parents didn't believe me. Or maybe it's the witch burnings in my cellular memory." I laughed.

"It'll come," Susan said confidently. "How's the book coming?"

My eyes were gritty from working so long on the computer the night before. "Slowly. A lifetime is a lot of material to distill. I've got to get it down from seven hundred pages. It's hard to go back through all those years, relive all that pain, see all my failures."

"Failures! Was Ulysses a failure? You were on a quest," Susan insisted, "You were an explorer in hostile territory. You life's a regular Odyssey."

I laughed ruefully. "Oh, it's been an Odyssey, all right. I've seen men turned into pigs. I've eaten with the lotus eaters." I got quiet, stirring lemon into my tea. "I know how lost he was, twenty years away from home. And I know how his heart ached with longing when the sirens sang."

I felt Susan's comforting acceptance in her silence. "So, what about it? Are you a multiple?"

"I don't worry much about it. Hume and Berkeley said the individual self is nothing but a cluster of different perceptions, right? So in some ways, everybody is a multiple. I just have to be careful to check in with mine once in awhile."

Then I unwrapped one end of my taco, held it up, and looked across it at Susan. "I went after a promotion and I got it. I'm a full professor now!" I took a big bite.

Susan raised her coffee and proposed a toast. "To Leda's daughter."

Shortly after, I was invited to do a workshop on healing at Itasca Women's Day in a large town in central Minnesota. About one hundred people, male and female, looked down from the tiered seats. Many of them were students in the local college. I swallowed as I recognized two newspaper people in the high back row, one from my own town. I had no idea what their interest here might be, but one had a reputation for defending the patriarchal status quo, including Freud.

"The truth will set you free," I thought to myself. Then I plunged in.

"Start with the premise that spiritual power grows from a ground of personal wholeness. Next, each human born comes into life as a whole being. Third, if the inner sense of wholeness is lost or discouraged from maturing, the individual becomes maimed and susceptible to indoctrination, manipulation and mastery. A philosopher named Elsa Gidlow said that a long time ago. My life illustrates the wisdom of her words." I briefly summarized my own story and traced my recovery.

One woman near the back was dabbing her eyes. I made a note to try and speak to her later.

"I'm sometimes bitter when I think about expensive Freudian therapists who told me I was a ball buster, a castrating woman, or that I suffered from penis envy. Until recently, no therapist ever went after the terror that caused my problems.

"The many women entering the field of psychotherapy have released the stranglehold of Freud. I believe his mistrust of the human soul has been destructive to both men and women. I believe that if the great poets Sylvia Plath and Anne Sexton had lived today, a good therapist could have prevented their suicides. Any questions before we start some simple exercises?"

After a silence, a hand came up, then another, and another. "Dr. Bonner, you said you did not think your parents were evil. Yet they both did dreadful things to you. How can you defend them?"

I thought about the question. "I have to be careful here, it's tricky territory. There is no defense for the abuse of children, and I don't defend their actions. But I believe even my parents thought they were good parents. People learn parenting from their parents; my father was disowned by his parents, and my mother had been abused by her father. My parents' parents had learned parenting in a culture that taught a child was little more than an uncivilized animal. Small wonder that our own parents had so little respect for us as children. Alice Miller is a good one to read about that."

Another hand came up, one that had been raised before.

"Dr. Bonner, I remember when I was a kid, hearing the grown-ups say, 'Children don't remember anyway.' Do you think most children just forget what's painful in their past?"

"Well, that's a question I feel particularly strong about. Children feel at least as acutely as adults, but they do learn very young when it is safe to have feelings and when it is not. When they are raised by trusting and trusted adults, then they can accept all their feelings, and believe in their own perceptions. Children raised that way do remember; often they remember incidents as early as their first weeks of life."

"Helen, don't you think some things are better forgotten? The past is the past."

"I am not an expert, except on my own experience. But I believe our memories, good or bad, give us a sense of continuity, a sense of the wholeness of our experience. I believe that trust is the natural relationship of the human being to itself and the world; chronic mistrust is the result of abuse of some kind, subtle or otherwise."

Other hands were up now. I felt their support, their good-heartedness. I chose a young man who looked scholarly and professional.

"Dr. Bonner, don't you feel we've learned a lot since then? That your kind of story is a thing of the past? Nobody's that hung up about sex anymore." Laughter.

"I hear more and more horror stories now that women are talking about their lives more freely. As for people not being hung up about sex anymore, I think we are extremely fixated on it." Laughter.

Another hand went up. "Are you saying that things will be better now that women are talking about their abuse and now that we have more women therapists?"

"Umm. I'm going to have to get political here. Mine is not just the story of an incest survivor. It is the story of many women who grew up in patriarchal times. Incest is only one of the many tyrannies of a culture that teaches men they have inborn privileges and prerogatives over women and children. We still tell every man he should be king, though every man can't be. I'm no psychologist, but I think this produces a desperate inadequacy in many men which results in turning against those who are weaker; women, children, the poor, the powerless. I believe we have the *knowledge* now to move toward cultural healing. Whether we will put our energy there remains to be seen."

One of the men in the back of the room stood to get my attention. He was a big man, with a loud imposing bass voice. I looked up at him, thinking, "Here it comes."

"Dr. Bonner, moved as I am by your personal testimony, is it not possible that you have simply been duped by your own very creative imagination? *Time* Magazine had a thorough article recently, debunking the so-called recovered memory accounts, "Lies of the Mind," I think it was called. Another recent article, "Dubious Memories," even blamed these so-called memories on therapists who need to drum up business. They're out there encouraging their clients to sue their own fathers! These are just popular articles, I realize; I'm not in the field, but the television investigative reporting program, *Sixty Minutes*, also did a segment on "Repressed Memories" recently, investigating two false claims and showing the terrible damage done to the accused."

I grappled with the familiar combination of rage and self doubt that came up when authority figures denied my experience. I calmed myself. "No one ever worked harder to discredit my own memories than I did. They emerged despite enormous resistance. I might not be able to take them to a court of law, but how many of your memories could you subject to legal verification? Yet you know what you know.

"I don't pretend to be purely objective, but the media does pretend objectivity. I read both of those articles and found them to be extremely biased; just look at the title, 'Lies of the Mind.'

"I believe there is a cultural denial of incest as strong as my personal one. Why did *Sixty Minutes* focus on a few dubious accounts, rather than on the thousands of verifiable ones? This cultural denial exists for many of the same reasons that my denial existed, to protect the perpetrators, to protect the power system, to protect ourselves from facing ugly truths, to create a comforting fantasy for ourselves that 'People don't do such things,' or 'We don't have these problems.'"

I heard my voice rising, worked to control it. "To those people who would deny the probability of repressed and recovered memories, I would like to say, read the professional literature. There is overwhelming evidence to support their validity. I am sure, as in all areas of life, there are people who fake claims, but statistics show those to be extremely rare, fewer than one percent."

I stopped, waiting for a rebuttal. An angry looking young woman waved her hand.

"But then anybody can claim anything. I know a girl who says her brother...." She couldn't bring herself to say the words. "Well, anybody can say anything."

"I hope my story has shown that no one who has been through incest or rape wants to claim a past that makes her feel so personally soiled and victimized. If anyone tells you she or he has memories you find difficult to believe, encourage that person to see a good therapist. Don't try to act as judge and jury." The clock showed the hour was up, and with relief, I watched the big journalist go out the door, engaged in good-natured dialog with a female student.

"I said my truth, and I wasn't struck down by lightning from the Big God," I told Glenda.

Glenda laughed with me. "Congratulations. That was a big one. How's everything else going?"

"The downs when they come usually last only a day, sometimes only an hour or so." I paused, evaluating the last few weeks since I'd seen her.

"No more nightmares, no flashbacks. Mostly good dreams now. The other night, there were dancers coming in through the ceiling of the old house, a man and a woman, so graceful I was touched."

A few days later, while my Jungian friend Carolyn was visiting, I had another dream:

There's been a turtle race. Riding a motor scooter, another woman and I are following the course of the race along zigzagging irrigation ditches, stopping occasionally to talk to someone and to look at the remains of the race. The turtles are the big kind like we saw the shells of at the fair, but we never see any real turtles. When I think I see one in the mud of the ditch, it is just an empty shell, and even that turns into pieces of segmented paper, plastic mailing labels.

There are men ahead of us on fast motorcycles. I get irritated with my companion because she is always holding me back. I will go on ahead and then stop and wait for her. Then the motor scooter won't start: I am irritated because she won't help me start it.

Carolyn asked me what I thought the dream meant.

"Well, I think there's more than one level. We women are definitely running behind. Men are ahead in life, going on faster, more powerful vehicles; our motor scooter is unreliable and hard to start. On a personal level, if everything in the dream is me, then my companion is me too. She is an older woman, single, trying to do new things very late in life. She takes on a lot, but she spends a lot of time getting there. I get irritated with her sometimes."

Carolyn nodded. "How did you feel when you woke up from that dream?"

"Angry, frustrated with my zigzag course, mucking in the muddy ditch for turtles and finding only empty shells or paper labels."

Carolyn thought about it a moment. "But the turtles must be you too. Those big old snapping turtles are ancient wise creatures. They do leave things behind that are valuable."

She laughed. "The dream sounds positive. That's how turtles race, and the turtles do win. The men speeding ahead are after trophies, shells. The good stuff is inside. And it's okay to ride a small vehicle." I found her interpretation empowering.

One of the students in Women's Studies asked me if I would do something for Women's History Month. I decided to read *Judges 19* in a new way.

I was wearing silk trousers and a vest like an Oriental watercolor. My hair was loosely tied back in a silk knot. I felt at home. The room was not large. Only thirty or so women were there. I realized once more how few women seemed to be willing to claim their own history. There were a few men there, too, I knew them, young, sensitive, raised by aware, hardworking mothers.

On each table were candles which had been carried on a night vigil through the streets. Faces moved in the shadows like flames themselves as I read to them the story, pausing occasionally to reach back to the past, to speak to that unnamed woman.

"When the stranger from another land came upon you, did you wear a crown of flowers in your hair? Did your dark lover demand you take off your moon pendant and replace it with a cross, and did you refuse? Was that your so called whoredom against your master? Did you toss your head in pride as you scorned his concubinage, asking equal or nothing?

"When months later, he came for you, speaking words of tenderness from his heart, did your young heart leap in triumph?

"When your father greeted him, took him into his house for five days of feasting and celebration, did your hands, and your mother's, joyfully prepare the bread and wine? Did you mount that donkey to return to his home in pride, his chosen first?

"When the host took you in on the road, and the shouts came from the evil men, 'Send out the Levite,' their hands groping their own inflamed bodies, did you tremble in fear for him, your new husband?

"Or did you know, as your silent mother must have known, as the host's virgin daughter must have known, the laws of the patriarch, the covenant of men—honor above all, the honor of the host, the honor of the husband, the honor of the tribe. Honor fed on your warm and trembling flesh."

The room hovered in silence. I uncovered a loaf of bread on the table before me, and took up a knife. I spoke now to the gathered solemn faces.

"He cut her body into twelve pieces. Twelve, a sacred number. I will cut this bread into twelve pieces in memory of the nameless one who, so very long ago, died for the sins of the fathers. Tonight, we take back the story of that dark night, and all of those like it. Tonight, in the retelling of her story, we grieve our sister as she was not grieved then. We commemorate her across the centuries as she was not commemorated then."

As my gaze swept across the still and shadowed faces, I felt as though they had indeed gone back in time. Candlelight caught the tears of one of the men, and the woman next to him reached for his hand.

"Let us grieve also for the virgin daughter, the invisible silent mother, and all the nameless ones."

I poured grape juice into small paper cups, broke the bread into pieces. Without a word they began to come forward, the women, the men, the young and old. Carrying their candles, they broke off pieces of bread, they drank the wine. After I took my own portion of bread, as I let the pure clear juice of the grape flow down my throat, I felt a healing in my own anguished heart.

Two years ago I had a dream:

I cut the heart out of something and I am putting it in a big wall-sized mural. It comes back to life when I put the new materials, paint or plaster, over it. It thaws, turns dark purple, and begins to beat again. The sculpture, or painting, is big, dark, and pretty ugly. When I am most discouraged that all my cutting and sculpting and painting is just creating a mess, I put something—a sheer thin sheet of paper?—over the whole thing, take it off, and lo, that is the masterpiece I've been trying to create, the imprinted paper. I go upstairs to show another artist, but he is looking through a dirty window and can't see how fine it is. I know it is though, and everyone else can see it is too, a truly wonderful creation. Clear and simple, yet strongly powerful and evocative, a real work of art.

The dream reflected my hope that from all the messy material of my life, I had somehow created a work of art, coming from my heart.

Months and then years went into the writing of this book, first cutting and shaping the mass of materials into something that had a form meaningful to others. Then I rewrote it as a novel, *Leda's Daughter*, as if it were fiction, under an anonymous name. Still hiding. But the book's authenticity came before my desire to remain anonymous or nice. The title had to be explicit; the autobiography had to be authentic. *Leda's Daughter* became *The Laid Daughter*, and I acknowledged it under my own name.

Sometimes you have to go a long way around to come a short distance correctly. I think that's a line from Albee's *Zoo Story*. My life has been like that, a long way around to come a short distance correctly, a long, long attempt to get away from, and then back to, the old wound, the split that divides one against oneself.

I believe we have a soul or a spirit that is our essential being; it is us as we were meant to be, as we were patterned to be, and that spirit will push us toward our fulfillment the way a young tree, bent under a limb, will push toward the sun. It will tell us what is wrong in dreams, in repetitious unconscious actions, in the stories we tell and the words we choose. At bottom, the self is not Freud's vicious untamed monster. The self is a spring, feeding into the rivers of our lives. As the Bible says, 'He restoreth my soul, he leadeth me beside the still waters.'

Making a journey like mine is surely what the old myths meant, the journeys to Hell or Hades or Purgatory, looking for some beloved woman or child. Orpheus goes after his beloved Eurydice in the underworld, hoping to charm his way with song, but he fails by looking back too soon. Demeter sends Hermes for her daughter, Persephone, when the king of the dead carries her off. There is always the danger of being lost there, in the twists and turns of hellish darkness, but in the myths, the heroes refuse to return to the light of the sun without the beloved.

So it was for me. But my trust that I would return with something of myself regained was stronger than the fear. The voice of the child, calling from the depths, gave me direction. My therapist was my spelunker's guide, handing down the ropes, holding the flashlight steady, reading the maps, calling encouragement.

Returning to the sunlight of a greening earth, I carry with me my recovered child. She has been in darkness a long while. Her legs are weak. She still does not laugh easily. But my, how she loves being out of that cave!

"I'm rewriting the myth," I told Susan. We were celebrating my birthday in a restaurant overlooking a lake now free of ice. She nodded. "Remember your poem about the suspension bridge?" Susan asked. "So far above the water you thought you could never get back to it?" She lay before me a beautifully wrapped present. "I think this speaks of where you are now." It was a framed poem by our favorite Minnesota poet, Susan Carol Hauser.

Sitting at the table, the white cloth strewn with spilled flowers and torn wrapping paper, I read the poem aloud. The words were solid and simple, as smooth as stones polished by the sea for a very long time.

Walking Lake Superior

The child removes
her shoes, her socks,

and cruises the cusp
between water
and shore.
Bent from the waist,
she draws her fingers
through pebbles
and stones,

chooses the ones
she knows
are hers,

and drops them
into
the stocking
she carries.

It swings from her hand,
a pendulum.

Afterword

by Glenda Parkinson,
Therapist

I knew from my first meeting with Helen that there was more to her than the intelligent, confident persona the world was accustomed to seeing. She was a college professor, a writer, a leader, and an achiever. She had a success identity. At 60, she was strikingly svelte and attractive. Age had only enhanced her inner and outer beauty. Her reason for seeking therapy was her fear of destroying her new marriage by her strange and unpredictable behaviors.

Helen didn't present with the overt symptomatology that you may have read about in "Three Faces of Eve," "Sybil," or "When Rabbit Howls." Her personalities were more camouflaged to outsiders, and usually unknown to herself. The trauma she experienced as a child was grave and horrifying. Creating them was how she survived.

Helen was a Multiple Personality Disorder (MPD). She was also plagued by Post-Traumatic Stress Disorder. Still, I struggled with labeling her as a Multiple Personality because of the societal perception that equates MPD with craziness. She was not nor is not crazy.

MPD is an extreme form of dissociation. To dissociate is to separate from the self momentarily. Only intelligent and creative children can cope with pervasive trauma and abuse by developing other selves to take some of the brunt of the pain. Children who learn to dissociate early in their lives develop a pattern for coping that can last a lifetime.

All people dissociate to some degree; multiples do it regularly and create "stand-ins" when pain or a sense of inadequacy requires more than they can bear. Helen's intelligence saved her from incapacitating mental illness and allowed her to use her inner resources for survival.

Guided all of her life by the occupants of her "house," Helen was bewildered by her actions and behaviors. Some of the occupants protected her; others were harmful. In therapy, Helen was able to identify and acquaint herself with half a dozen primary personalities; the Caretaker, Passive Woman, Sneaky Snake, Creepy Crawly, the Bandaged Child, and the Bitch Queen. Therapy began to clarify former inconsistencies for Helen and promote a lifestyle which made sense.

Helen spent only a year in intense psychotherapy with me. The average length of treatment time is somewhere between five and ten years. She was highly motivated and followed her gut instincts in making therapeutic decisions for herself. She read. She wrote. She practiced suggestive directives. She attended a national conference for adult survivors. Her art work was another vehicle for self-understanding. She used relaxation techniques when feeling panicky. She begin to fill her new "house" by acknowledging and fulfilling the needs of her integrating selves. Decisions Helen made for herself rather than against herself were the catalyst toward wholeness.

Helen will continue to grow and develop. Life will be less fragmented for her. Merely existing is in the past. She has always been strong and emotionally healthy, considering her experience with parents who had tried to break her spirit. She no longer has to run from herself but can, instead, revel in the peace that comes from self-acceptance.

According to the media, "false memory syndrome" is rampant in our society, fueled by greedy psychotherapists who feed off power. I've never seen it. What I have seen are women and men riddled with fear and confusion, trying to cope with crippling emotional pain, shattered self-esteem, decaying egos, and incapacitating symptomatology, both emotional and physical. Professionals aren't always professional in any field. I regret that there are some people who have been victimized by unprofessional psychotherapists. However, far more women and men will have their healing jeopardized by their inability to trust the therapeutic process because of recent sensationalism by the media of a small minority of "false memory" victims. My hope is that those deserving of psychotherapy will not be hampered in their quest for good health because of it. The reality is that the majority of adult survivors of incest have learned to survive and even flourish with therapeutic guidance—people like Helen who have gone through this painstaking process called healing.

What we did, we did together. A good therapeutic process involves both the client and the therapist experiencing a unique interpersonal relationship. Helen has every hope of being able to live a healthier life. As for me, my life is richer because of the relationship we shared.

Glenda Parkinson, Therapist
Bemidji, MN.

About the Author

Dr. Helen Bonner is a Professor of Women's Studies, Literature, and Creative Writing at Bemidji State University, Bemidji, Minnesota, where she is also Editor of *Dust & Fire, Women's Stories*. She does monthly *Commentaries* for KCRB radio, and has published many short stories, both commercial and literary. A Northern Californian, she reared a family and worked as a secretary, a reporter, and a social worker before getting her Ph.D. She has taught in California, Texas, Ohio, and Minnesota, and has traveled widely. Her greatest interest is the healing of all people; her greatest faith is that possibility.

About the Kairos Center

The Kairos Center was founded to explore the integration of body and soul, mind and matter.

If you want to be on the Kairos Center mailing list for news about workshops, classes, or spiritual tools, call, write or FAX to:

Kairos Center

4608 Finley Drive
Austin, Texas 78731
Phone 1-800-624-4697
FAX: 512-453-8378